Ramses

The Lady of Abu Simbel

Also by Christian Jacq

The Son of the Light
The Temple of a Million Years
The Battle of Kadesh

About the translator
Dorothy Blair is the author of critical works on the history of
literature in French from Africa and the Caribbean. She has
published translations of some two dozen works written in
French from or about Africa and the Middle East.

Ramses

The Lady of Abu Simbel

Christian Jacq

Translated by Dorothy S. Blair

SIMON & SCHUSTER
A VIACOM COMPANY

First published in Great Britain by Simon & Schuster Ltd, 1998
A Viacom company

Copyright © Éditions Robert Laffont, S.A., Paris, 1996
English translation copyright © Dorothy S. Blair, 1998

1 3 5 7 9 10 8 6 4 2

Simon & Schuster UK Ltd
Africa House
64-78 Kingsway
London WC2B 6AH

Simon & Schuster Australia
Sydney

A CIP catalogue record for this book is available
from the British Library.

Hardback: 0-684-82139-7
Trade paperback: 0-684-82122-2

Typeset by SX Composing DTP, Rayleigh, Essex
Printed and bound in Great Britain by
The Bath Press, Bath

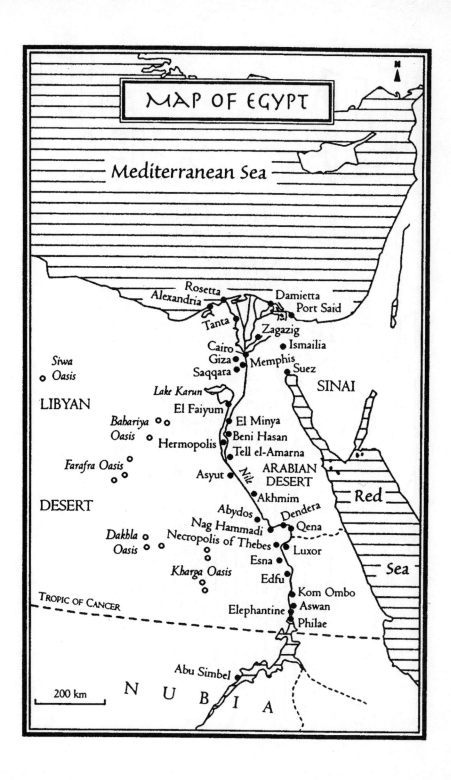

MAP OF EGYPT

Mediterranean Sea

Rosetta
Alexandria
Damietta
Port Said
Tanta
Zagazig
Cairo
Ismailia
Giza
Memphis
Saqqara
Suez
SINAI
Siwa
Oasis
LIBYAN
Lake Karun
El Faiyum
Bahariya
El Minya
Oasis
Beni Hasan
Hermopolis
Tell el-Amarna
Farafra Oasis
Asyut
ARABIAN
DESERT
Akhmim
DESERT
Abydos
Dendera
Nag Hammadi
Qena
Dakhla
Necropolis of Thebes
Oasis
Luxor
Esna
Kharga Oasis
Edfu
Kom Ombo
TROPIC OF CANCER
Elephantine
Aswan
Philae
Abu Simbel
N U B I A
200 km
Red
Sea
Nile

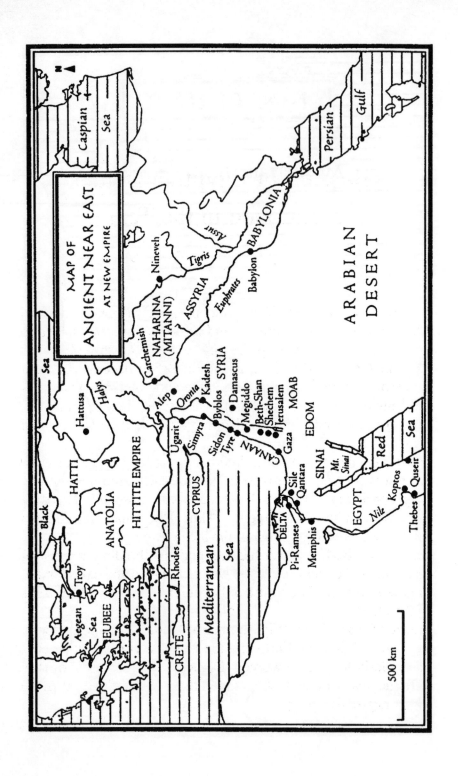

MAP OF
ANCIENT NEAR EAST
AT NEW EMPIRE

500 km

Glossary of Egyptian Deities
mentioned in the Text

Amon (also **Amun**). The 'hidden god', originally a local Theban deity, god of fertility and reproduction, then taken up widely as a war-god, procuring victory to the pharaohs. Assimilated with Ra (q.v.), as Amon-Ra, to become the most powerful god in the Egyptian pantheon, sometimes known as the King of the Gods, with temples at Karnak, Luxor, Memphis. Portrayed as a ram or a handsome young man with a plumed crown.

Aton (also **Aten** or **Adon**). Another name for Ra, the sun-god. Aton was the one, or universal, god of Akhenaton, the 'heretic king', probably the pharaoh whose dreams Joseph interpreted, thereby gaining his favour. Akhenaton may have been influenced by Joseph to adopt the idea of one god.

Bastet (or **Bast**). A cat-headed goddess holding a musical instrument, the guardian of the Delta, of music and dance and of pregnant women. The centre of her cult was the city of Bubastis in the Delta.

Hathor (or **Hather**). Wife/mother of Horus. A major goddess, the Lady of Heaven, Earth and the Underworld, a gentle deity, particularly helpful to women. Depicted as a cow or a woman with the head of a cow. Also given the name of Sekhmet (q.v.) in her aggressive form.

Horus. The son of Osiris (q.v.), the hawk-god and special protector of kings.

Isis. The wife of Osiris; had a reputation as a sorceress, but also represented the rich plains fertilized by the annual flooding of the Nile.

Ma'at. The wife of Thoth (q.v.); goddess of truth and justice, who presided over the judgment of the dead. She was regarded as a moral concept of reason, harmony and the right attitude of individuals to others.

Mut. The goddess-mother, wife of Amon-Ra, depicted as vulture-headed; the centre of her cult was a splendid temple in Thebes.

Osiris. The most widely worshipped of all the Egyptian gods. Identified with the fertile black soil of the Nile Valley, the annual cycle of flooding and new growth corresponding to the cycle of his life, death and rebirth.

Ptah. The local god of Memphis, regarded as the creator of all things, the source of moral order, the Lord of Truth and Justice. The patron of artisans and builders.

Ra. A sky-god, identified with the sun, the oldest and one of the greatest in the Egyptian pantheon. The centre of Ra's cult was Heliopolis (Greek: 'sun-city'). Akhenaton's universal god, Aton, was linked to Ra.

Sekhmet. The wife of Ptah, a lioness-headed goddess of war and healing, associated with Memphis; a figure to be placated. Took the form of a lioness to attack men who turned against Ra.

Set (**Seth**; also **Setekh**). One of the principal gods, sometimes seen as a Satan figure, representing powers of evil and destruction, requiring respect and placating. Storms, thunder, whirlwinds and hail were his instruments.

Thoth. The scribe of the gods, the god of wisdom and patron of science, literature and inventions and of the scribes in the temple. The inventor of writing, language and magic. Depicted as a man with the head of an ibis or as a baboon or dog-headed ape.

D. S. Blair

1

Invincible, Ramses' lion, gave a terrifying roar which froze the blood in the veins of Egyptians and rebels alike. The enormous beast, decorated by the pharaoh with a fine gold collar for his good and loyal services at the battle of Kadesh against the Hittites,* weighed as much as three big men and measured more than eight cubits from head to tail. His thick, resplendent mane was so luxuriant that it covered the top of his head, his jowls, neck, part of his shoulders and his chest. His sleek coat was a burnished tawny hue.

Invincible's anger could be felt by everyone within half a day's march, and everyone was aware that it also expressed that of Ramses, who, since his victory at Kadesh, had become known as Ramses the Great.

Was this greatness real, though, when the Pharaoh of Egypt could not succeed, in spite of his prestige, in imposing his will on the barbarians from Anatolia? The Egyptian army had proved a great disappointment when it came to the battle. The generals, through either cowardice or incompetence, had deserted Ramses, leaving him alone to face hundreds of thousands of adversaries who were certain of victory. But the god Amon, hidden in the Light, had heard his son's prayer and lent the pharaoh's arm supernatural strength.

* Distant ancestors of the Turks.

After five years of a turbulent reign, Ramses had believed that his victory at Kadesh would prevent the Hittites from showing signs of rebellion for a long time to come and that the whole region was entering a period of relative peace.

He had been grossly mistaken, he the Strong Bull, the Beloved of Ma'at, the Son of the Light, the Protector of Egypt. Did he deserve these coronation titles, given the sedition that was brewing up in the traditional protectorates, Canaan, and southern Syria? Not only were the Hittites not giving up the fight, but they had launched a vast offensive, allying themselves with the Bedouin, who were looters and murderers and who had long coveted the fertile lands of the Delta.

The general of the army's Ra division approached the king. 'Majesty, the situation is more critical than we thought. This is no ordinary revolt. According to our scouts, the whole land of Canaan is rising up against us. If we overcome this first obstacle, there will arise a second, then a third, then . . .'

'And you don't think we'll win?'

'Our losses could be heavy, Majesty, and the men have no wish to get killed for nothing.'

'Isn't the survival of Egypt a good enough motive?'

'I didn't mean—'

'But that's what you were thinking, General! So the lesson of Kadesh was in vain. I am doomed to be surrounded by cowards, who lose their lives because they want to save them.'

'My obedience and that of the other generals is absolute, Majesty. We merely wished to warn you.'

'Have our espionage services obtained any information about Ahsha?'

'Unfortunately not, Majesty.'

Ahsha, Ramses' childhood friend, now minister for foreign affairs, had been captured while visiting the Prince of Amurru.*

* Modern-day Lebanon.

Had he been tortured? Was he still alive? Did his jailors consider that the diplomat had an exchange value?

As soon as he heard the news, Ramses had mobilised his troops, who had scarcely had time to recover from the shock of Kadesh. To save Ahsha it was necessary to cross territories which were now hostile. Once more, the local princes had broken their oaths of allegiance to Egypt and had sold themselves to the Hittites, in exchange for a bit of precious metal and some false promises. Which of them did not dream of invading the land of the pharaohs and enjoying its reputedly inexhaustible wealth?

Ramses the Great had so much work still to complete: his Temple of a Million Years at Thebes, the House of Ramses, Karnak, Luxor, Abydos, his House of Eternity in the Valley of the Kings; and Abu Simbel, the stone dream he wished to offer to his beloved wife, Nefertari . . . And here he was, on the border of the land of Canaan, on top of a hill, gazing down on an enemy fortress.

'Majesty, if I dared . . .'

'Take courage, General!'

'Your show of strength is very impressive. I'm convinced Emperor Muwatallis will have understood the message and will see that Ahsha is freed.'

Muwatallis, the Hittite emperor, was a determined and cunning man, aware that his tyranny rested only on force. At the head of a vast coalition, he had nevertheless failed in his enterprise to conquer Egypt, but he was launching a new assault, using the Bedouin and the rebels as his instruments.

Only the death of Muwatallis or that of Ramses would put an end to a conflict whose outcome would be decisive for the future of many peoples. If Egypt were defeated the military might of the Hittites would impose a cruel dictatorship which would destroy an age-old civilization, developed since the reign of Meni, the first of the pharaohs.

For a moment Ramses thought of Moses. Where was he

hiding, this other childhood friend, who had fled from Egypt after killing a man? Searches had been in vain. Some claimed that the Hebrew, who had given invaluable help in building Pi-Ramses, the new capital in the Delta, had been swallowed up by the desert sands. Had Moses joined the rebels? No. He would never have become his enemy.

'Majesty . . . Majesty, are you listening to me?'

The sight of the plump, frightened face – this officer thought only of his own comfort – reminded Ramses of the man he hated more than anyone in the world, Shaanar, his elder brother: the scoundrel had allied himself with the Hittites, in the hope of seizing the throne of Egypt. Shaanar had disappeared, taking advantage of a sandstorm, while being transferred from the great jail in Memphis to the prison settlement in the oases, but Ramses was convinced he was still alive and still firmly intent on harming him.

'Prepare the troops for battle, General.'

The shamefaced general slipped away.

How Ramses would have loved to be enjoying the delights of a garden in the company of Nefertari and his son and daughter; how he would have savoured day-to-day happiness, far from the clash of arms. But it was his duty to save his country from the bloodthirsty hordes, who would not hesitate to destroy the temples and ride roughshod over the laws. What was at stake was greater than his own person. He had no right to think of his own peace of mind and his family; he must make a stand against the evil, even at the cost of his life.

Ramses gazed at the fortress which barred the road leading into the heart of the protectorate of Canaan. More than twelve cubits high, the double slopes of its walls sheltered an important garrison. There were archers on the battlements. The moats were filled with sharp potsherds which would cut the feet of the footsoldiers responsible for raising the scaling-ladders.

A sea breeze refreshed the Egyptian soldiers massed

between two hills, on which a relentless sun beat down. They had arrived there by forced marches, enjoying only brief halts and makeshift camps. Only the well-paid mercenaries were resigned to doing battle; the young recruits, already deeply unhappy at the idea of leaving their country for an indefinite period, were afraid of dying in terrible battles. Everyone hoped that Pharaoh would simply reinforce the north-east border, instead of throwing himself into a venture which risked ending in disaster.

Not long ago, the Governor of Gaza, the capital of Canaan, had given the Egyptian high command a splendid banquet, swearing that he would never ally himself with the Hittites, those barbarians from Asia, of legendary cruelty. His blatant hypocrisy had sickened Ramses. Today, his treachery did not surprise the twenty-seven-year-old monarch, who was beginning to understand the secret workings of men's hearts.

The lion grew impatient and roared again.

Invincible was no longer the young cub Ramses had found one day dying in the Nubian savannah, bitten by a snake and with almost no chance of surviving. A deep empathy had immediately been established between the great cat and the man. Fortunately, Setau the healer, also a childhood friend and university comrade of Ramses, had been able to find the right antidotes. The beast's tremendous stamina had helped him to overcome the ordeal and become an adult of terrifying strength. The king could not have dreamt of a better body-guard.

Ramses stroked Invincible's mane, but this did not calm him.

Setau was climbing up the hill, clad in an antelope-skin tunic, with many pockets filled with drugs, pills and phials. He was black-haired, unshaven, of stocky build and average height, with a forthright expression. He had a passion for snakes and scorpions, from whose venom he prepared potent remedies. He pursued his researches untiringly, together with his wife, Lotus, a ravishingly beautiful Nubian, the very sight of whom was enough to rejoice the hearts of the soldiers.

Ramses had entrusted Setau and Lotus with overseeing the army's health care and the couple had taken part in all the king's campaigns, not through love of war but in order to capture fresh reptiles and tend the wounded. And Setau thought no one better placed than himself to come to the assistance of his friend Ramses, in case of trouble.

'The troops' morale isn't too good,' he declared.

'The generals want to retreat,' Ramses admitted.

'Given the behaviour of your soldiers at Kadesh, what can you expect? When it comes to a headlong flight and a rout, they're unequalled. You'll make the decision alone, as usual.'

'No, Setau, not alone. With the advice of the sun, the winds, the heart of my lion, the spirit of this land . . . They don't lie. It is up to me to understand their message.'

'There's no better council of war.'

'Have you talked to your snakes?'

'They, too, are messengers of the invisible. Yes, I've questioned them and they've replied, unequivocally, "Do not retreat." Why is Invincible so restless?'

'Because of that oak wood on the left of the fortress, halfway between it and ourselves.'

Setau looked at it, chewing on the stem of a reed. 'You're right: it doesn't look good. A trap, as at Kadesh?'

'That one worked so well that the Hittite stategists have thought of another, hoping it will be equally effective. When we attack, our momentum will be broken, while the archers from the fortress will decimate us at their leisure.'

Menna, Ramses' armour-bearer, bowed to the king. 'Your chariot is ready, Majesty.'

The monarch stood for a while making a fuss of his two horses, whose names were Victory at Thebes and The Goddess Mut is Content. Apart from the lion, they had been the only ones not to betray him at Kadesh, when the battle seemed lost.

Ramses took the reins, under the incredulous gaze of his armour-bearer, the generals and the elite chariot regiment.

'Majesty,' cried Menna anxiously, 'you're not going to—'

'We shall bypass the fortress and go straight for the oak wood.'

'Majesty, you've forgotten your coat of mail! Majesty!'

Brandishing a corslet covered with small metal plates, Menna ran in vain behind Ramses, who had launched his chariot, alone, towards the enemy.

2

As he stood in his chariot, driving at full speed, Ramses the Great resembled a god rather than a man. Tall, with a broad, open forehead, bushy eyebrows, the piercing eyes of a falcon, a long, thin, slightly hooked nose, round, delicately lobed ears, strong jaw, fleshy lips, and wearing the close-fitting Blue Crown, he was the very embodiment of power.

At his approach the Bedouin hidden in the oak wood emerged from their hiding-place. Some bent their bows, others brandished their javelins.

As at Kadesh, the king was swifter than a tornado, more quick-witted than a jackal, covering immense distances in an instant; like a sharp-horned bull which fells its enemies, he crushed the first attackers who advanced towards him, and he shot arrow after arrow, piercing the chests of the rebels.

The leader of the Bedouin raiders managed to avoid the monarch's furious charge and, with one knee on the ground, prepared to hurl a long dagger at his back.

Invincible made a leap which rooted the amazed rebels to the spot. In spite of his weight and size, the lion seemed to fly through the air. His claws out, he felled the leader of the Bedouin, buried his fangs in his head, and closed his jaws.

The horror of the scene was such that a number of the warriors dropped their weapons and fled to escape from the huge beast, which was already mauling two other Bedouin, who had run in vain to the rescue.

The Egyptian chariots, followed by several hundred foot-soldiers, joined Ramses and had no difficulty in destroying the last pocket of resistance.

Now Invincible quietly licked his blood-stained paws and gazed lovingly at his master. The gratitude he read in Ramses' eyes elicited a growl of pleasure. The lion lay down near the right wheel of the chariot, his eyes alert.

'This is a great victory, Majesty!' declared the commander of the Ra division.

'We have barely avoided a disaster. Why didn't one of the scouts point out the enemy gathered in the wood?'

'We . . . we neglected this spot, which seemed unimportant to us.'

'Must I depend on a lion to teach my generals the profession of arms?'

'Your Majesty no doubt wishes to call his council of war to prepare the attack on the fortress . . . ?'

'We attack immediately.'

By the expression in his master's voice, Invincible understood that it was the end of his rest. Ramses patted his two horses on the rump and they exchanged looks as if to encourage each other.

'Majesty! Majesty, I beg you!' The armour-bearer, Menna, arrived breathlessly, holding out the king's metal-plated corslet.

Ramses agreed to don this coat of mail, which did not detract too much from the elegance of his wide-sleeved linen robe. On his wrists the sovereign wore two bracelets of gold and lapis-lazuli, each depicting the heads of two wild ducks, the symbol of the royal couple, like two migrating birds, taking flight towards the mysterious regions of heaven. Would Ramses see Nefertari again before undertaking the great journey to the other side of life?

Victory in Thebes and The Goddess Mut is Content pawed the ground impatiently. Their heads were adorned with a panache of scarlet plumes, tipped with blue, and their backs protected by scarlet and blue caparison. They were anxious to gallop off towards the fortress.

There arose on the lips of the footsoldiers a song created spontaneously after the victory at Kadesh, whose words reassured the cowards among them: 'Ramses' arm is powerful, his heart is valiant. He is a peerless archer, a strong bulwark protecting his soldiers, a flame which consumes his enemies.'

Menna nervously filled the king's two quivers with arrows.

'Have you checked them?'

'Yes, Majesty. They are light and strong; you alone will be able to reach the enemy archers.'

'Don't you know that flattery is a serious fault?'

'Yes, but I'm so frightened! If it hadn't been for you, the barbarians would have wiped us out.'

'Prepare a good feed for my horses. When we return they will be hungry.'

As soon as the Egyptian charioteers approached the stronghold, the Canaanite archers and their Bedouin allies shot several volleys of arrows, which fell harmlessly at the feet of the horses. The horses whinnied and some of them reared up, but the king's calm prevented his elite troop from giving way to panic.

'Bend your bows,' he ordered, 'and wait for my signal.'

The Pi-Ramses arsenal had produced a quantity of bows made from acacia wood, with ox sinews for tightening cords. The meticulously studied curve of the weapon allowed an arrow to be shot from more than two hundred paces and travel in a parabola to meet its target with precision. This technique made a mockery of the sheltering battlements behind which the besieged archers sought protection.

'All together!' thundered Ramses in a voice which released every man's pent-up energy.

The majority of the arrows reached their mark. Countless enemy archers fell dead or seriously wounded, hit in the head, pierced through the eye or the throat. Those who replaced them suffered the same fate.

Now assured that his footsoldiers would not perish under the rebels' arrows, Ramses ordered them to hurl themselves at the wooden gate of the fortress, and demolish it with their battle-axes. The Egyptian chariots drove up. Pharaoh's archers adjusted their aim even more precisely, preventing any resistance. The sharp potsherds that filled the moats served no purpose as, contrary to custom, Ramses was not going to have the scaling-ladders raised, but was going to storm the main entrance.

The Canaanites massed behind the gate could not repel the Egyptians. The encounter was terrifyingly violent. Pharaoh's soldiers climbed over a heap of corpses and flooded into the interior of the fortress like a devastating tidal wave. The besieged men gradually gave ground. They collapsed on top of one another, their long scarves and fringed robes stained with blood. Egyptian swords pierced helmets, broke bones, slashed sides and shoulders, cut tendons, burrowed into entrails.

Then a sudden silence fell over the stronghold. Women begged the victors to spare the survivors assembled on one side of the central courtyard.

Ramses' chariot made its entrance into the reconquered citadel.

'Who is in command here?' the king asked.

A man in his fifties, who had lost his left arm, stepped out of the wretched crowd of defeated rebels. 'I am the oldest of the soldiers. All my superior officers are dead. I beseech the Lord of the Two Lands to show mercy.'

'Those who break their word cannot expect mercy.'

11

'May Pharaoh at least grant us a swift death.'

'My verdict, Canaanite, is this. The trees of your province will be cut down and the wood transported to Egypt. The prisoners – men, women and children – will be sent to the Delta and put to work for the benefit of the state. Canaan's cattle and horses are now our property. The surviving soldiers will be recruited into my army and will fight in future under my command.'

The vanquished rebels prostrated themselves, only too happy to be still alive.

Setau was not dissatisfied. The number of seriously wounded had not turned out to be significant, and he had enough fresh meat and honey dressings to stop the bleeding. With nimble, careful fingers, Lotus closed wounds with strips of sticky material placed in a cross. The pretty Nubian's smile made the men forget their pain. The stretcher-bearers carried the wounded to the hospital, where they were treated with salves, ointments and potions, before being repatriated to Egypt.

Ramses addressed the men who had been wounded in the defence of their country. Then he summoned the senior officers, to whom he revealed his intention to proceed to the north, in order to recapture, one by one, the fortresses of Canaan which had passed into Hittite control, with the collaboration of the Bedouin. The pharaoh's enthusiasm was contagious. Fear was banished from their hearts and they rejoiced at the day and night of rest he granted them.

Later, Ramses dined with Setau and Lotus.

'How far do you intend to go?' asked the healer.

'At least as far as northern Syria.'

'As far as . . . Kadesh?'

'We shall see.'

'If the expedition lasts too long we shall run out of remedies,' observed Lotus.

'The Hittites' reaction was swift. Ours must be even swifter.'

'Will this war end one day?'

'Yes, Lotus, on the day when the enemy is totally defeated.'

'I hate talking politics,' grumbled Setau. 'Come on, dearest. Let's go and make love before setting out to look for some snakes. I feel that tonight will be favourable for a good collection.'

Ramses celebrated the dawn rites in the little shrine set up near his tent in the middle of the camp. A most modest sanctuary compared with the temples in Pi-Ramses, but the fervour of the Son of the Light was undiminished. His father Amon would never reveal his true nature to humans, would never be confined in any form whatsoever; yet all could sense the presence of the Invisible.

When the sovereign left the shrine, he noticed a soldier who was holding an oryx on a leash and having difficulty in controlling the animal.

A strange soldier in truth, with his long hair, coloured tunic, pointed beard and shifty eyes. And why had this wild creature been introduced into the camp, so close to the royal tent?

The king had no time to ponder the question any longer. The Bedouin released the oryx, which charged Ramses, its horns aimed at the belly of the unarmed sovereign.

Invincible struck the antelope on its left side and planted his claws in the back of its neck; it was killed immediately and collapsed under the lion.

The Bedouin was rooted to the spot; he drew out a dagger from his tunic but did not have time to use it. A violent pain in his back, followed immediately by a blinding icy fog, made him drop his weapon. He fell headlong, mortally wounded, with a lance planted between his shoulder-blades.

Calm and smiling, Lotus had shown astonishing agility. The lovely Nubian didn't even seem perturbed.

'Thank you, Lotus.'

Setau emerged from his tent, followed by some soldiers. They saw the lion devouring its prey, and discovered the body of the Bedouin.

Menna was shattered; he threw himself at Ramses' feet. 'I am devastated, Majesty! I promise to identify the sentinels who let this criminal into the camp, and punish them severely.'

'Summon the trumpeters and order them to sound the call for departure.'

3

Ahsha was growing more and more irritated, especially with himself, as he spent his days gazing at the sea, from the first-floor window of the palace where he was imprisoned. How could he, head of the Egyptian intelligence service and minister for foreign affairs, have fallen into the trap laid for him in the province of Amurru?

The only son of a wealthy, noble family, Ahsha had been a brilliant student at the Royal Academy of Memphis at the same time as Ramses. He was elegant and refined, and as much in love with the ladies as they were with him. He had a long face, slender, delicate hands and feet, eyes sparkling with intelligence, and a spellbinding voice. He loved to be in the front rank of fashion, but the arbiter of elegance hid a man of action and a top-flight diplomat who spoke several foreign languages and had specialized knowledge of the Egyptian protectorates and the Hittite Empire.

After the victory at Kadesh, which seemed to have finally curbed Hittite expansion, Ahsha had thought good to proceed urgently to the province of Amurru, in the land of Canaan languishing along the Mediterranean to the west of Mount Hermon and the trading city of Damascus. He wished to make this province into a fortified base from which elite raiding parties would set out to counter any attempt by the Hittites to advance towards Palestine and the Marches of the Delta.

When he entered the port of Beirut, aboard a vessel loaded with gifts for the Prince of Amurru, the venal Benteshina, the Egyptian diplomat had not suspected that he would be welcomed by Hattusilis, brother of the Hittite emperor, Muwatallis, who had just seized the region.

Ahsha had sized up his opponent: small, puny-looking, but intelligent and cunning, Hattusilis was a formidable enemy. He had forced his prisoner to compose an official letter to Ramses, in order to lure Pharaoh's army into a trap. But Ahsha, thanks to the use of a code, hoped to have awakened the pharaoh's suspicions.

How would Ramses react? Reasons of state demanded he leave his friend in the hands of the enemy, and hasten towards the north. Knowing Pharaoh, Ahsha was convinced that he would not hesitate to strike at the Hittites with the utmost violence, whatever the risks. But the head of the Egyptian diplomatic service was an excellent bargaining counter. Benteshina would wish to sell Ahsha to the Egyptians for a good weight of precious metal.

In truth his chances of survival were slender, but Ahsha had no other hope. This enforced inactivity made him irritable. Since his adolescence he had always taken the initiative, and he found it intolerable to have to wait on events in this way. He had to act in one way or another. Perhaps Ramses thought Ahsha was dead; perhaps he had equipped his troops with new weapons and then tried to launch a large-scale offensive.

The more Ahsha pondered, the more he was convinced that there was no solution but for him to free himself.

At noon, as every day, a servant brought him a hearty meal; he had no complaints about the palace staff, who treated him like a distinguished guest. He was enjoying a piece of grilled beef when he heard the heavy footsteps of the master of the palace himself.

'How is our great Egyptian friend?' asked Benteshina,

Prince of Amurru, an obese man of some fifty years, with a bushy black moustache.

'Your visit is an honour.'

'I felt like drinking wine with the head of Ramses' diplomatic service.'

'Why is Hattusilis not with you?'

'Our great Hittite friend is busy elsewhere.'

'It must be very good to have only great friends. When shall I see Hattusilis again?'

'I have no idea.'

'So Canaan has become a Hittite base?'

'Times are changing, my dear Ahsha.'

'Are you not afraid of Ramses' anger?'

'Insurmountable ramparts will now rise between Pharaoh and my principality.'

'Could it be that the whole of Canaan is under Hittite control?'

'Don't ask me too many questions. You must know that I intend to trade your precious life for some riches. I hope nothing untoward will happen to you in the course of the exchange, but . . .' Benteshina's leer indicated to Ahsha that he might well be dispatched before telling what he had seen and heard in Amurru.

'Are you sure you have chosen the right side?'

'Certainly, friend Ahsha! To tell the truth, the Hittites have imposed the law of the strongest. And then, there is talk of many worries which prevent Ramses from ruling with peace of mind. Either a plot or a military defeat – or both together – will result in his death or replacement by a more conciliatory monarch.'

'You know little about Egypt, Benteshina, and even less about Ramses himself.'

'I am a good judge of men. In spite of the reversal at Kadesh, Emperor Muwatallis will triumph.'

'A risky gamble.'

'I love wine, women and gold, but I am not a gambler. The Hittites have war in their blood, the Egyptians do not.' Benteshina gently rubbed his hands. 'If you wish to avoid a regrettable accident when the exchange takes place, my dear Ahsha, you ought to think seriously of changing sides. Suppose you gave Ramses false information . . . After our victory, you would be rewarded.'

'You are asking me, the head of the Egyptian diplomatic service, to be a traitor!'

'It's all a question of circumstances. I had sworn loyalty to Pharaoh . . .'

'This isolation stops me thinking clearly.'

'Would you like a woman?'

'A refined, cultivated woman, very understanding.'

Benteshina drained his cup of wine and wiped his damp lips with the back of his right hand. 'To help you think clearly, I'd agree to almost any sacrifice.'

Night had fallen. Two oil lamps cast a dim light in Ahsha's chamber, where he lay on his bed, dressed only in a short kilt.

One thought obsessed him: Hattusilis had left Amurru. This departure did not tally with Hittite expansion into the protectorates of Palestine and Phoenicia. If the Anatolian warriors had made a spectacular advance, why had Hattusilis abandoned his Canaanite base from where he could control the situation? He could not have run the risk of going further south; he had probably returned to his own country. But why?

'My lord . . .' A faint, trembling voice disturbed Ahsha.

He sat up and saw, in the half light, a young woman, barefoot, dressed in a short tunic, her hair loose.

'Prince Benteshina sent me. He ordered me . . . he insists . . .'

'Come and sit down beside me.'

She obeyed reluctantly. She was about twenty, blonde, plump, very appetizing.

Ahsha stroked her shoulder. 'Are you married?'

'Yes, my lord, but the prince promised me my husband wouldn't know anything.'

'What work does he do?'

'A customs officer.'

'And you, have you a job?'

'I file the dispatches at the courier service's main office.'

Ahsha slipped the straps of the tunic off the young woman's shoulders, kissed her on the neck, then pushed her down on her back on the bed. 'Do you get news from the capital of Canaan?'

'Sometimes. But I'm not allowed to talk about it.'

'Are there many Hittite soldiers here?'

'I'm not allowed to talk about that either.'

'Do you love your husband?'

'Oh yes, my lord!'

'Does it disgust you to make love to me?'

She turned her head away.

'Answer my questions and I won't touch you.'

She looked at the Egyptian with eyes full of hope. 'I have your word?'

'I swear by all the gods of the province of Amurru.'

'There aren't yet very many Hittites here; a few score drill-officers are training our soldiers.'

'Has Hattusilis left?'

'Yes, my lord.'

'Where has he gone?'

'I don't know.'

'What's the situation in Canaan?'

'Uncertain.'

'Isn't the province under Hittite control?'

'There are contradictory rumours circulating. Some people claim that Pharaoh has seized Gaza, the capital of Canaan, and that the governor of the province was killed in the attack.'

Ahsha felt a new breath of hope fill his breast, as if he were being reborn. Not only had Ramses deciphered the message but he had also counter-attacked, preventing the Hittites from deploying. That was why Hattusilis had left: to warn the emperor.

'I'm sorry, my girl.'

'You . . . you're not going to keep your promise?'

'Yes, I am, but I have to take certain precautions.'

Ahsha tied her up and gagged her. He needed a few hours before she gave the alarm. Finding her cloak, which she had dropped in the doorway of the room, he saw a way of getting out of the palace. He wrapped himself in the garment, pulled down the hood and dashed down the stairs.

There was a banquet in progress on the ground floor. Some of the guests were asleep, dead drunk. Others were indulging in feverish lovemaking. Ahsha stepped over two naked bodies.

'Where do you think you're going?'

Ahsha could not run: several armed men guarded the palace door.

'You've finished with the Egyptian already? Come here, girl.'

A few more steps, then freedom.

Benteshina's sticky hand pulled back the hood.

'Bad luck, my dear Ahsha.'

4

Pi-Ramses, the capital built by Ramses in the Delta, was known as 'the Turquoise City' because of the blue glazed tiles which adorned the façades of the houses. Any stroller through the streets of Pi-Ramses would be filled with wonder at the sight of the temples, the royal palace, the boating lakes, the port, and go into raptures over the orchards, canals abounding in fish, the nobles' villas with their gardens, the flower-lined avenues. There were apples, pomegranates, olives and figs to be savoured, fruity vintage wines to be enjoyed, and one could join in singing the popular song 'Happy is the one who dwells in Pi-Ramses, where the humble are as respected as the great, where acacias and sycamores dispense their shade, where buildings are ablaze with turquoise and gold, where the breeze blows gently and birds frolic round the ponds.'

But Ahmeni, the king's private secretary, his university friend and trusted servant, did not share in this general light-heartedness. He felt, as did many other inhabitants of the town, that the usual gaiety no longer reigned there, because Ramses was absent. Absent and in danger.

Listening to no advice about the need for caution, tolerating no procrastination, Ramses had set out post-haste for the north to reconquer Canaan and Syria, dragging his troops along with him in a venture whose outcome was uncertain.

21

Officially Ramses' sandal-bearer, Ahmeni was small, slight, thin and almost bald; weak-boned, of pale complexion, with long, delicate fingers, capable of tracing the finest hieroglyphs, this plasterer's son had invisible links with Ramses. He was, in the ancient phrase, 'the eyes and ears of the king', and remained in the background, at the head of a service comprising a score of devoted and competent officials. An untiring worker, sleeping little and eating much, without ever putting on weight, Ahmeni seldom left his office, where a brush-holder of gilded wood, a gift from Ramses, enjoyed the place of honour. As soon as he touched this object, which was shaped like a column topped by a lily, he was reinvigorated and set to again to tackle the huge pile of dossiers which would have discouraged any other scribe. In his office, which no one but he was allowed to tidy up, the papyri were carefully arranged in wooden chests and jars or tightly packed in leather cases placed on shelves.

'An army courier,' announced one of his assistants.

'Show him in.'

The soldier was covered with dust and looked exhausted. 'I bring a message from Pharaoh.'

'Show it to me.'

Ahmeni identified Ramses' seal. Although short of breath, he ran all the way to the palace.

Queen Nefertari was seeing the vizier, the principal steward of the Royal House, the accounts scribe, the table scribe, the senior ritualist, the head of secrets, the director of the House of Life, the chamberlain, the director of the Treasury, the manager of the grain stores, and a number of other high officials. They wished to receive precise directives, so as to avoid taking any initiative which did not have the approval of the Great Royal Wife, who was responsible for ruling the country in the absence of Ramses. Fortunately, Ahmeni was always available to give his assistance and Tuya, the king's mother, helped with her valuable advice.

Lovelier than the loveliest, with black, glossy hair, green-blue eyes, a countenance as radiant as a goddess's, Nefertari was facing the ordeal of power and solitude. A musician, dedicated to the temple, devoted to the writings of the sages, she had wished for a career of meditation. But Ramses' love had transformed the shy girl into an Egyptian queen, resolved to carry out her duties without weakening.

The administration of the Queen's House alone exacted a heavy burden of work: this age-old institution consisted of a boarding school for the education of Egyptian and foreign girls, a weaving school and workshops for the manufacture of jewellery, mirrors, vases, fans, sandals and ritual objects. Nefertari reigned over a large staff of priestesses, scribes, administrators of the land revenues, workmen and peasants, and had made a point of getting to know the principal people responsible for each sector of activity. She was a stickler for justice and accuracy.

During these anxious days, when Ramses was risking his life to defend Egypt from a Hittite invasion, the Great Royal Wife had to double her efforts and rule the country, no matter how great her fatigue.

'Ahmeni, at last! You have news?'

'Yes, Majesty! A papyrus brought by an army courier.'

The queen had not moved into Ramses' office, which would remain empty until his return, but worked in a large room, decorated with light blue ceramics, and overlooking the garden where Wideawake, the king's yellow dog, slept under an acacia.

Nefertari broke the seal of the papyrus and read the text written in cursive script and signed by Ramses himself.

No smile lit up the queen's grave face. 'He is trying to comfort me,' she admitted.

'Has the king made progress?'

'Canaan has been subdued and the traitor king killed.'

'That's a fine victory!' cried Ahmeni enthusiastically.

'The king is continuing to the north.'

'Why are you so sad?'

'Because he will go on to Kadesh, whatever the risks. Before that he will try to free Ahsha and will not hesitate to risk his own life. And suppose fortune abandons him?'

'His magic will not desert him.'

'How would Egypt survive without him?'

'First of all, Majesty, you are the Great Royal Wife, and you rule extremely well. And then, Ramses will return, I'm certain.'

From the corridor came the sound of hurried footsteps. There was a knock at the door. Ahmeni opened it.

A midwife appeared in a state of great excitement. 'Majesty, Iset is in labour and is asking for you!'

Iset the Fair had eyes of an alluring green, a small nose and delicate lips. Her face was usually infinitely appealing. Even in these hours of pain, she retained her youthful charm, which had enabled her to captivate Ramses and become his first love. She often thought of the reed hut at the edge of a cornfield where she and Prince Ramses had consummated their passion.

But then Ramses had fallen in love with Nefertari, and now Nefertari alone reigned in his heart. Fair Iset had been eclipsed, because for her neither ambition nor jealousy had any meaning. Neither she nor any other woman could compare with Nefertari. Power frightened Iset; only one emotion persisted in her heart: the love she bore Ramses.

In a moment of folly, she had been tempted to plot against him out of resentment, but she had been incapable of harming him and had quickly turned aside from the forces of evil. Her greatest claim to glory was the fact that she had given birth to Kha, a boy of exceptional intelligence.

After bringing a daughter, Meritamon, into the world,

Nefertari could not have any more children. The queen had then insisted that Iset bear the monarch a second son and more descendants. But the king had created the institution of 'Royal Children' which would allow him to choose, from different levels of society, girls or boys who would be brought up in the palace. Their number would be proof of the inexhaustible fertility of the royal couple and prevent any difficulty over the succession.

But Iset was to relive her passion for Ramses by bearing him another child. The results of the traditional tests* had told her she would be delivered of a boy.

She was giving birth standing up, assisted by four midwives who were known as 'the gentle ones' and 'the ones with strong thumbs'. The ritual formulas had been recited in order to ward off the spirits of darkness who would try to prevent the birth. Fumigations and potions had eased the pains. Iset the Fair felt the infant emerge from the beneficent pool of waters where he had been growing for nine months.

The touch of a soft hand and the scent of lilies and jasmine gave Iset the impression that she had entered a heavenly garden where there was no more pain. Turning her head to one side, she saw that Nefertari had taken the place of one of the midwives. With a damp cloth, the queen wiped the brow of the woman struggling to give birth.

'Majesty . . . I did not think you would come.'

'You called for me; here I am.'

'Have you any news of the king?'

'Excellent news. Ramses has reconquered Canaan and will soon subdue the other rebels. He is outstripping the Hittites.'

'When will he return?'

'He'll be impatient to see his child.'

---

* For example, if the pregnant woman's urine made barley sprout, she would have a boy; if it made wheat germinate, she would have a girl; if neither germinated, the child would be still-born.

'This child . . . you will love him?'

'I shall love him like my own daughter, like your son, Kha.'

'I was afraid that . . .'

Nefertari clasped Iset's hands tightly. 'We are not enemies, Iset. You must win the battle you are waging.'

Suddenly the pain grew greater. She cried out. The principal midwife bustled around. Iset wished she could forget the fire which racked her and sink into a deep sleep, cease from the struggle and dream of Ramses. But Nefertari was right: she had to finish the mysterious work which had begun in her womb.

Nefertari held out her hands to receive Iset's child, while one of the midwives cut the umbilical cord.

The new mother closed her eyes. 'It really is a boy?'

'Yes, Iset. A fine, strong boy.'

5

Kha, the son of Ramses and Iset the Fair, was copying on to a blank papyrus the maxims of the old sage Ptah-hotep, who, at the age of one hundred and ten, had decided to set down some advice to future generations on how to lead a well-ordered and balanced life. Kha was only ten, but he hated childish games and spent his time studying, in spite of the gentle reprimands of Nedjem, the minister for agriculture, who was worried about the youngster's education: although fascinated by Kha's intellectual aptitude, Nedjem would have preferred him to spend more time in recreation. Kha learned quickly, remembered everything, and could already write like an experienced scribe.

Not far from him, Meritamon, the pretty daughter of Ramses and Nefertari, was playing the harp. At six, she already showed remarkable musical talent, as well as a genuine gift for flirtation. While he traced his hieroglyphs, Kha loved to listen to his sister strumming tunes and singing sweet songs. The king's dog, Wideawake, sighed with pleasure, his head resting on the feet of the little girl, who bore a startling likeness to Nefertari.

When the queen came into the garden, Kha stopped writing and Meritamon stopped playing. The two children ran to her, anxious and impatient.

Nefertari embraced them. 'Everything has gone well; Iset

has given birth to a boy.'

'You and my father must have made provision for his name.'

The queen smiled. 'Do you think we can make provision for everything?'

'Yes, because you are the royal couple.'

'Your little brother is called Meneptah, "the beloved of the god Ptah", the patron of artisans and the master of the creative Word.'

Dolora, Ramses' elder sister, was tall and dark with greasy skin that obliged her to make much use of salves. Perpetually weary, she had long led a life of leisure, prey to the boredom of a wealthy young noblewoman. Then she had found a cause when the Libyan magus Ofir told her of the beliefs of the heretic king Akhenaton, the supporter of the One God, Aton. True, the magus had been forced to kill in order to preserve his freedom, but Dolora had approved of his action and had agreed to help him, come what may.

On the advice of the magus, who had found refuge in Egypt itself, Dolora had returned to the palace and lied to Ramses, in order to obtain his pardon: she had been kidnapped by the magus and he had used her in order to get out of the country. Dolora had professed her joy at having escaped from the worst and been able to rejoin her family.

Had Ramses believed this version of the facts? On his orders, Dolora had to remain at the court of Pi-Ramses. That was what she hoped for, so as to be able to pass information to Ofir as soon as the opportunity arose. As the king had left to fight in the northern protectorates, she had not been able to see him again to strengthen his trust. She spared no effort to win over Nefertari, of whose influence over her husband she was well aware.

As soon as the queen left the council chamber, where she had been talking to the men in charge of the canals, Dolora bowed to her.

'Majesty, allow me to attend Iset.'

'What exactly do you wish to do, Dolora?'

'Supervise her household, purify her chamber every day, use a soap made from the bark and pith of the balanite tree* to wash the mother and child, clean every object with a mixture of ashes and soda. And I have prepared for her a toilet case containing pots of cosmetics, jars filled with delicate essences, khol and stylets to apply it. Iset must retain her beauty!'

'She will appreciate your devotion.'

'If she agrees, I will see to her make-up myself.'

Nefertari and Dolora walked a short way together along a corridor decorated with paintings of lilies, cornflowers and mandrakes.

'The baby is said to be magnificent,' said Dolora.

'Meneptah will grow to be a very strong man.'

'Yesterday I wanted to play with Kha and Meritamon, but I was not allowed to. I was deeply hurt, Majesty.'

'Those are my orders, and the orders of Ramses, Dolora.'

'How long will you go on mistrusting me?'

'This shouldn't surprise you. After the trouble you got into with the magus, his support for Shanaar—'

'I've had more than my share of misfortune, Majesty. My husband was killed by Moses, that accursed magus nearly got me completely in his power, Shanaar has always hated and humiliated me, and I'm the one who's always found to be in the wrong! I only wish for peace and I so long to regain the affection and trust of my family. I've made serious mistakes, I admit, but shall I always be judged a criminal?'

'You plotted against Pharaoh!'

Dolora knelt before the queen. 'I've been the slave of

* A tree rich in saponin.

wicked men and under their influence. Now all that is finished. I wish to live alone, in the palace, as Ramses insisted, and forget the past. Shall I ever be pardoned?'

Nefertari was moved. 'Take care of Iset, Dolora; help her preserve her beauty.'

Meba, the deputy minister for foreign affairs, entered Ahmeni's office. A career diplomat, heir to a wealthy family of ambassadors, Meba was by nature haughty and condescending. After all, he belonged to a high caste, which possessed power and riches and which did not permit him to compromise himself with lesser folk. However, Meba had been sorely tried when Shanaar, the king's elder brother, had ousted him from his post as head of the Egyptian diplomatic service. Humiliated, kept out of things, he had thought he would never return to the forefront of affairs, until the day when he had been contacted by the Hittite spy ring which had been set up in Egypt.

To betray . . . Meba had not had time to think about it. Rediscovering his taste for intrigue and his talent for wheeling and dealing, he had managed to win the trust of the authorities and obtain new duties. From being Ahsha's former superior, he had become, in appearance, his loyal assistant. In spite of his acute mind, the young minister had been taken in by Meba's feigned humility; to have as his collaborator an experienced man, and one who, moreover, had been made a scapegoat by Shanaar, had encouraged Ahsha to lower his guard.

Since the disappearance of the magus Ofir, the head of the Hittite spy ring, Meba had been waiting for instructions; they did not come. He was delighted by this silence, and made the most of it to consolidate his network of friendships in the secretariat and in high society, while taking care to spread his venom. He told himself he had been the victim of injustice, and that Ahsha was a brilliant intellectual, but dangerous and inefficient. Eventually, Meba forgot the Hittites and his own treachery.

Ahmeni was chewing a dried fig, while composing a letter of reprimand to be sent to the managers of the grain stores and, at the same time, reading a provincial chief's complaint about the shortage of firewood.

'What's going on, Meba?'

The diplomat detested this abrupt, ill-bred little scribe. 'Are you sure you aren't too busy to listen to me?'

'I've a little bit of ear left, providing you make it brief.'

'In Ramses' absence, aren't you the one who runs the country?'

'If you're dissatisfied with anything, ask for an audience with the queen. Her Majesty in person approves my decisions.'

'Don't try to outsmart me. The queen will send me back to you.'

'What's your complaint?'

'The lack of clear directives. My minister is abroad, the king is waging war, my administration is a prey to uncertainty and doubt.'

'Wait for the return of Ramses and Ahsha.'

'And what if . . . ?'

'If they don't return?'

'Shouldn't we be considering that terrible possibility?'

'No.'

'You're sure about that?'

'I am.'

'Then I shall wait.'

'That's the best thing for you to do.'

To have been born in Sardinia, to have been the leader of a notorious gang of pirates, to have confronted Ramses, to owe his life to him and to have become the commander of his personal bodyguard: such was the extraordinary destiny of

31

Serramanna, a giant of a man with a swaggering mustachios. Ahmeni had once suspected him of treachery, before making amends and winning back his friendship.

The Sardinian would have loved to fight against the Hittites, break a few skulls and pierce a few chests. But Pharaoh had charged him with the protection of the royal family, and Serramanna had buckled down to this task with the same zeal as he had formerly shown in boarding rich merchant vessels.

In his eyes, Ramses was the greatest warlord ever, and Nefertari the most beautiful woman and the most inaccessible. The royal couple were a daily miracle and to serve them was now indispensable to the former pirate. Well paid, enjoying plentiful good food and the company of splendid women, he was ready to give his life for the continuity of the kingdom.

However, there was one shadow in the picture: his hunter's instinct gave him no peace. The return to the court of the king's sister seemed to him a move that might harm Ramses and Nefertari. He considered Dolora a liar and mentally unstable. In his opinion, the magus who had been manipulating her was still making use of her – though he had no proof of this.

Serramanna was making inquiries about the blonde woman whose body had been found in a house belonging to that traitor Shanaar, who had disappeared in a sandstorm while being transferred to the Khargeh prison settlement.

Dolora's explanations had been somewhat vague. The Sardinian knew that the murdered woman had been acting as the magus's medium, but it seemed improbable that Dolora could say no more about the unfortunate woman. Why this silence? Because she was trying to hide the truth. Dolora was playing at being the persecuted victim, the better to hide important facts. But, as she was once more in Nefertari's good books, Serramanna could not accuse her simply on the basis of suspicion.

Stubborn determination was one of a pirate's essential qualities. The sea could remain empty for days on end and then, suddenly, the prey would appear. But you still had to be sailing in the right direction, criss-crossing the areas abounding in booty. That was why he had sent out his sleuths, to Memphis as well as in Pi-Ramses, armed with faithful portraits of the young blonde woman who had been murdered.

Eventually, somebody was bound to talk.

6

The City of the Sun,* built by order of the heretic pharaoh Akhenaton, was now no more than a ghost town. The palaces, the nobles' dwellings, the workshops, the artisans' houses, all empty, the temples silent for ever, not a soul in the grand avenue along which the chariot of Akhenaton and Nefertiti used to drive, or in the formerly busy shopping streets and alleyways of the workers' district. All were now deserted.

On this desolate site, in the vast plain bordering the Nile, sheltered by the arc of a mountain range, Akhenaton had offered a domain to the One God, Aton, who was symbolized by the disc of the sun.

Now no one visited the forgotten capital any more. After the death of the king the inhabitants had returned to Thebes, taking with them precious objects, furniture, cooking utensils, archives . . . Here and there pieces of pottery lay around and, in a sculptor's studio, an unfinished head of Nefertiti.

As the years went by, the buildings became more and more dilapidated, the white paint flaked off, the plaster crumbled. The City of the Sun, built too quickly, could not stand up to

* Akhetaton, 'Land of the Light of Aton', in Middle Egypt, halfway between Memphis to the north and Thebes to the south. Its modern name is (Tell) el-Amarna.

the rain and sandstorms. The inscriptions on the stelae, carved by Akhenaton to proclaim the limits of the area sacred to Aton, were obliterated; the weather would render the hieroglyphs illegible and reduce to nothing the mystic's mad enterprise.

Tombs of the dignitaries of the regime had been hollowed out of the cliff, but no mummies rested in them. The sepulchres, like the city, had been abandoned, left without souls and without protection. No one dared venture there, since it was said that ghosts had taken possession of the place and would break the necks of any visitors who showed too much curiosity.

That was where Shanaar and the magus Ofir had found a hiding-place. They had made their home in the High Priest of Aton's tomb, whose hall of pillars had proved quite comfortable. On its walls were depicted temples and palaces, preserving the image of the lost splendour of the City of the Sun. The sculptor had immortalized Akhenaton and Nefertiti worshipping the sun disc, from which long rays fanned out, ending in hands offering life to the royal couple.

Shanaar often sat staring at the bas-reliefs representing Akhenaton, the incarnation of the sun in triumph. Shanaar was thirty-five, with a round, almost moon-shaped face, little brown eyes, podgy cheeks, thick lips and heavy bones. He hated this sun, the protector of his brother, Ramses. Ramses, the tyrant whom he had sought to bring down with the help of the Hittites; Ramses, who had sentenced him to exile in the prison settlement of the oases; Ramses, who wanted him to appear before a court of justice, from which he would emerge only to go to his death.

During his transfer from prison in Memphis to the oases, a sandstorm on the desert road had offered Shanaar the opportunity to escape. The hatred he felt for his brother, and his desire for revenge, had given him the strength to survive the ordeal. Shanaar had made his way to the only place where he would be safe, the heretic king's deserted city.

He had been welcomed there by his accomplice Ofir, head of the Hittite spy ring: Ofir, with his hawk-like profile, high cheekbones, prominent nose, thin lips, jutting chin, the man who was to make Shanaar the successor to Ramses.

He picked up a stone and threw it angrily at the statue of Akhenaton, damaging the monarch's crown.

'Curse him! And may all the pharaohs and their kingdom disappear for ever!'

Shanaar's dream had been shattered. He, who should by rights have reigned over an immense empire, was reduced to the condition of a pariah in his own country. Ramses should have been defeated at Kadesh, the Hittites should have invaded Egypt, Shanaar should have mounted the throne of the Two Lands, collaborated with the occupying force, then got rid of the Hittite emperor and become the sole master of all the lands from Anatolia to Nubia. Ramses the wrecker, Shanaar the saviour: that was what would have made the people of the region believe.

Shanaar turned to Ofir, who was sitting in the inner recesses of the tomb. 'Why did we fail?'

'A run of bad luck. Our fortunes will turn.'

'That's hardly a satisfactory answer, Ofir.'

'Although magic is an exact science, it cannot exclude the unpredictable.'

'And the unpredictable element was Ramses himself.'

'Your brother possesses exceptional qualities and a rare and fascinating capacity for resistance.'

'"Fascinating"? Are you perhaps falling under the spell of that despot?'

'I simply study him, the better to destroy him. Did not the god Amon come to his assistance during the battle of Kadesh?'

'Do you really believe that nonsense?'

'The world is not built solely of what is visible. Secret

forces circulate within it, and form the web of reality.'

Shanaar punched the wall where the sun disc, Aton, was depicted. 'Look where all your fine words have brought us! Here, in this tomb, far from power! We're alone and doomed to perish in poverty.'

'Not quite, since Aton's supporters feed us and guarantee our safety.'

'Aton's supporters! A band of madmen and mystics, prisoners of their illusions.'

'You're right, but they're useful to us.'

'Are you going to form them into an army capable of defeating Ramses?'

Ofir traced strange geometric figures in the dust.

'Ramses has defeated the Hittites,' Shanaar insisted. 'Your spy ring has been dismantled and I no longer have a single supporter. Apart from stagnating here, what future have I got?'

'Magic will help you to change it.'

Shanaar shrugged. 'You didn't succeed in doing away with Nefertari, and you weren't able to weaken Ramses.'

'You are unjust,' stated the magus. 'The ordeal I subjected the queen to left its scars.'

'Iset the Fair will bear Ramses another son and the king will adopt as many heirs as he wishes. No family worries will prevent my brother from reigning.'

'Blows will eventually wear him down.'

'Aren't you aware that a Pharaoh of Egypt is regenerated at the end of thirty years of his reign?'

'We haven't got there yet, Shanaar. The Hittites haven't given up the fight.'

'But the coalition they formed was destroyed at Kadesh.'

'Emperor Muwatallis is cunning and cautious; he knew the right moment to retreat and he'll organize a counter-offensive which will take Ramses by surprise.'

'I've had enough of dreaming, Ofir.'

In the distance, the sound of galloping horses could be heard.

Shanaar seized a sword. 'This isn't the time when the Atonians usually bring us food.' He rushed to the entrance of the tomb, which overlooked the ghost city and the plain. 'Two men.'

'Are they coming our way?'

'They've left the town and are making for the cliff – towards us! We'd better get out of this tomb and hide somewhere else.'

'No need to be precipitate; there are only two of them.' Ofir rose to his feet. 'Perhaps it is the sign I was waiting for, Shanaar. Take a good look.'

Shanaar recognized one of the supporters of Aton; the presence of his companion astounded him. 'Meba . . . Meba here?'

'He's my assistant and your ally.'

Shanaar put down the sword.

'No one at Ramses' court suspects Meba; today we must forget our differences.'

Shanaar did not reply. He felt nothing but contempt for Meba, whose sole ambition was to preserve his fortune and his comfort. When the diplomat had introduced himself as the new Hittite agent, Shanaar had not believed in the sincerity of his commitment.

The two horsemen dismounted at the foot of the path leading to the tomb of the High Priest of Aton. The supporter of the Sun God held the horses. Meba made his way to his accomplices' hideout. Anxiety nearly choked Shanaar. Suppose this man had betrayed them and was being closely followed by Pharaoh's police? But the horizon remained empty.

Meba was very tense and omitted the normal polite formulas. 'I'm taking a great risk in coming here. Why did you send me that message insisting that I meet you?'

38

Ofir's retort was stinging: 'You're under my orders, Meba. You will go where I tell you to go. What is the news?'

Shanaar was astonished. So, from the depths of his lair, the magus was continuing to direct his network.

'Nothing extraordinary. Frankly, the Hittite counter-attack hasn't been a success. Ramses has reacted vigorously and retaken Canaan.'

'Is he heading towards Kadesh?'

'I don't know.'

'You must be efficient, Meba, much more efficient, and give me more information. Have the Bedouin fulfilled their promises?'

'The rebellion seems general. But I have to be very cautious, so as not to arouse Ahmeni's suspicions.'

'You work at the Foreign Affairs secretariat, don't you?'

'Caution . . .'

'Is there a chance that you could get near little Kha?'

'Ramses' son? Yes, but why?'

'I need an object which is particularly dear to him, Meba, and I need it urgently.'

7

With his wife and son, Moses had left the land of Midian, which lay to the south of Edom and east of the Gulf of Aqaba. The Hebrew had been hiding there for a long time, and had emerged from this refuge to return to Egypt, against the advice of his father-in-law. Since he had been accused of murder, he was mad to give himself up to Pharaoh's police! He'd be imprisoned and condemned to death.

But no argument could shake Moses' determination. God had spoken to him and had commanded him to lead his Hebrew brethren out of Egypt, so that they could live by the true faith, in their own land. The task seemed impossible, but the prophet would have the strength to accomplish it.

His wife, Zipporah, had also tried to dissuade him. In vain. And so the little family had set out to travel towards the Delta. Zipporah followed her husband, who walked calmly, leaning on a large gnarled staff, never hesitating over the path to take.

When a cloud of sand announced the approach of a troop of horsemen, Zipporah clutched her son tightly in her arms and sheltered behind Moses. He was tall, bearded and broad-shouldered, with the build of an athlete.

'We must hide,' she begged him.

'It wouldn't be any use.'

'If they're Bedouin, they'll kill us; if they're Egyptians, they'll arrest you!'

40

'Don't be afraid.'

Moses stood still, thinking of the years he had spent studying at the Royal Academy in Memphis, when he had been taught the wisdom of the Egyptians and become a close friend of Prince Ramses, the future pharaoh. After holding a not unimportant post at the Mer-Ur harem, the Hebrew had been appointed overseer of the building site of Pi-Ramses, the new capital of the Two Lands. By entrusting Moses with this post, Ramses had made him one of the foremost personalities of the kingdom.

But Moses' mind was in turmoil. Ever since his youth, a fire had smouldered within him; and it was only when he encountered the burning bush, burning yet not consumed, that the pain had vanished. The Hebrew had finally discovered his mission.

The horsemen were Bedouin. At their head were Amos, bald and bearded, and Baduch, tall and thin: they were the two tribal chiefs who had lied to Ramses on the site of the battle of Kadesh, to lure him into a trap. Their men ranged themselves in a ring round Moses.

'Who are you?'

'My name is Moses. This is my wife and my son.'

'Moses ... Are you the friend of Ramses, the high dignitary who committed a crime and fled into the desert?'

'I am indeed.'

Amos leaped from his horse and embraced the Hebrew. 'Then we're on the same side! We too are fighting against Ramses, the man who was your friend and who now wants your head!'

'The king of Egypt is still my friend,' said Moses firmly.

'You're out of your mind! He's pursuing you with unrelenting hatred. Bedouin, Hebrews and nomads must ally themselves with the Hittites to bring down this despot. His strength has become the stuff of legend, Moses. Come with us and help us harass the Egyptian troops who are trying to invade Syria.'

'I am not travelling northwards, I'm going to the south.'

'To the south?' exclaimed Baduch suspiciously. 'Where do you want to go?'

'To Egypt, to Pi-Ramses.'

Amazed, Amos and Baduch exchanged glances.

'Are you joking?' asked Amos.

'No, that's the truth.'

'But you'll be arrested and executed!'

'Yahveh will protect me. I must deliver my people out of Egypt.'

'The Hebrews, out of Egypt . . . Have you gone mad?'

'That is the mission Yahveh has entrusted to me, and that is the mission I shall accomplish.'

Baduch dismounted in his turn. 'Don't move, Moses.'

The two chiefs moved away, to talk out of earshot of the Hebrew.

'He's crazy,' decided Baduch. 'He's gone mad from being too long in the desert.'

'You're wrong.'

'Wrong? Moses is a madman – it's obvious!'

'No, he's cunning and determined.'

'This poor wretch, lost in the desert with a wife and child . . . What a splendid dodge!'

'Yes, Baduch, splendid. Who'd ever suspect a wretch like him? But Moses is still very popular in Egypt, and he intends to stir up rebellion among the Hebrews.'

'He hasn't a hope of succeeding! Pharaoh's police will stop him.'

'If we help him, he could be useful to us.'

'Help him? How?'

'By getting him across the border and helping him obtain weapons for the Hebrews. They'll probably be wiped out but they'll have caused trouble in Pi-Ramses.'

Moses breathed deeply and filled his lungs with the Delta air;

although this land had become his enemy, it still cast its spell over him. He should by rights have hated it, but the fresh green of the farmlands and the pleasant palm groves filled him with wonder, reminding him of the dream he'd had as a young man, when he'd been the friend and confidant of the future Pharaoh of Egypt, the dream of spending a lifetime near Ramses, serving him, helping him to hand down the ideal of truth and justice that had nurtured the dynasties. But that ideal belonged to the past; from now on it was Yahveh who would guide Moses' steps.

Thanks to Baduch and Amos, the Hebrew and his wife and child had entered Egypt during the night, eluding the soldiers who patrolled the border between two forts. In spite of her fear, Zipporah had expressed neither criticism nor objections. Moses was her husband: she owed him obedience and would follow him wherever he wished to go.

At sunrise, as nature came back to life, Moses felt his hopes grow stronger. This was where he would wage his battle, whatever the forces ranged against him. Ramses would have to understand that the Hebrews demanded their freedom and were making manifest their wish to form a nation, in accordance with the will of God.

The little family halted in villages where, as was the custom, travellers were received kindly. The way Moses spoke proved he was of Egyptian stock, and this made contacts with the villagers easier. Travelling in stages, they eventually reached the outskirts of the capital.

'I built a good part of this city,' Moses told his wife.

'How big and beautiful it is! Are we going to live here?'

'For a time.'

'Where shall we lodge?'

'Yahveh will provide.'

Moses and his family entered the artisans' district, where intense activity reigned. The maze of alleyways astonished Zipporah, who was already missing the peaceful life of her oasis. People shouted to each other on all sides; carpenters, tailors and sandal-makers worked energetically. Donkeys laden with jars of meat, dried fish or cheeses passed by unhurriedly.

Beyond this district were the houses of the Hebrew brickmakers. Nothing had changed. Moses recognized every house, heard the familiar songs, and felt memories of rebellion and the enthusiasm of youth surging up within him. As he was lingering in a little square in the middle of which a well had been dug, an old brickmaker came and looked up into his face.

'You, fellow, I've seen you before. But . . . it's impossible! You can't be . . . not the famous Moses?'

'Yes, indeed I am.'

'Everyone thought you were dead!'

'They were wrong,' said Moses with a smile.

'In your time we brickmakers were better treated. Now those who work badly are made to go and find their own straw themselves. You'd have protested, you would! Just imagine having to go and find straw! And what argument it takes to get more pay!'

'Have you at least got somewhere to live?'

'I'd like a bigger place, but the Administration is slow in dealing with my request. In your day, you'd have helped me.'

'I will help you.'

The brickmaker looked at him suspiciously. 'Weren't you accused of some crime?'

'Yes, I was.'

'They say you killed the husband of Ramses' sister.'

'A blackmailer and a torturer,' Moses reminded him. 'I didn't mean to kill him but the quarrel got out of hand.'

'So, you really did kill him . . . But *I* understand, you know.'

'Will you agree to give me and my family shelter for the night?'

'You're welcome.'

*

As soon as Moses and his wife and child were asleep, the old brickmaker left his bed and walked in the dark to the door which opened on to the street.

It creaked as he opened it. The brickmaker stood still anxiously for several minutes. As soon as he was sure that Moses had not woken up, he slipped outside. By denouncing the criminal to the police, he would obtain a big reward.

He had gone only a few yards along the alleyway when a powerful hand pinned him against a wall.

'Where are you going, you bastard?'

'I . . . I was stifling, I needed air.'

'You intended to sell Moses, didn't you?'

'No, of course not!'

'I ought to strangle you.'

'Leave him,' ordered Moses, who had appeared in the doorway of the house. 'He's a Hebrew like us. Who are you, who comes to my assistance?'

'My name is Aaron.' The man was old but strong. His voice was deep and resonant.

'How did you know I was here?'

'Who wouldn't recognize you, in this district? The council of elders wishes to see you and to hear what you have to say.'

8

Benteshina, Prince of Amurru, was having a delightful dream. A young noblewoman from Pi-Ramses, completely naked, perfumed with myrrh, was creeping up his thighs like a voluptuous liana. Suddenly she hesitated and began to pitch and toss, like a ship about to capsize. Benteshina gripped her by the neck.

'My lord, my lord! Wake up!'

Opening his eyes, the prince discovered he was about to strangle his head steward. The first faint glow of dawn lit up the room.

'Why are you disturbing me so early?'

'Get up, I beg you, and look out of the window.'

Reluctantly Benteshina did as his servant recommended. He could scarcely heave his mass of flabby flesh across the room.

There was not a trace of mist over the sea; it promised to be a magnificent day.

'What is there to see?'

'At the entrance to the port, my lord!'

Benteshina rubbed his eyes. At the entrance to the port of Beirut, he saw three Egyptian warships.

'What about the land routes?'

'Blocked as well; an enormous Egyptian army is deployed. The city is besieged.'

'Is Ahsha in good condition?' asked Benteshina.

The steward looked down. 'He's been thrown into a dungeon, on your orders.'

'Bring him to me.'

Ramses himself had fed his two horses, Victory in Thebes and The Goddess Mut is Content. The two superb animals were never parted, associated in battle as in peace. Both enjoyed the monarch's caresses and unfailingly whinnied with pride when he congratulated them on their courage. They felt not the slightest fear in the presence of Invincible, the Nubian lion: hadn't they faced thousands of Hittite soldiers in the company of the great cat?

The general in command of the army's Ra division bowed to the king. 'Majesty, our plan of action has been carried out. Not a single inhabitant of Beirut will escape. We are ready to attack.'

'Intercept all the caravans that were intending to enter the city.'

'Are we to prepare for a siege?'

'Possibly. If Ahsha is still alive, we shall free him.'

'That would be fortunate, Majesty, but the life of one man . . .'

'The life of one man is sometimes very precious, General.'

Ramses spent the whole morning with his horses and his lion. Their calm seemed to him a good omen. In fact, before the sun reached its zenith, an officer brought the king the news he had been waiting for.

'Benteshina, Prince of Amurru, requests an audience.'

Benteshina wore an ample robe of multicoloured silk, which masked his portly figure, and he was perfumed with attar of roses. He was smiling and relaxed.

'Greetings to the Son of the Light, to the—'

'I do not feel inclined to listen to flattery from a traitor.'

The Prince of Amurru did not lose his apparent good humour. 'Our conversation must be constructive, Majesty.'

'In selling yourself to the Hittites, you made a bad choice.'

'I still have one decisive argument: your friend Ahsha.'

'Do you think that his presence in a dungeon will stop me sacking this city?'

'I'm sure of it. All peoples praise Ramses the Great's sense of friendship. Besides, a pharaoh who betrayed those close to him would provoke the wrath of the gods.'

'Is Ahsha still alive?'

'He is.'

'I demand proof.'

'Your Majesty will see his friend and minister for foreign affairs appear at the top of the main tower of my palace. I do not deny that Ahsha's stay in prison, for attempted flight, may have had some unfortunate physical consequences for him, but nothing serious.'

'What do you ask in exchange for his freedom?'

'Your pardon. When I hand over your friend, you will forget that I betrayed you a little bit, and you will issue a decree stating that you maintain your trust in me. That's asking a lot, I admit, but I must save my throne and my modest possessions. And oh, if you had the regrettable idea of keeping me prisoner, your friend would of course be executed.'

Ramses was silent for several minutes. Then, 'I need to think about it,' he said calmly.

Benteshina had only one fear: that reasons of state would come before friendship. Ramses' hesitation made him tremble.

'I need time to convince my generals,' the king explained. 'Do you think it easy to give up a victory and pardon a criminal?'

Benteshina was reassured. '"Criminal"? Isn't that putting it rather too strongly, Majesty? The politics of alliances is a difficult art. Since I am making honourable amends, why not forget the past? Egypt represents my future, and you can be sure I shall give proof of my loyalty. If I dared, Majesty . . .'

'What now?'

'I and the inhabitants of the city would look unfavourably on a blockade. We are accustomed to living well and the delivery of provisions is part of our pact. While waiting to be freed and for your decree to be drawn up, wouldn't Ahsha like to be well fed?'

Ramses rose to his feet. The interview was at an end.

'Ah, Majesty . . . if I might know how long it will take you to reflect . . . ?'

'A few days.'

'I am convinced we can come to an agreement which will be favourable to Egypt as well as to the province of Amurru.'

Ramses stood facing the sea, deep in meditation, with his lion at his feet. The waves broke near the king; dolphins sported far out to sea. The south wind blew strongly.

Setau sat down on the king's right.

'I don't like the sea,' he complained. 'There are no snakes and you can't even see the other shore.'

'Benteshina is trying to blackmail me.'

'And you're hesitating between Egypt and Ahsha.'

'Do you blame me?'

'I'd blame you if you weren't, but I know the solution you must choose, and I don't like it.'

'Have you got a plan in mind?'

'Would I disturb the meditations of the Lord of the Two Lands if I hadn't?'

'There mustn't be any risk to Ahsha.'

'You're asking a lot.'

'Have you a real chance of succeeding?'

'One, perhaps.'

*

Benteshina's steward saw to it that his master's endless wishes were satisfied. The Prince of Amurru drank heavily and would tolerate none but the finest wines. Although the palace cellars were constantly restocked, the countless banquets rapidly depleted them. So the steward waited impatiently for every delivery.

When the Egyptian troops besieged Beirut, he had been hoping for the arrival of a caravan delivering to the palace a hundred giant amphorae of red Delta wine. That was what Benteshina insisted on and nothing else would do. So the steward was delighted to see entering the main courtyard a stream of wagons loaded with giant wine amphorae. The blockade must have been raised. Thanks to his blackmail, Benteshina had defeated Ramses.

The steward hurried to meet the driver of the first wagon and give him his instructions: some of the jars to the cellar, others to the storeroom near the kitchen, the rest to an outhouse adjoining the banqueting hall. The unloading began, accompanied by songs and joking.

'Do you think we might perhaps have a taste?' the steward suggested to the leader of the convoy.

'Good idea.'

The two men entered the cellar. The steward bent over a jar, already imagining the fruity taste of the fine vintage wine. As he was stroking the round belly of the vessel, a violent blow on the back of his neck felled him to the ground.

The leader of the convoy, an officer of Ramses' army, helped Setau and the other members of the raiding party out of the jars. Armed with light battle-axes with hollowed-out backs, made from three jutting tenon joints sunk into the handles and solidly tied, they dispatched the Canaanite guards, who were not expecting an attack from inside.

While some of the raiders opened the main gate of the city to let in the footsoldiers of the Ra division, Setau hurried to Benteshina's apartments. When two Amurrites tried to bar his way, he freed some vipers, which were maddened by being long enclosed in a sack.

At the sight of the reptile Setau waved in front of him, Benteshina broke out in a cold sweat.

'Set Ahsha free or you die.'

Benteshina didn't need to be told twice. Shaking like a jelly and panting like an ox, he went himself to open the door of the room where Ahsha was imprisoned.

When he saw that his friend was in good health, Setau was so excited that he clumsily unclenched his fist, freeing the viper, which darted at Benteshina.

9

Tuya, the Mother of Pharaoh, was slender, with a thin, straight nose, an almost square chin, and large, stern, piercing almond eyes. She was nearing her fiftieth year but remained the guardian of tradition and the conscience of the kingdom of Egypt. As the head of a large staff, she gave advice rather than orders, but saw to it that everyone respected the values that had made the Egyptian monarchy a stable regime, the link between the visible and the Invisible. The official inscriptions referred to her as 'Mother of the God, She who Gave Birth to the Strong Bull, Ramses'. She lived for the memory of her dead husband, the Pharaoh Seti. Together they had built a strong, peaceful Egypt, which it was their son's duty to maintain on the path of prosperity.

Ramses had the same energy as his father, the same faith in his mission; and nothing mattered to him more than the happiness of his people. To save Egypt from invasion, he had had to resign himself to waging war against the Hittites. Tuya had approved her son's decision, for to compromise with evil led only to disaster. Fighting was the only acceptable stand. But the conflict was continuing and Ramses was taking endless risks.

Tuya prayed that Seti's soul, which had become a star, would protect the pharaoh. In her right hand she held a mirror, whose handle was shaped like a papyrus, the hieroglyph signifying 'to be verdant, young, in full bloom'. When this precious object was placed in a tomb, it ensured that its owner's soul would enjoy eternal youth. Tuya faced the bronze disc towards the sky and asked the mirror the secret of the future.

'May I trouble you?'

The Mother of Pharaoh turned round slowly. 'Nefertari.'

The Great Royal Wife, wearing a long white gown caught at the waist by a red girdle, was as beautiful as the goddesses painted on the walls of the eternal abodes in the Valleys of the Kings and Queens.

'Nefertari, do you bring me good news?'

'Ramses has freed Ahsha and retaken the province of Amurru. Beirut is once more under Egyptian control.'

The two women embraced.

'When will he return?'

'I don't know,' replied Nefertari.

While they talked, Tuya sat down at her dressing-table. With the tips of her fingers she massaged her face with a cream whose principal components were honey, red natron, powdered alabaster, ass's milk and seeds of fenugreek. This treatment removed wrinkles and toned up and rejuvenated the skin.

'You look worried, Nefertari.'

'I'm afraid that Ramses may decide to continue further.'

'Further north, towards Kadesh . . .'

'Towards a new trap laid for him by Muwatallis. By letting Ramses reconquer more or less easily the territories belonging to our zone of influence, he may be luring our army into that trap.'

The heads of the Hebrew tribes met in Aaron's large house, which was built of unbaked bricks. He had sworn everyone to silence; Moses' safety was at stake, as the Egyptian police must not know of his return.

Moses had remained popular; many hoped he would be able to restore some of their former pride to the little nation of brickmakers. But that was not the opinion of Libni, the leader appointed by his peers to maintain relative cohesion between the clans.

'Why have you returned, Moses?' asked the rough-voiced old man.

'On the mountain, I saw a bush that burned and yet was not consumed.'

'An illusion.'

'No, a sign of the divine presence.'

'Are you losing your mind, Moses?'

'God called to me from the midst of the bush and He spoke to me.'

The elders murmured.

'What did He say to you?'

'God has heard the cries and complaints of the children of Israel, who are in bondage.'

'Really, Moses, we are free workers not prisoners of war!'

'The Hebrews cannot conduct their affairs freely.'

'Of course we can! What are you getting at?'

'God said to me, "When you have led the people out of Egypt, you will worship the Lord your God on this mountain."'

The heads of the tribes exchanged looks of consternation.

'Out of Egypt!' exclaimed one of them. 'What does that mean?'

'God has seen the affliction of his people in Egypt. He wishes to deliver them and lead them to a vast and fertile land.'

Libni grew angry. 'Your exile has made you lose your reason, Moses. We have been settled here for years – you yourself were born in Egypt – and this has become our fatherland.'

'I spent several years in the land of Midian, I kept the flocks there, I got married there and had a son. I was convinced that my life had taken a definite turn, but God decided otherwise.'

'You were in hiding after committing a crime.'

'I killed an Egyptian, it is true, because he himself was threatening to kill a Hebrew.'

'We have nothing to reproach Moses with,' interrupted the head of one of the tribes. 'It's up to us to protect him now.'

The other members of the council approved.

'If you wish to live here,' declared Libni, 'we will hide you. But you must give up your crazy plans.'

'I shall find a way to convince you, one by one if necessary, for such is the will of God.'

'I have no intention of leaving Egypt,' declared the young head of one tribe. 'We own houses and gardens here; the pay of the best brickmakers has just been increased, everyone has enough to eat. Why should we give up this comfort?'

'Because I must lead you to the Promised Land.'

'You aren't our leader,' objected Libni, 'and you're not going to tell us what to do.'

'You will obey, because God insists.'

'Do you know who you're speaking to?'

'I didn't mean to offend you, Libni, but I have no right to hide my intentions. What man would be vain enough to believe that his will is stronger than the will of God?'

'If you really are his messenger, you'll have to prove it.'

'There will be plenty of proof. Have no doubt about that.'

Ahsha lay on a soft couch, letting Lotus massage him, her gentle touch dispelling his aches and pains. In spite of her apparent frailty, the pretty Nubian was surprisingly energetic.

'How do you feel now?' she asked.

'Much better. But towards my lower back the pain is still unbearable.'

'You'll just have to bear it,' growled Setau, who had just entered Ahsha's tent.

'Your wife is divine.'

'Maybe, but she *is* my wife.'

'Setau! You weren't imagining—'

'Diplomats are cunning liars, and you're the worse of the lot. Get up. Ramses is waiting for you.'

Ahsha turned to Lotus. 'Will you help me?'

Setau grabbed Ahsha's arm and hauled him roughly to his feet. 'You are completely better. No more massage needed!' The snake-charmer held out a kilt and a shirt to the diplomat. 'Hurry up. The king hates being kept waiting.'

After appointing a new Prince of Amurru, a Canaanite educated in Egypt, whose loyalty would perhaps not be as fickle as Benteshina's, Ramses had proceeded to a series of appointments in Phoenicia and Palestine. He insisted that the princes, mayors and village chiefs should be natives, who had to swear an oath to respect their alliance with Egypt. If they went back on their word, the Egyptian army would intervene immediately. To this end, Ahsha had drawn up a system of observation and information-gathering on which he pinned great hopes: a light military presence, but a network of well-paid correspondents. As head of the Egyptian diplomatic service, he was a great believer in espionage.

On a low table, Ramses had unrolled a map of the whole region. The efforts of his troops had been rewarded: Canaan, Amurru and southern Syria once more formed a vast buffer zone between Egypt and Hatti. This was Ramses' second victory over the Hittites. It remained for him to make a vital decision about the future of the Two Lands.

Setau and Ahsha, the latter less elegant than usual, made their entrance into the council tent, where the generals and senior officers had already taken their places.

'Have all the enemy strongholds been dismantled?'

'Yes, Majesty,' said the commander of the Ra division. 'The last one, Shalom, fell yesterday.'

'"Shalom" means "peace",' explained Ahsha. 'And at present peace reigns in the area.'

'Should we press on to the north,' asked the king, 'seize Kadesh and strike a fatal blow at the Hittites?'

'Such is the wish of the senior officers,' declared the general. 'We must complete our victory by exterminating the barbarians.'

'We have no chance of succeeding,' advised Ahsha. 'The Hittites once again retreated as fast as we advanced. Their troops are still intact and they are preparing traps from which we'd escape much weakened.'

'With Ramses at our head,' exclaimed the general enthusiastically, 'we shall conquer.'

'You know nothing about the terrain. The Hittites would crush us on the high plateaux of Anatolia, in the gorges, in the forests. At Kadesh, thousands of footsoldiers would die and we could not even be sure of seizing the fortress.'

'The unfounded fears of a diplomat. This time we are prepared!'

'You may withdraw,' ordered Ramses. 'You will know my decision tomorrow.'

10

Thanks to Aaron's hospitality, Moses spent several peaceful weeks in the brickmakers' district. His wife and son went about freely and were intrigued to discover the bustling life of the Egyptian capital. They quickly fitted into the Hebrew tribe and before long were meeting Egyptians, Asians, Palestinians, Nubians and other inhabitants of Pi-Ramses, who endlessly rubbed shoulders in the narrow streets of the city.

Moses, for his part, lived as a recluse. He had asked several times to be heard again by the council of elders and had not repudiated his original declarations in the face of the incredulity and criticisms of the tribal elders.

'Is your soul still tormented?' asked Aaron.

'Not since the burning bush appeared to me.'

'No one here believes you have encountered God.'

'When a man knows the mission he must accomplish on this earth, he is no longer assailed by doubt. From now on, my path is laid down, Aaron.'

'But you are alone, Moses!'

'It only seems that way. My convictions will eventually change people's minds.'

'In Pi-Ramses, the Hebrews want for nothing. Where will you find food in the desert?'

'God will provide.'

'You have the calibre of a leader, but you are on the wrong track. Change your name and your appearance, forget your crazy plans, resume your place among your people. You will grow old in peace, honoured and untroubled, at the head of a large family.'

'That is not my destiny, Aaron.'

'Then change the one that you've dreamed up.'

'I am not responsible for it.'

'Why ruin your life like this, when happiness is within your reach?'

There was a knock at the door of Aaron's home. 'Open up! Police!'

Moses smiled. 'You see, Aaron? I'm not being given the choice.'

'You must run!'

'This door is the only way out.'

'I'll defend you.'

'No, Aaron.'

Moses opened the door himself.

Serramanna, the Sardinian giant, looked in astonishment at the Hebrew. 'So, the man wasn't lying. You really are back!'

'Do you want to come in and share our meal?'

'A Hebrew denounced you, Moses, a brickmaker who was afraid of losing his job because of your presence in this district. Follow me. I have to take you to prison.'

Aaron intervened. 'Moses must be tried.'

'He will be.'

'Unless you do away with him before the trial.'

Serramanna seized Aaron by the collar of his tunic. 'Are you calling me a murderer?'

'You have no right to lay a hand on me!'

The Sardinian let him go. 'That's true. But neither have you the right to insult me.'

'If Moses is arrested, he'll be executed.'

'The law applies to everyone, even to Hebrews.'

'You must flee, Moses, return to the desert!' begged Aaron.

'You know very well that we shall leave together.'

'You'll never get out of that prison.'

'God will help me.'

'That's enough. Come on,' demanded Serramanna. 'Don't make me tie your hands.'

Seated in a corner of his prison cell, Moses watched the ray of light which filtered through the bars, shining on the floor of beaten earth trampled by prisoners' feet. Thousands of motes of dust danced in the sunbeam.

The fire of the burning bush, the energy of Yahveh's mountain, would burn for ever in Moses. His past was forgotten, forgotten his wife and child; the only thing that now counted was the exodus, the departure of the Hebrew people for the Promised Land.

A crazy hope for a man locked up in a cell in the great prison of Pi-Ramses, a man whom Egyptian justice would condemn to death for premeditated murder, or, at best, to forced labour in the oasis prison settlement. In spite of his confidence in Yahveh, Moses occasionally found himself doubting. How would God set about freeing him to allow him to carry out his mission?

The Hebrew was dozing when distant shouts roused him from his torpor. They grew louder by the minute, until they became deafening. The whole city seemed in an uproar.

Ramses the Great was back.

No one had been expecting him for several weeks, but it was indeed him, superb in his chariot drawn by Victory in Thebes and The Goddess Mut is Content, whose heads were adorned with red plumes tipped with blue. On the right of his chariot walked Invincible, gazing at the citizens who crowded along the route like curious animals. Wearing the Blue

Crown, with the golden uraeus at the front, and the ritual tunic on which were painted blue-green wings that placed the sovereign under the protection of Isis, the female falcon, Ramses was radiant.

With one voice, the footsoldiers struck up the song that had become traditional: 'Ramses' arm is powerful, his heart is valiant. He is a peerless archer, a strong bulwark protecting his soldiers, a flame which consumes his enemies.' He appeared as the one chosen by the Divine Light, the falcon who had won impressive victories.

Generals, officers of the chariot corps and infantry, army scribes, private soldiers – all had donned their ceremonial uniforms to parade behind the standard-bearers. Acclaimed by the crowd, the soldiers' thoughts were of their leave and the extra pay which would let them forget the rigours of war. In military life, there was no better moment than the return home, especially when it was in triumph.

Caught unawares, the gardeners had not had time to deck with flowers the grand avenue of Pi-Ramses leading to the temples of Ptah, the god of creation through the Word, and of Sekhmet, the terrifying goddess who had the power both to destroy and to heal. But the cooks were bustling around roasting geese, joints of beef and pork, filling baskets with dried fish, vegetables and fruit. Jars of beer and wine were being brought out of storerooms. Pastrycooks were hurriedly baking cakes. Fashionable folk had put on festive garments and servants were perfuming their mistresses' hair.

At the end of the procession walked several hundred prisoners, Asians, Canaanites, Palestinians and Syrians; some had their hands tied behind their backs, others walked freely, their wives and children at their sides. Donkeys were loaded with bundles containing their meagre possessions. The prisoners were to be taken to the employment secretariat in the capital, which would allocate them to the lands and building sites of the temples. They would serve their term of imprisonment as workmen or agricultural labourers, and then be allowed to choose whether to become part of Egyptian society or return to their own countries.

Was this peace or merely a truce? Had Pharaoh finally crushed the Hittites, or had he returned to gather his strength in order to leave again for the war? Those who knew nothing were the ones with the most to say: according to them, Emperor Muwatallis was dead, the citadel of Kadesh had been captured, the Hittite capital destroyed . . . Everyone was now waiting for the reward ceremony, when Ramses and Nefertari would appear at the window of the palace to distribute gold necklaces to the brave soldiers.

To everyone's astonishment, Ramses avoided the palace and made his way to the Temple of Sekhmet. He alone had observed in the sky a tiny cloud which was rapidly growing bigger and blacker. The horses became nervous, the lion growled. A storm was brewing.

Joy gave way to fear. If the terrifying goddess was unleashing the wrath of the clouds, it must be a sign that war threatened the realm of Egypt and that Ramses must leave again without delay for the battlefield. The soldiers stopped singing. Everyone was aware that Pharaoh was beginning a new fight to appease Sekhmet and prevent her from sending a wave of calamities and hardships to flood the country.

Ramses alighted, patted the heads of his horses and his lion and then stood meditating in the courtyard of the temple. The cloud had split apart and multiplied tenfold – a hundredfold. The whole sky grew dark and the light of the sun was gradually hidden.

Putting aside the fatigue of his journey, forgetting the festivities which Pi-Ramses was making ready to celebrate, the monarch prepared to meet the Terrifying One. He alone could dispel her anger.

Ramses pushed open the great gate of gilded cedar and entered the Hall of Purity, where he set down the Blue Crown.

Then he advanced slowly between the pillars of the first hall, crossed the threshold of the Hall of Mysteries and continued towards the innermost shrine.

And then he saw her, luminous in the half-darkness. Her long white gown shone like a sun, the perfume of her ritual wig delighted the heart, the nobility of her posture equalled that of the stones of the temple.

Nefertari's voice rang out, sweet as honey. She uttered the words of veneration and appeasement, dating from the earliest days of Egyptian civilization, which transformed the Terrifying One into the Mild and Loving One. Ramses raised his hands, palms up, towards the lion-headed statue and read the incantations carved on the walls.

When the litany was over the queen, the magical being through whom the transmutation had been performed, presented the king with the Red Crown of Lower Egypt, the White Crown of Upper Egypt and the sceptre called 'Mastery of Power'. Wearing the double crown and holding the sceptre in his right hand, Ramses bowed to the beneficial energy present in the statue.

When the royal couple emerged from the temple, strong sunlight flooded the sky and the Turquoise City. The storm had been dispelled.

11

Immediately after the golden necklaces for bravery had been distributed, Ramses went to visit Homer, the Greek poet who had decided to settle in Egypt to compose his great works and end his days there. His comfortable home, near the palace, was surrounded by a garden, whose finest ornament, a lemon tree, delighted the failing eyes of the white-bearded old man. When the king approached him, Homer was smoking, as was his wont, sage leaves stuffed into a pipe made from a large snail shell, and was drinking a cup of wine flavoured with aniseed and coriander.

The poet rose, leaning on a gnarled staff.

'Don't get up, Homer.'

'When people no longer greet Pharaoh correctly, it will be the end of civilization.'

The two men sat down on garden chairs.

'Majesty, tell me if I was correct to write these lines: "Whether one fights zealously in the forefront of the battle or remains in the background, the benefit is the same. The same honour is reserved for the craven as for the brave. Is it for nothing that my heart has so often been exposed to such great danger? Is it for nothing that I have risked my life in so many battles?"'

'No, Homer.'

'So, you have returned as a conqueror.'

'The Hittites have been pushed back to their traditional positions. Egypt will not be invaded.'

'Let us celebrate the event, Majesty. I have had a remarkable wine delivered to me.'

Homer's cook brought out a Cretan amphora with a narrow neck, which let out only a thin trickle of wine, mixed with sea water which had been collected at night at the summer solstice when a north wind was blowing, and kept for three years.

'The text of *The Battle of Kadesh* is finished,' said Homer. 'Your private secretary, Ahmeni, took it down from dictation and gave it to the sculptors.'

'It will be engraved on the walls of the temples and will proclaim the victory of order over chaos.'

'Alas, Majesty, the fight must be endlessly renewed. It is in the nature of chaos to want to devour order.'

'That is the reason why the Pharaonic institution was established. It alone can consolidate the reign of Ma'at.'

'Whatever you do, don't modify it. I fully intend to live a long and happy life in this country.'

Hector, Homer's black and white cat, jumped on to the poet's lap and sharpened his claws on his tunic.

'Many, many days' march separate your capital from that of the Hittites. Will that distance be sufficient to keep the shadows at bay?'

'As long as the breath of life sustains me, that is what I shall strive to do.'

'War is never over. How many times will you still have to ride out to battle?'

When Ramses left Homer's dwelling, he found Ahmeni waiting for him. Paler than usual, thinner, with a little less hair, Ahmeni looked so frail that he seemed to be falling apart. Stuck behind his ear was a writing-brush he had forgotten.

'I would like to consult you most urgently, Majesty.'

'Is there a problem with one of your dossiers?'

'Not with a dossier, no . . .'

'Give me a few minutes to see my family.'

'I'm prepared to accept that your first priority is a certain number of ceremonies and audiences laid down by protocol, but there is something much more important: *he* has returned.'

'Are you talking about . . . ?'

'Yes, about Moses.'

'Is he in Pi-Ramses?'

'You must admit that Serramanna was right to arrest him. If he had left him at liberty, it would have made a mockery of justice.'

'Are you saying that Moses has been imprisoned?'

'He had to be.'

'Bring him to me immediately.'

'Impossible, Majesty. Pharaoh cannot intervene in a judicial matter, even if a friend is incriminated.'

'But we have proof of his innocence!'

'It is essential to go through the normal procedure. If Pharaoh were not the first servant of Ma'at and of justice, there would be nothing but disorder and confusion in this land.'

'You are a true friend, Ahmeni.'

Young Kha was copying a celebrated text which generations of scribes before him had copied:

By way of heirs, scribes who have attained knowledge leave behind books of wisdom. The writing-palette is their beloved son. Their books are their pyramids, their brush is their child, the stone covered with hieroglyphs their wife. Monuments disappear, sand covers the stelae, tombs are forgotten; but the names of the scribes who have lived with wisdom endure because of the influence of their works. Become a scribe, and engrave on your heart this thought: a book is more use than the most solid wall. It will serve you as a temple even after your death; your name will live on in men's mouths through the book; it will be stronger than a well-built house.

The youngster did not entirely agree with the author of these maxims; true, what is written passes down the ages, but that was also the case with the abodes of eternity and the stone sanctuaries that master craftsmen had built. The scribe who wrote these lines had lavished excessive praise on the excellence of his own profession. So Kha had sworn to be both a scribe and a master builder, so as not to limit his mental faculties.

Since Ramses had made him confront death in the shape of a cobra, Kha had greatly matured and had finally put away childish games for good. What interest did a wooden horse on wheels have, compared with the mathematical problem set down by the scribe Ahmes in a fascinating papyrus, given him by Nefertari? Ahmes likened the circle to a square of which one side represented $\frac{8}{9}$ of its diameter, thus obtaining a harmonic mean based on the value 3.16.* As soon as he had the opportunity, Kha was going to study the geometry of monuments, to be able to understand the secrets of the master builders.

'May I interrupt Prince Kha's reflections?' asked Meba.

The boy did not look up. 'If you think fit . . .'

For some time now, the deputy minister for foreign affairs had been coming often to talk with Kha, who detested his haughty, aristocratic manner and sophisticated appearance, but appreciated his culture and knowledge of literature.

* The practical application of the famous *pi* (π) according to the Rhind papyrus.

'Working again, Prince?'

'What better way of developing the mind?'

'That's a very serious question on such young lips! Basically, you are right. As a scribe and the king's son, you will give orders to dozens of servants, you will handle neither plough nor pick, your hands will always remain soft, you will never have to undertake hard tasks or bear heavy burdens. You will live in a magnificent villa, your stables will be full of splendid horses, every day you will change into fresh luxurious garments; you will travel in a comfortable litter and you will enjoy Pharaoh's trust.'

'Many lazy, well-to-do scribes live like that, it is true; but I hope to be able to read difficult texts, help in drafting the rituals and be admitted as bearer of offerings in the processions.'

'Those are modest ambitions, Prince Kha.'

'On the contrary, Meba, they demand long, hard work.'

'Surely a greater destiny is promised to Ramses' first-born son?'

'The hieroglyphs are my guide; they have never lied.'

Meba was worried by the words of this twelve-year-old. He felt as though he were talking to an experienced scribe, sure of himself and indifferent to flattery. He said, 'Life is more than just work and austerity.'

'I don't see my life as any different, Meba. Are you saying that's wrong?'

'No, of course not.'

'You occupy an important post. Do you enjoy so much spare time for recreation?'

The diplomat avoided Kha's eyes. 'I am kept very busy, since Egypt's international policies demand great competence.'

'But my father makes the decisions, doesn't he?'

'True, but my colleagues and I work hard to facilitate his task.'

'I'd like to know the details of your work.'

'It's very complicated and I don't know if—'

'I'll try to understand.'

The arrival of Meritamon, Kha's lively little sister, who came skipping merrily along, relieved the diplomat.

'Are you playing with my brother?' the child asked.

'No, I came to bring him a present.'

Kha looked up, showing interest. 'What are you talking about?'

'About this brush-holder, Prince.'

Meba produced a pretty miniature pillar of hollowed-out gilded wood, containing twelve brushes of different sizes.

'That's . . . that's very beautiful!' observed the prince, putting down on a stool the worn brush he was using.

'Can I see?' asked Meritamon.

'You must be very careful,' Kha said seriously. 'These things are very fragile.'

'Will you let me write with it?'

'Providing you pay attention and take pains not to make mistakes.'

Kha gave his sister a piece of used papyrus and a new brush, which he had dipped in the ink, and watched the little girl carefully trace the hieroglyphs. Occupied with their task, the two children forgot about Meba.

This was the moment he had been waiting for. He stole Kha's used brush and slipped away.

12

The whole night through, Iset the Fair had dreamed of the reed hut where she and Ramses had first made love. That was where they had concealed their passion, with no thought for the future, living only for the moment in the enjoyment of their insatiable desire.

Iset had never wished to become Queen of Egypt. The duties were beyond her: Nefertari alone was capable of carrying them out. But how could she forget Ramses? How could she forget the love that continued to blaze in her heart? While he was away waging war, she was worried to death. She could not concentrate, she had no inclination to put on her make-up, she wrapped herself in any old dress and went barefoot.

No sooner was he back than this worry disappeared. And with her beauty regained, Iset would have seduced the most indifferent man who caught sight of her, trembling and anxious, in the palace corridor which led from Ramses' office to his private apartments. When he passed that way, she would dare to address him . . .

No, she felt like running away. If she troubled Ramses, he would send her back to the provinces and she would be condemned never to see him again. That punishment would be unbearable.

When the king appeared, Iset's legs nearly gave way

beneath her. She did not have the strength to run away and could not take her eyes off Ramses, whose power and imposing presence were those of a god.

'What are you doing here, Iset?'

'I wanted to tell you, I have borne you another son.'

'The nurse has shown him to me: Meneptah is a fine child.'

'I shall love him as much as Kha.'

'I am sure of it.'

'For you, I shall always be the plot of earth which you till, the lake in which you bathe . . . Do you want more sons, Ramses?'

'The institution of Royal Children will provide them.'

'Ask me for anything you wish. My body and soul belong to you.'

'You are wrong, Iset. No human being can be the owner of another human being.'

'Nevertheless, I am yours and you can take me in the hollow of your hand like a fledgling fallen from its nest. Deprived of your warmth, I would wither away.'

'I love Nefertari, Iset.'

'Nefertari is a queen, I am only a woman. Could you not love me with a different love?'

'With her, I am building a world. Only the Great Royal Wife shares this secret.'

'Will you allow me to stay here in the palace?' Iset's voice had become very faint. Her whole future depended on Ramses' answer.

'You will bring up Kha, Meneptah and my daughter Meritamon here.'

The Cretan, one of the body of mercenaries under Serramanna's command was making inquiries in the villages of Middle Egypt near the deserted city of the heretic pharaoh. Akhenaton, a former pirate like his chief, was growing used to Egyptian life and the material advantages it offered.

Although he missed the sea, he consoled himself by sailing up and down the Nile in fast little boats and amused himself by dodging the snares of the river with its sudden, unpredictable reactions. Even an experienced sailor had to show humility in the face of the current, the sandbanks hidden under shallow water and the herds of angry hippopotami.

The Cretan had shown hundreds of villagers the portrait of the young blonde woman who had been murdered. Without success. To tell the truth, he was carrying out his mission without enthusiasm, convinced that the victim came from Pi-Ramses or Memphis. Seramanna had sent his emissaries to all the provinces, in the hope that one of them would pick up a vital clue, but luck hadn't favoured the Cretan. He was simply taking advantage of the peaceful countryside, living according to the rhythm of the seasons. He wouldn't be the one to receive the reward promised by the Sardinian; nevertheless he carried out his task conscientiously, delighted to be able to spend many hours in welcoming taverns. Another two or three days of investigation and he would return to Pi-Ramses, unsuccessful, but pleased with his stay.

Seated at a good table, the Cretan watched the girl who was serving the beers. Laughing and saucy, she liked to provoke the customers. He decided to try his luck.

He caught at the sleeve of her tunic. 'I fancy you, my dear.'

'And who might you be?'

'A man.'

She burst out laughing. 'That's what you all boast of!'

'But I can prove it.'

'Oh, yes? How?'

'In my own way.'

'That's what you all say.'

'Ah, but I can act.'

The serving-girl ran a finger over her lips. 'You'd better look out. I don't like braggarts and it takes a lot to satisfy me.'

'That's lucky; that's my worst fault too.'

'You almost tempt me, fellow.'

'Suppose we did something about it?'

'What do you take me for?'

'For what you are: a pretty girl who'd like to make love to an enterprising man.'

'Where were you born?'

'On the island of Crete.'

'Are you . . . a decent fellow?'

'In love, I give as much as I take.'

They found themselves in a barn in the middle of the night. Neither of them had much use for preliminaries, so they flung themselves at each other with a passion that was appeased only after several assaults. Sated at last, they lay side by side.

'You remind me of someone,' he said. 'Your face is like that of a person I'd very much like to find.'

'Who's that?'

The Cretan showed the serving-girl the portrait of the young blonde woman.

'I know her.'

'Does she live around here?'

'She used to live in the little village at the edge of the abandoned city, near the desert. I saw her at the market, many months ago.'

'What's her name?'

'I don't know. I never spoke to her.'

'Did she live alone?'

'No, there was an old fellow with her, a sort of sorcerer who still believed in the accursed pharaoh's lies. Nobody went near them.'

Unlike the other villages in the area, this one could hardly be described as neat and tidy: squalid houses, cracked façades, flaking paint, neglected gardens. Who could possibly want to live here? The Cretan ventured down the main street, which was filled with refuse on which goats were feeding.

A wooden shutter banged. A little girl ran off, clutching a rag doll. She stumbled, and the Cretan caught her by the wrist.

'Where does the sorcerer live?'

The child struggled.

'If you don't answer me, I'll take your dolly away.'

She pointed to a low house with wooden bars over the windows; the door was shut. Letting go of the little girl, the Cretan ran towards the wretched house and shoved the door open with his shoulder.

The square room with its floor of beaten earth was plunged in semi-darkness. An old man lay dying on a bed of palm leaves.

'Police,' said the Cretan. 'You've nothing to fear.'

'What . . . what do you want?'

'Tell me who this young woman is.'

The policeman showed the old man the portrait.

'Lita . . . it's my little Lita . . . She believed she belonged to the heretic's family . . . and he took her away.'

'Who are you talking about?'

'A foreigner . . . a foreign sorcerer who stole Lita's soul.'

'What's his name?'

'He's come back . . . hiding in the tombs . . . in the tombs, I'm sure.'

The old man's head rolled to one side. He was still breathing, but he could no longer speak.

The Cretan was daunted. The dark entrances to the abandoned tombs looked like the mouths of hell. You'd surely have to be some sort of demon to decide to take refuge here. Perhaps the old man had lied to him? But it was his duty to follow up this trail. With a little luck he'd lay his hands on Lita's murderer, take him back to Pi-Ramses and get the reward.

In spite of that pleasant prospect, the Cretan felt uneasy. He would have preferred to fight in the fresh air, confront several pirates out at sea, lay about him out in the open. The thought of having to enter these sepulchres was unnerving, but he didn't draw back.

He climbed up a steep slope and ventured into the first tomb, which had a fairly high ceiling and walls decorated with figures paying tribute to Akhenaton and Nefertiti. Step by step he advanced to the end of the cave, but discovered neither mummy nor any trace of human presence. No demons attacked him.

Reassured, he explored a second tomb, as disappointing as the first. The rock, of poor quality, was crumbling. The scenes carved here would certainly not last for centuries. Bats were disturbed and flew off.

The old man who had informed him must have been delirious. Nevertheless, he decided to examine another two or three large tombs before leaving this deserted site. Here, everything was well and truly dead.

He walked along below the cliff overhanging the plain where the City of the Sun had been built, then entered the tomb of Merire, the High Priest of Aton. The reliefs here were well cared for; the Cretan stood admiring the depictions of the royal couple, lit up by the rays of the sun.

Behind him came a slight sound of footsteps. Before the policeman had time to turn round, the magus Ofir slit his throat.

13

Meba had closed his eyes. When he opened them he saw the Cretan's body lying on the ground.

'You had no right, Ofir, you had no right—'

'Stop moaning, Meba.'

'You've just killed a man!'

'And you're witness to a murder.'

Ofir's look was so full of menace that the diplomat shrank back into the recesses of the tomb. He wanted to escape from those incredibly cruel eyes, which followed him into the darkness.

'I know who this snooper is,' declared Shanaar. 'He's one of the mercenaries paid by Serramanna to protect Ramses.'

'A policeman on our track . . . The Sardinian must have been wondering about Lita and trying to discover her identity. The fact that this sleuth turned up here proves that a vast search operation is in progress.'

'We're no longer safe in this accursed city,' concluded Shanaar.

'Don't let's be pessimistic. This busybody won't talk.'

'All the same, he did manage to get to us. Serramanna will do the same.'

'Only one person could have let on about where we were hiding: Lita's guardian, the man the villagers think is a sorcerer. The old fool is dying, but he's still strong enough to betray us. I'll see to him this evening.'

Meba felt obliged to intervene. 'You're not going to commit another murder!'

'Come here out of the shadows,' ordered Ofir.

Meba hesitated.

'Hurry up.'

The diplomat approached. A nervous tic twisted his lips. 'Don't touch me, Ofir!'

'You are our ally and under my orders, and don't you forget it.'

'True, but these murders . . .'

'We aren't in your comfortable secretariat now. You're part of a spy ring whose mission is to oppose Ramses' power – to destroy it, in fact, and allow the Hittites to conquer Egypt. Do you really think a bit of diplomatic play-acting is all that's needed? One day you too may have to kill an opponent who threatens your safety.'

'I'm a high official and I—'

'You're an accessory to the murder of this policeman, Meba, whether you like it or not.'

Once more the diplomat found himself looking at the Cretan's body. 'I never thought it would come to this.'

'Well, now you know.'

'We were interrupted by this snooper,' Shenaar reminded them. 'Did you succeed, Meba?'

'That's why I took the risk of coming back to this accursed city! Yes, I succeeded.'

The magus's voice became soft and winning. 'Nice work, my friend. We're proud of you.'

'I keep my promises. Don't forget yours.'

'The future power will not forget you, Meba. Show us the treasure you stole.'

The diplomat produced Kha's brush. 'The prince used this to write with.'

'Excellent,' pronounced Ofir, 'really excellent.'

'What are you going to do with it?'

'With this object, I shall be able to tap into Kha's energy and turn it against him.'

'Surely you don't mean—'

'Ramses' elder son is one of our direct opponents. Every ordeal which weakens the royal couple is good for our cause.'

'Kha is only a child!'

'He's the pharaoh's elder son.'

'No, Ofir, not a child!'

'You have chosen your side, Meba. It's too late now to draw back.' The magus held out his hand. 'Give me that.'

The diplomat's hesitation amused Shanaar. He hated this coward so much that he was ready to strangle him with his own hands.

Meba slowly handed the brush to Ofir. 'Is it really necessary to take it out on the youngster?'

'Go back to Pi-Ramses,' ordered the magus, 'and don't ever come here again.'

'Will you be staying long in this tomb?'

'As long as I need to make the spell work.'

'And then?'

'Don't be too inquisitive, Meba. I'll contact you.'

'I'm worried that my position in the capital may become untenable.'

'Just keep your head and all will be well.'

'What must I do?'

'Do your usual work. My instructions will arrive when the time comes.'

The diplomat made to leave the tomb, then turned round again. 'Think about it, Ofir. If his son is touched, Ramses will be furious and—'

'Go, Meba.'

From the entrance to the sepulchre, Ofir and Shanaar watched their accomplice descend the slope and mount his horse which had been hidden behind a ruined villa.

'We can't rely on that coward,' said Shanaar. 'He's like a maddened rat, trying in vain to find the way out of its cage. Why not get rid of him immediately?'

'As long as Meba occupies an official position, he'll be useful to us.'

'And what if it occurs to him to reveal the place where we are hiding?'

'Do you suppose I haven't thought of that?

Since Ramses' return Nefertari had had but few moments of intimacy with her husband. Ahmeni, the vizier, ministers and high priests had laid siege to the sovereign's office, and the queen herself continued to reply to the petitions of scribes, heads of workshops, tax collectors and other officials belonging to her House.

She was often sorry that she had not become a musician in the service of a temple; there she would have lived peacefully, far from the turmoil of day-to-day existence; but the Queen of Egypt had no right to seek that refuge and must carry out her duties with no thought for her fatigue or the burden of trying events.

Thanks to Tuya's constant assistance, Nefertari had learned the art of government. During the seven years of his reign, Ramses had spent many months in foreign parts and on fields of battle. The young queen had had to draw on her own unsuspected inner ressources in order to support the weight of the crown and celebrate the rites that maintained the essential link between the fraternity of the gods and the community of men.

The fact that she had no time to think of herself did not displease Nefertari; the day consisted of more tasks than there were hours, and it was well thus. True, she rarely saw Kha and Meritamon and she missed those irreplaceable moments in which a child's awareness developed. Although Kha and Meneptah were the children of Ramses and Iset the Fair, she loved them as much as her own daughter, Meritamon. Ramses had been right to ask Iset to supervise the upbringing of the three children. Between the two women there was neither rivalry nor enmity; not being able to bear more children herself, Nefertari had begged Ramses to lie with Iset, so that the latter could bear him offspring from among whom he could choose his successor. But after the birth of Meneptah, Ramses had decided to have no more intercourse with Iset and to adopt an unlimited number of 'Royal Children', who would proclaim the fertility of the royal couple.

The love the queen felt for Ramses far surpassed their physical union and its pleasures. It was not only the man who had charmed her, but above all his radiance. They formed one being and she was certain that they were in communication at every moment, even when far from each other.

The weary queen put herself in the expert hands of her manicurist and chiropodist; at the end of a long day's work, she indulged in the requirements of her beauty, which had to make her seem calm on all occasions, whatever her worries might be.

Then came the exquisite moment of the bath: two servants poured hot perfumed water over the queen's naked body. Then she lay down on the warm tiles and there began a long massage with a salve made from incense, terebinth balm, sweet oil and citron, which would get rid of tension and relieve her aching limbs before she slept.

Nefertari thought of the shortcomings for which she was responsible, of the mistakes she had made, of her useless fits of anger. The way of righteousness was to act on behalf of those who needed help, for just deeds enriched the Rule of Ma'at and protected the country from chaos.

Suddenly the hand which was massaging her changed its rhythm and became more of a caress.

'Ramses!'

'Will you let me replace your servant?'

'I must think about it.' She turned over, very slowly, and saw him looking lovingly at her. 'Didn't you have an interminable meeting with Ahmeni and the administrators of the granaries?'

'This evening and this night belong to us.'

She unfastened his kilt.

'What is your secret, Nefertari? Sometimes I find myself thinking that your beauty is not of this world.'

'Is our love?'

They embraced on the warm tiles, their perfumes mingled, their lips met, then their desire carried them away over the waves.

Ramses wrapped Nefertari in a large shawl which, when unfolded, represented the wings of the goddess Isis, endlessly in movement to give the breath of life.

'This is magnificent!' she said.

'A new masterpiece from the weavers of Sais, so that you need never feel cold again.'

She nestled close to the king. 'May the gods grant that we are never parted again.'

14

Ramses' office was as bare as that of his father, Seti. Lit by three large stone-framed windows, it had unadorned white walls, one large table, a straight-backed chair for the monarch, straw-seated chairs for his visitors, a cupboard for papyri which contained magic incantations intended to protect the royal person, a map of Egypt and the neighbouring countries, and a statue of the late pharaoh, whose eternal gaze watched over his son's work. Near the king's writing materials lay two acacia branches tied tightly together at one end by a linen thread: Seti's divining rod, which Ramses had already had occasion to use.

'When will Moses' trial take place?' the king asked Ahmeni.

'In two weeks' time.'

The pale scribe was, as usual, loaded down with a quantity of papyri and inscribed tablets. In spite of his weak back, he insisted on carrying confidential documents himself.

'Have you warned him?'

'Of course.'

'And what was his reaction?'

'He seemed calm.'

'Did you tell him we have proof of his innocence?'

'I gave him to understand that his case wasn't hopeless.'

'Why are you being so cautious?'

'Because neither you nor I can know the verdict.'

'No one can be blamed for acting in self-defence!'

'Moses killed a man – and what's more, the man was your sister's husband.'

'I shall intervene to say what I think of that scoundrel.'

'No, Majesty, you cannot intervene in any way. Since the pharaoh ensures the presence of Ma'at on earth, and the impartiality of justice, he must not interfere in judicial procedures.'

'Do you think I don't know that?'

'I wouldn't be a real friend if I didn't help you to fight against your worst self.'

'That's a very hard task, Ahmeni!'

'I'm stubborn and persistent.'

'Moses came back to Egypt of his own accord, didn't he?'

'That doesn't wipe out either his fault or what he did.'

'Are you siding against him?'

'Moses is my friend too. I shall give evidence in his defence. But will it convince the vizier and the judges?'

'Moses was very highly thought of at court. Everyone will understand the chain of events that led him to kill Sary.'

'Let us hope so, Majesty.'

Despite an agreeable night spent in the company of two very cooperative Syrian ladies, Serramanna was in a bad mood. So, before the breakfast which the Egyptians called 'rinsing the mouth', he dismissed the two girls.

In spite of all his efforts, the murdered girl had still not been identified. He had believed that the portrait of the victim would help his investigators to get quickly on the right track. But nobody in either Memphis or Pi-Ramses knew the blonde. There was only one possible conclusion: she had been hidden away in the strictest secrecy.

One witness ought to know a great deal about it: Ramses' sister. Alas, Serramanna could not question her as he'd have liked to. By making honourable amends and swearing loyalty to the royal couple, Dolora had won their confidence again, at least partially.

His patience becoming sorely tried, Serramanna consulted the reports drawn up by his agents on their return from the provinces. Elephantine, el-Kab, Edfu, the Delta towns . . . nothing. One detail surprised him when he checked the list of his instructions concerning the mission: a Cretan had not reported back. Yet this former pirate was avaricious and he knew the penalty for lack of discipline.

He dressed hurriedly, without stopping to shave, and went to see Ahmeni. The twenty elite officials who made up the administrative staff were not yet on duty, but Ramses' private secretary and sandal-bearer had made short work of some barley gruel, figs and dried fish, and was already filing papyri. No matter how much he ate, Ahmeni never put on weight.

'Problems, Serramanna?'

'A report missing.'

'Is that so worrying?'

'When it concerns the Cretan, yes. He's very fussy about things being done correctly.'

'Where did you send him?'

'To Middle Egypt, to the province of el-Nersheh. To be precise, not far from Akhenaton's deserted city.'

'That's a pretty isolated spot.'

'I've learned from you to be conscientious.'

Ahmeni smiled. The two men had not always been friends, but since their reconciliation they felt real respect for each other.

'Perhaps he's simply been delayed a bit.'

'He should have been back more than a week ago.'

'Frankly, this incident doesn't seem to me all that important.'

'On the contrary, my instinct tells me it's very serious.'

'Why are you telling me about it? You have all the necessary powers to clear up the mystery.'

'Because nothing is going right, Ahmeni, nothing at all.'

'What do you mean?'

'The magus who disappeared, Shanaar's body, which can't be found, this blonde girl we can't identify . . . I don't like it.'

'Ramses rules and is in control of the situation.'

'We aren't at peace, as far as I know, and the Hittites haven't given up the idea of destroying Egypt.'

'So you think the Hittite spy ring wasn't completely destroyed.'

'The calm before the storm, that's what I feel. And my instinct has rarely deceived me.'

'What do you suggest?'

'I'm leaving for this lost city, I want to know what has become of the Cretan. Watch over Pharaoh until I get back.'

Dolora was a prey to doubt. The tall brunette had resumed her existence as a wealthy, idle aristocrat, going from banquet to banquet, from reception to reception, in the whirl of social life. She exchanged empty talk with empty-headed women of fashion, while insupportable old fops and young seducers, whose talk was as vapid as their thoughts, paid court to her.

Since becoming a supporter of Aton, the One God, Dolora had been obsessed with one thing only: to encourage the spread of the truth, to let its radiance finally dawn over the land of Egypt, driving out the false gods and those who worshipped them. But Dolora met only people who were blind to the truth, content with their lot. Deprived of Ofir's presence and advice, she was like someone shipwrecked in a storm. Week by week, her courage grew less. How was she to preserve a faith which nothing and no one fostered? Dolora despaired of a future which she felt to be dead.

Her maid of the bedchamber, a bright-eyed brunette, had changed the sheets and was sweeping the room.

'Are you unwell, Princess?'

'Who could envy my fate?'

'Fine gowns, walks in dream gardens, meeting wonderful men . . . I envy you a bit.'

'Are you unhappy?'

'Oh, no! I have a nice husband and two healthy children, and we earn a good living. Soon my husband will have finished building our new house.'

Dolora dared to ask the question which obsessed her. 'And God? Do you think about him sometimes?'

'God is everywhere, Princess: you only have to worship the gods and look at nature.'

Dolora did not insist. Ofir was right: the true religion had to be imposed by force and could not wait for people to be converted. Once forced to accept the dogma, they would renounce their former errors.

'Princess, do you know what people say?'

The maid's bright eyes were filled with an overwhelming desire to gossip. Perhaps Dolora would gather some interesting information.

'They whisper that you intend to remarry and that a number of suitors are competing for this honour.'

'People will say anything.'

'What a pity. You have worn mourning long enough. In my opinion, it's not good for a woman of your rank to suffer loneliness like this.'

'This life suits me.'

'You seem so sad sometimes. But that's normal, of course. You must be thinking about your husband. That poor man, murdered! How would Osiris and his tribunal have judged his soul? With respect, Princess, it's rumoured that your husband did not always behave decently.'

'That is the sad truth.'

'Then why shut yourself away with bad memories?'

'A new marriage doesn't tempt me.'

'Happiness will return, Princess! Especially if your husband's killer is condemned.'

'What do you know about it?'

'Moses is going to be brought to trial.'

'Moses? But he fled!'

'It's still a secret, but my husband is a friend of the chief jailor of the great prison: the Hebrew's imprisoned there. He's certain to be condemned to death.

'Can anyone see him?'

'No, he's being kept in secret, because of the seriousness of the accusations against him. You'll certainly be summoned to the trial and you'll have the chance to get your revenge.'

Moses back, Moses, the man who believed in the One God. This must be a sign intended for Dolora!

15

The trial of Moses took place in the Great Hall of Justice, and was presided over by the vizier, the servant of Ma'at, clad in a heavy starched gown. His sole ornament was a heart, the symbol of man's conscience which, when he came to judgment at the time of his death, would be weighed in the scales of the hereafter.

Before the hearing opened, the vizier had met Ramses in the Temple of Ptah, to renew the oath he had sworn to him on the occasion of his investiture: namely, to respect the goddess of justice and show favour to none. The king had been careful not to give him any advice, simply noting his commitment.

The Great Hall was full. Not a single member of the court wanted to miss the event.

The chiefs of some of the Hebrew tribes were present. Opinions varied: some people were convinced of Moses' guilt, others were expecting revelations which would justify his return. Everyone knew of his strong character and no one imagined that he had acted naively.

The vizier opened the hearing by extolling Ma'at, the Rule which would outlive the human race. He had had placed on the tiled floor forty-two strips of leather, a reminder that the judgment would be applicable in the forty-two provinces of Egypt.

Two soldiers brought in Moses. All eyes converged on the

Hebrew, Ramses' former high dignitary, with his craggy, bearded face and impressive build; he showed amazing calm. The soldiers led him to his place facing the vizier.

The fourteen-member jury, seated on either side of the minister for justice, consisted of a surveyor, a priestess of the goddess Sekhmet, a physician, a carpenter, a housewife, a peasant, a treasury scribe, a court lady, a construction manager, a female weaver, the general of the Ra division, a stone-cutter, a granary scribe and a seaman.

'Your name is Moses?'

'It is.'

'Do you object to any member of this jury? Look at them carefully and take your time to think.'

'I have confidence in the justice of this country.'

'Isn't this your own country?'

'I was born here, but I am a Hebrew.'

'You are an Egyptian and you will be judged as such.'

'Would the procedure and the verdict be any different if I were a foreigner?'

'Certainly not.'

'What is the importance in this case?'

'It is up to the court to decide. Are you perhaps ashamed to be an Egyptian?'

'It is up to this court to decide, as you have just said.'

'You are accused of killing an overseer by the name of Sary, then fleeing. Do you admit these facts?'

'I do, but they need explanation.'

'That is the object of this trial. Do you find the terms of the accusation inaccurate?'

'No.'

'Then you will understand that, in accordance with the law, I must demand the death sentence.'

Murmurs ran through the audience. Moses remained impassive, as if these terrifying words did not concern him.

'Given the seriousness of the facts,' the vizier went on, 'I am fixing no limit for the duration of this trial. The accused will have all the time he needs for his defence and to explain the reasons for his criminal action. I insist on absolute silence and I shall suspend the proceedings at the slightest disorder; any guilty person will be punished by a heavy fine.'

The magistrate addressed Moses. 'At the time of this tragedy, what position did you hold?'

'I was a dignitary at the court of Egypt and head overseer of the building site of Pi-Ramses. In particular, I was in charge of the teams of Hebrew brickmakers.'

'To everyone's satisfaction, according to my dossiers. You were a friend of Pharaoh, were you not?'

'True.'

'You studied at the Royal Academy of Memphis, your first official post was at the harem of Mer-Ur, then foreman at Karnak, then head overseer in Pi-Ramses. A brilliant career, which had only just begun. The victim, Sary, went the opposite way. He had been Ramses' tutor, hoped to become the head of the Academy of Memphis, but had been forced into an inferior occupation. Were you informed of the reasons for this demotion?'

'I had my opinion.'

'May we know what it was?'

'Sary was a vile creature, ambitious and greedy. Fate struck at him through my hand.'

Ahmeni asked the vizier for permission to speak. 'I can provide details: Sary plotted against Ramses. The king showed him mercy because he was his sister's husband.'

A number of courtiers seemed surprised.

'Let the Princess Dolora appear before this court,' ordered the vizier.

The tall dark woman came forward hesitantly.

'Do you agree with what Moses and Ahmeni said?'

Dolora looked down. 'Their words are moderate, much too moderate. My husband had turned into a monster. When he understood that his career was definitely over, he harboured a greater and greater hatred of his subordinates, and ended up behaving with intolerable cruelty towards them. During the last months of his life, he persecuted the team of Hebrew brickmakers under him. If Moses hadn't killed him, someone else would have done so.'

The vizier looked puzzled. 'Aren't your words somewhat excessive?'

'I swear they are not! My husband made my life torture.'

'Were you perhaps glad at his death?'

Dolora bent her head even lower. 'I was. I felt a kind of relief and I was ashamed of myself – but how could I mourn such a tyrant?'

'Have you anything further to add, Princess?'

'No, nothing.' She returned to her seat among the courtiers.

'Does anyone wish to defend Sary's memory and contradict his wife's version?'

Not one voice was raised. The scribe responsible for registering the depositions noted them in a fine, rapid script.

'What is your version of events?' the vizier asked Moses.

'It was a sort of accident. Although my relationship with Sary was strained, I didn't mean to kill him.'

'Why was there this animosity between you?'

'Because I discovered that Sary was a blackmailer and was persecuting the Hebrew brickmakers. I killed Sary unintentionally, trying to defend one of them and to save my own life.'

'So you maintain that you acted in self-defence?'

'That is the truth.'

'Why did you flee?'

'I gave way to panic.'

'That's strange, for an innocent man.'

'Killing a man causes a terrible shock. You instantly lose your head and react as if you were drunk. Then you realize you've committed a terrible deed and you have only one wish: to escape from yourself, disappear, forget and be forgotten. That's why I hid in the desert.'

'When you got over this fright, you should have returned to Egypt and presented yourself for trial.'

'I had taken a wife and we had a child. Egypt seemed very distant.'

'Why did you return?'

'I had a mission to accomplish.'

'What was that?'

'Today it is still my secret – nothing to do with this trial. Tomorrow everyone will know.'

Moses' replies irritated the vizier. 'Your version of events is not very convincing. You behaviour does not plead in your favour and your explanations are somewhat confused. I believe you had every intention of murdering Sary because he was behaving unjustly towards the Hebrews. Your motives are understandable, but nevertheless a crime was committed. When you returned to Pi-Ramses, you remained in hiding. Is that not an admission of your guilt? A man whose conscience is clear does not act like that.'

Ahmeni thought it was time for him to strike the decisive blow. 'I have proof of Moses' innocence.'

'Unless you have significant new facts to present, I shall charge you with contempt of court,' the vizier retorted severely.

'The Hebrew brickmaker whose defence Moses undertook is called Abner. Sary was blackmailing him. Abner complained to Moses, and Sary wanted to get his own back on Abner by harassing him. Moses arrived in time and prevented Sary from ill-treating his victim. But the quarrel turned nasty and Moses killed Sary unintentionally and in self-defence. Abner was a witness, and his evidence has been recorded. It is available to you.'

Ahmeni passed the document to the vizier, who noted that

the papyrus did indeed bear the seal of a judge. He broke the seal, checked the date and read the contents.

Moses dared not show his joy, but exchanged meaningful glances with Ahmeni.

'This document is authentic and admissible,' the vizier concluded.

The trial was over, Moses cleared of the charge. The jury would pronounce an acquittal.

'Before the jury deliberates,' the vizier resumed, 'I would nevertheless like to make a final verification.'

Ahmeni frowned.

'Let this Abner appear before us,' the vizier demanded, 'and confirm his deposition verbally.'

16

Ramses vented his anger to Ahmeni. 'Irrefutable proof, an authenticated document and yet Moses is still in prison!'

'The vizier is meticulous,' Ahmeni suggested cautiously.

'But what more does he need?'

'I've told you, he wants to see this Abner.'

Ramses had to face the facts: the vizier's demands had to be met. 'Has this man been summoned?'

'Yes, and there's the rub.'

'Why?'

'Abner can't be found. The chiefs of the tribes maintain he's been missing for several months. No one knows what's become of him.'

'Lies! They want to harm Moses.'

'Possibly. But what's to be done?'

'Let Serramanna be personally responsible for finding him.'

'We shall have to wait a bit. Serramanna's following up a trail in Middle Egypt, near the heretic's deserted city. He's obsessed with the need to identify the murdered blonde. And to tell the truth, he's convinced the Hittite spy ring hasn't been destroyed.'

The king's anger subsided. 'And what do you think, Ahmeni?'

'That Shanaar is dead, and his accomplices have fled or are

no longer in a position to do any harm. But Serramanna trusts his instinct.'

'Perhaps he's right. Instinct is a direct way of understanding beyond reason, which can lead us astray or raise false hopes. My father transformed instinct into intuition and used it with genius.'

'Seti wasn't a pirate!'

'Serramanna comes from the world of darkness and has a good knowledge of its tactics. It would be a mistake not to listen to him. Get in touch with him urgently and order him to return to Pi-Ramses.'

'I'll send messengers after him.'

'And transmit my request to the vizier: I wish to see Moses.'

'But . . . he's in prison!'

'The trial has taken place, the facts are known: such an interview cannot influence the course of justice.'

A violent wind swept the plain around the City of the Sun, whose ruins were an eyesore. As Serramanna was walking down one street, a length of wall collapsed. Although he had frequently faced danger, he was uneasy. Dangerous shadows lurked in these palaces and abandoned houses. Before questioning the villagers, he wanted to get at the truth about the place, meet its ghosts, measure the extent of the tragedy that had unfolded under the sun of Aton.

As nightfall approached Serramanna made his way to the neighbouring village to find some refreshment and sleep for a few hours before continuing his search. The village seemed deserted: not a donkey about, not a goose, not a dog. The doors and shutters of the houses were open; nevertheless, the Sardinian unsheathed his short sword. Caution should have advised him not to venture alone into a place where danger lurked, but he relied on his experience and his strength.

On the beaten-earth floor of a wretched hovel, an old

woman was sitting with her head on her knees, looking grief-stricken.

'You can kill me if you like,' she said in a broken voice. 'There's nothing left to steal here.'

'Don't worry, I'm a member of Ramses' police.'

'Go away, stranger. This village is dead, my husband is dead, and I only want to die.'

'Who was your husband?'

'An honest man, whom they accused of being a sorcerer when he actually spent his life helping others. By way of thanks, that accursed magus murdered him!'

Serramanna sat down beside the widow with her soiled gown and dusty hair. 'Describe this magus to me.'

'What's the use?'

'He's a criminal and I'm looking for him.'

The widow looked at him in astonishment. 'You're joking!'

'Do I look as if I'm joking?'

'It's too late. My husband's dead.'

'I shan't bring him back to life – the gods will do that. But I fully intend to get my hands on this magus.'

'He's tall, dried-up, with a face like a hawk and cold eyes.'

'What's his name?'

'Ofir.'

'Egyptian?'

'Libyan.'

'How do you know all these details?'

'For several months he used to come to our house, to talk to our adopted daughter, Lita. Poor child, she had visions and believed she was related to the heretic king's family. My husband and I tried to bring her to her senses, but she preferred to believe the magus. One night she vanished and we never saw her again.'

Serramanna showed the widow the portrait of the young woman murdered by Ofir. 'Is that her?'

'Yes, that's my daughter, Lita. Is she . . . ?'

The Sardinian didn't believe in hiding the truth. He nodded in reply. 'When did you last see Ofir?'

'A few days ago, when he came to see my sick husband. It was he, Ofir, who made him drink a deadly potion!'

'Is he hiding hereabouts?'

'In the tombs in the cliffs, haunted by demons. Cut his throat, policeman, trample on his dead body and burn it!'

'You must leave this place, widow. One mustn't live with ghosts.'

Serramanna left the hovel, leaped on to his horse and galloped off towards the cliffs. It was already growing dark.

Abandoning his mount at the bottom of the slope, he ran towards the tombs with his sword in his hand. He would not have the advantage of surprise, but he preferred to act immediately. He chose the tomb with the largest entrance and rushed inside.

Everywhere was empty. The only inhabitants of these sepulchres were the figures carved on the walls, the last survivors of a past era.

Meritamon was playing the harp to the royal couple with a skill which astonished the monarch. Seated hand in hand on folding chairs at the edge of a pool where blue water-lilies flourished, Pharaoh and the Great Royal Wife were enjoying a moment of happiness. Not only was the little eight-year-old already a virtuoso but, what is more, she showed surprising sensitivity. Invincible, the enormous lion, and Wideawake, the golden-yellow dog lying between its fore-paws, seemed under the spell of the tune Meritamon was playing.

The last notes softly died away, leaving a faint echo behind.

The king kissed his daughter.

'Are you satisfied?' she asked.

'You're a very gifted musician, but you still have a lot to learn.'

'Mother promised to have me admitted to the Temple of Hathor, and there they'll teach me wonderful things.'

'If that is your wish, it shall be granted.'

The little girl was as dazzlingly beautiful as Nefertari, with the same light in her eyes. 'If I become a temple musician, will you come and visit me?'

'However could I do without your playing?'

Kha approached, looking grumpy.

'You seem upset,' the queen commented.

'Something of mine has been stolen.'

'Are you sure?'

'I always put my things away every evening. Someone has stolen one of my old brushes that I liked writing with.'

'Perhaps you've just mislaid it.'

'No, I've looked everywhere.'

Ramses took his son by the shoulders. 'You're making a serious accusation.'

'I know one mustn't speak lightly. That's why I've given it a lot of thought before complaining.'

'Whom do you suspect?'

'For the moment, nobody. But I'm going to try to find out. I was very fond of that brush.'

'You've got others.'

'True, but that one was special.'

The lion raised its head, the dog pricked up its ears. Someone was coming.

Dolora appeared, looking unconcerned. She was wearing a large wig with long plaits and a green gown which suited her dull complexion.

'His Majesty wished to see me?'

'At Moses' trial,' declared Ramses, 'your behaviour was remarkable.'

'All I did was tell the truth.'

'It took courage to describe your husband so clearly.'

'One does not lie when faced with Ma'at and the vizier.'

'Your statements were a great help to Moses.'

'I only did my duty.'

The palace cupbearer brought fresh wine and the conversation turned to the work the two children would have to undertake to achieve wisdom.

When she left the garden Dolora was convinced she had regained the king's trust. Surface kindness tinged with suspicion had given way to liking.

She dismissed her litter-bearers. She preferred to take a little stroll and return on foot.

No one would have recognized, in the modestly garbed water-carrier who approached her, Shanaar, now much thinner and with a moustache and beard.

'Satisfied, dear sister?'

'Your plan was excellent.'

'My brother is blinded by friendship. By coming to Moses' aid, you have become Ramses' ally.'

'Now that Ramses believes me to be sincere, he's vulnerable. What must I do next?'

'Keep your ears open. The smallest piece of information might be valuable. I shall contact you in the same way.'

17

Ramses and Ahmeni listened attentively to Serramanna's long tale. Ramses' office was illuminated by a soft light which was in strong constrast to the tension reigning in the room. It was the end of the hot season, when Egypt was arrayed in soothing shades of gold.

'Ofir, a Libyan magus,' Ahmeni repeated, 'and Lita, a poor mad girl he manipulated. Must we really worry about that? This sinister individual has fled, he has no support in the country, and he's probably already across the border.'

'You undestimate the seriousness of the situation,' reckoned Ramses. 'Have you forgotten that he was hiding in the City of the Sun?'

'It's been abandoned for so long—'

'But its founder's pernicious ideas continue to cloud certain minds! This Ofir aimed to use them to set up a network of sympathizers.'

'A network . . .' mused Ahmeni. 'Could Ofir possibly be a Hittite spy?'

'I'm convinced of it.'

'But the Hittites don't care a rush about Aton and the One God!'

'The Hebrews do,' Serramanna put in.

Ahmeni had dreaded hearing him bring this up, but the Sardinian hadn't learnt the art of diplomacy and continued to speak his mind as bluntly as ever.

'We know that Moses was contacted by a false architect,' he reminded them, 'and the description of this impostor corresponds exactly with that of the magus. Isn't that a conclusive argument?'

'Calm down,' suggested Ahmeni.

'Go on,' ordered Ramses.

'I don't know anything about religion,' the Sardinian continued, 'but I do know the Hebrews talk about "One God". Must I remind you, Majesty, that I suspected Moses of treachery?'

'Moses is our friend!' protested Ahmeni. 'Even if he did meet Ofir, why should he plot against Ramses? The magus must have contacted a number of notables.'

'What's the good of blinding ourselves?' asked the Sardinian.

The pharaoh rose and looked into the distance through the central window of his office. The green and pleasant countryside of the Delta was the very expression of the sweetness of life.

'Serramanna is right,' he said. 'The Hittites have launched a double offensive, attacking us simultaneously from without and within. We have won the battle of Kadesh, driven their troops back beyond our protectorates and eliminated a spy ring. But these victories are illusory. The Hittite army hasn't been destroyed and this Ofir is still at large. A man like that, who doesn't shrink from committing crimes, won't give up trying to harm us. But Moses can't be an accomplice. He's loyal, a person incapable of acting in the dark. When it comes to him, Serramanna's wrong.'

'I hope so, Majesty.'

'I have a fresh mission for you, Serramanna.'

'I'm to arrest Ofir?'

'First find the Hebrew brickmaker Abner.'

*

Nefertari had decided to celebrate her birthday at a large estate in the heart of the Delta, near the capital, which had been put in the charge of the minister for agriculture, Nedjem. He was of an amiable disposition, always delighted with nature's works, and now presented the royal couple with a new type of plough, better adapted to the rich, loamy soil of the Delta. He himself enthusiastically demonstrated it, digging a furrow of the correct depth with no damage to the soil.

The estate workers could not hide their delight. To see the king and queen so close was a veritable boon which would fill the coming year with a thousand and one blessings. The crops would be abundant, magnificent fruit would grow in the orchards, the flocks and herds would produce countless young.

Nefertari sensed, though, that Ramses was not sharing in this joyful day's festivities. At the end of a hearty meal, she took advantage of a moment's respite.

'Your heart is weighed down by anxiety. Is it because of Moses?'

'It's true that I'm worried about his fate.'

'Has Abner been found?'

'Not yet. If he doesn't appear in court, the vizier won't pronounce the acquittal.'

'Serramanna won't disappoint you. But I sense that something else is worrying you.'

'The rule of the pharaohs makes it incumbent on me to protect Egypt from her internal as well as external enemies and I'm afraid I have failed.'

'Since the Hittites are keeping their distance, the enemy you fear must be on our own soil.'

'We shall have to wage a war against the sons of darkness who wear masks and move in a false light.'

'Strange words, but they do not surprise me. Yesterday, during the celebration of the evening rites in the Temple of

Sekhmet, the granite statue's eyes shone with a disquieting brightness. We know that look well: it presages some calamity. I immediately pronounced the incantations to ward off harm, but when peace returns to the shrine, will it spread to the external world?'

'The ghosts of Akhetaton are returning to haunt people's consciences. Nefertari.'

'Didn't Akhenaton set the limits of his experiment in space and time?'

'Yes, he did, but he released forces he could not control. And Ofir, a Libyan magus in the service of the Hittites, has awakened demons which were slumbering in the deserted city.'

Nefertari was silent for a long moment, with her eyes closed. Freeing herself from her links with the ephemeral, her thoughts soared towards the Invisible, seeking a truth hidden in the complexities of the future. The practice of rites had developed in the queen a capacity for clairvoyance, a direct contact with the powers which, at every moment, were creating life. Occasionally, intuition succeeded in lifting the veil.

Ramses anxiously awaited the Great Royal Wife's verdict.

'The confrontation will be fearsome,' she said as she opened her eyes. 'The armies Ofir has prepared are no less violent than those of the Hittites.'

'Since you confirm my fears, we must act as speedily as possible. Let us deploy the forces of the kingdom's principal temples and cover them with a protective net woven by the gods and goddesses. I cannot do without your help.'

Nefertari threw her arms round Ramses in a gesture of infinite love. 'Do you need to ask me for it?'

'We are going to undertake a long journey and face countless dangers.'

'Our love would have little meaning, if it weren't given to Egypt. Egypt gives us life: we shall offer our lives to Egypt.'

Young bare-breasted peasant girls, wearing headdresses

made of reeds and kilts of various plants, danced in honour of the earth's fertility and threw little cloth balls to each other to ward off the evil eye. Thanks to their skill, heavy, clumsy, misshapen evil spirits would not be able to find their way into the cultivated fields.

'If only we had their skill,' sighed Nefertari.

'You too have a secret worry, haven't you?'

'I'm anxious about Kha.'

'Has he done something wrong?'

'No, it's because of his brush that was stolen. Do you remember my favourite shawl disappearing? There's no doubt that this magus used it to cast a spell, to ruin my health and weaken us as a couple. Thanks to Setau's treatment, I was able to give birth to Meritamon and escape death, but I dread a new attack – and this time one against a child, against your first-born son.'

'Is he ill?'

'Doctor Pariamaku has just examined him and found nothing abnormal.'

'His diagnosis isn't enough for me. You must call on Setau and ask him to set up a magic wall round Kha. As from today he must let us know of even the slightest incident. Have you warned Iset?'

'Of course.'

'The thief must be found, and we must know if we are being betrayed by someone inside the palace. Serramanna must question all the staff.'

'I'm afraid, Ramses, afraid for Kha.'

'We must control our fear, or it may harm him. The one who is working with the forces of darkness will use our slightest weakness.'

Equipped with a scribe's palette and some brushes, Kha entered the laboratory of Setau and Lotus. The pretty Nubian was milking venom from a a black cobra, while her husband was preparing a potion for treating digestive troubles.

'Are you the person who's going to teach me magic?' asked Kha.

'Your only teacher will be the magic itself,' said Setau. 'Are you still scared of snakes?'

'Oh yes!'

'Only fools aren't afraid of reptiles. They were born before us and know secrets we need. Have you noticed how they slither their way across worlds?'

'Ever since my father made me meet the great cobra, I have known that I shall avoid a bad death.'

'You still need to be protected, it seems.'

'Someone has stolen one of my brushes and a magus wants to use it against me. The queen told me the truth.'

The boy's gravity and maturity astonished Setau.

'As snakes cast a spell on us,' he explained, 'so do they teach us how to fight against spells. That's why every morning I'm going to give you a drink made of a mixture of ground onions, snakes' blood and nettles. In two weeks' time I shall add some copper filings, red ochre, alum and rust from lead; then Lotus will give you a remedy which she has invented.'

Kha grimaced. 'That doesn't sound very nice.'

'A little wine will take away the bad taste.'

'I've never drunk any wine.'

'That's another lack to be remedied.'

'Wine clouds the minds of scribes and prevents them having a steady hand.'

'Too much water prevents the heart from dilating; don't give in to that failing. To learn to distinguish fine vintages, you have to start tasting them early.'

'Will they protect me against the bad magic?'

Setau stirred a pot of greenish ointment. 'A passive subject has no chance of resisting bad magic. Only intensive work will allow you to ward off the assaults of the unseen.'

'I'm ready,' declared Kha.

18

It had been raining for the last ten days in Hattusa,* the capital of the Hittite Empire, built on the central Anatolian plateau where arid plains alternated with gorges and ravines.

Emperor Muwatallis had a bent back and short legs; his brown eyes were ceaselessly alert. He was weary now and, as usual, felt the cold, so he stayed close to the fire and did not take off his woollen cap or his long red and black cloak.

In spite of the defeat at Kadesh and the failure of his counter-offensive, Muwatallis felt safe in his mountain city, which consisted of a lower town and an upper town, dominated by a citadel where the imperial palace stood. Gigantic fortifications, following the lines of the hills, made Hattusa an impregnable stronghold.

However, in that proud, invincible city, critical voices were being raised against the emperor. For the first time, his acute sense of strategy had not resulted in victory for his army. Soldiers mounted vigilant guard along the ramparts, which bristled with towers and crenellations; but they all wondered whether tomorrow Muwatallis would still be presiding over the empire's destiny. Up till now, he who was known familiarly as 'the Great Chief' had thwarted any attempts to seize power, by eliminating anyone who showed

* Present-day Bogazköy, in Turkey, about 95 miles east of Ankara.

ambition. But recent events had weakened his position.

Two men coveted the throne: his son, Uri-Teshup, backed by the elite of the army, and Hattusilis, the emperor's brother, a shrewd diplomat who had set up a coalition against Egypt. A coalition which Muwatallis was trying to maintain by offering a quantity of expensive gifts to his allies.

Muwatallis had just spent a soothing half-day in the company of a ravishing young woman, both amusing and cultured, who had let him forget his worries. He would have preferred, like her, to devote his time to love poetry, forgetting military parades. But that was only a dream, and a Hittite emperor had neither the leisure nor the right to dream.

Muwatallis warmed his hands. He was still undecided: should he do away with his brother or his son, or both of them? A few years previously, violent intervention would have been imperative; countless schemers, and even sovereigns, had succumbed to poison, which was much appreciated at the Hittite court. At present, the hostility between the two pretenders could be useful to him. After all, they cancelled each other out, allowing him to appear as an indispensable mediator.

And his conduct was constrained by another distressing fact: the empire was on the point of breaking up. Repeated military failures, the financing of the war, and problems of international trade could well make the giant totter.

Muwatallis had meditated in the Temple of the God of Storms, the finest in the whole of the lower town, which contained no fewer than twenty-one shrines dedicated to the gods. Like every priest, the emperor had broken three loaves and poured wine on a block of stone, while uttering the ritual words 'May it endure for all eternity'. It was for his country that the emperor formed this wish; in his nightmares, he saw himself conquered by Egypt and betrayed by his allies. How long would he be able to gaze down from the top of his citadel on the terraces built of close-set rocks, the notables' fine dwellings and the monumental gates allowing access to his capital?

The emperor's chamberlain informed him that his visitor had arrived. The latter had passed through the many guardrooms before arriving at the emperor's dwelling, which was surrounded by water-tanks, stables, an armoury and barracks. Muwatallis liked to receive his guests in a cold, austere, pillared hall decorated with weapons commemorating the Hittite army's victories.

Uri-Teshup's heavy, martial tread could be recognized out of a thousand. He was tall, hairy, muscular and vigorous, with long red hair, the very embodiment of the fearsome warrior, ever ready to set off to do battle.

'Are you well, my son?'

'No, father.'

'You seem in excellent health.'

'Have you summoned me in order to mock me?'

'Remember to whom you are speaking!'

Uri-Teshup shed a little of his arrogance. 'Forgive me. My nerves are on edge.'

'Why?'

'I was the commander of a victorious army, and here I'm reduced to the rank of a subordinate and under the orders of Hattusilis, who was defeated at Kadesh! It's such a waste of the energy I could use in the service of my country.'

'Without Hattusilis, the coalition would never have been set up.'

'What use has that been? If you'd trusted me, I'd have triumphed over Ramses!'

'You persist in your mistake, my son. What's the good of endlessly harping on the past?'

'Get rid of Hattusilis and give me back a real command.'

'Hattusilis is my brother. Besides, our allies appreciate him and he has the ear of the merchants, without whom our war effort would be interrrupted.'

'So what do you suggest?'

'That we let bygones be bygones and join forces to save Hatti.'

'Save Hatti? But who's threatening our country?'

'Around us, the world is evolving. We haven't crushed Egypt, and certain alliances may change more quickly than I thought.'

'I don't understand what you're getting at. I was born to fight, not to hatch intrigues that won't result in Hatti becoming any greater.'

'You're jumping to conclusions, my son, and to wrong ones at that. If we wish to establish our supremacy in the whole of this region, let us begin by forgetting our internal differences. There's one useful and indispensable step to be taken: you and Hattusilis must be reconciled.'

Uri-Teshup struck one of the pillars of the fireplace with his clenched fist. 'Never! I'll never agree to humiliate myself in front of that second-rater!'

'Let us put an end to our divisions and we shall be all the stronger.'

'Shut your brother and his wife up in a temple and give me the order to attack Egypt: that's a useful step.'

'Do you reject any form of reconciliation?'

'I do.'

'Is that your last word?'

'If you get rid of Hattusilis, I shall be your loyal supporter. With the army.'

'Does a son bargain with the love he bears his father?'

'You are far more than a father, you are Emperor of Hatti. The interests of Hatti, and nothing else, must dictate our decisions. My position is the right one: you will eventually recognize that.'

The emperor seemed weary. 'You may be right. I must think about it.'

On leaving the audience chamber, Uri-Teshup was certain

he had convinced his father. Soon the ageing emperor would have no choice but to grant him full powers, before giving up the throne to him.

Putuhepa, Hattusilis's wife, wearing a scarlet gown, a gold necklace, silver bracelets and leather sandals, was burning incense in the underground chamber of the Temple of Ishtar. At this late hour, the citadel was silent.

Two men descended the stairs: Hattusilis, followed by the emperor. The former, a small man, had his hair tied back by a bandeau, and was draped in a thick length of multicoloured cloth; he wore a bracelet on his left forearm.

'How cold it is,' complained Muwattalis, pulling his woollen cloak tightly round him.

'This room is not particularly comfortable,' Hattusilis agreed, 'but it has the advantage of being completely quiet.'

'Do you wish to be seated, Majesty?' asked Putuhepa.

'This stone bench will suit me. In spite of his long journey, my brother seems less tired than I am. What important facts have you gleaned, Hattusilis?'

'I'm worried about our coalition. Certain of our allies seem about to forget their commitments. They are getting increasingly greedy. I've managed to satisfy them, but you must know that this coalition is becoming very expensive. However, there's a greater worry.'

'Speak, I beg you.'

'The Assyrians are becoming a threat.'

'That petty nation?'

'They have followed our example and they believe us to be falling into decline, because of our recent defeats and our internal dissension.'

'We could crush them in a few days!'

'I don't think so. And would it be wise to divide our forces just when Ramses is preparing to attack Kadesh?'

'Have you got precise information?'

'According to our spies, Ramses' army is about to resume the offensive. This time, the Canaanites and the Bedouin won't oppose the King of Egypt. Tomorrow their road to Hatti will be clear. To open a second front against the Assyrians would be folly.'

'What do you recommend, Hattusilis?'

'That we make our internal unity a priority. The quarrel between me and your son has lasted too long and is weakening us. I am ready to meet him to make him aware of the gravity of the situation. If we go on distrusting each other, we are lost.'

'Uri-Teshup rejects any reconciliation and insists he be given command of all our troops.'

'So that he can rush headlong against the Egyptians and be routed!'

'According to him, a head-on clash is our only solution.'

'You are the emperor: it is up to you to choose between me and him. If you adopt your son's policy, I will withdraw.'

Muwattalis paced up and down a little, to get warm.

'There is only one reasonable solution,' Putuhepa declared calmly. 'You, Majesty, being the emperor, must put the greatness of Hatti before anything else. The fact that Hattusilis is your brother and Uri-Teshup your son is of no importance when faced with our people's safety, and you know very well that Uri-Teshup's belligerence will lead us to disaster.'

'What is this "reasonable solution" of yours?'

'No one can convince a madman. Therefore we must get rid of him. Neither you nor Hattusilis must be compromised by his disappearance, so I will see to it myself.'

19

Moses rose to his feet. 'You? Here?'

'The judge gave me permission to visit you.'

'Does Pharaoh have to ask permission to visit his prisons?'

'In your case, yes, since you are accused of murder. But you are first of all my friend.'

'So, you do not reject me . . .'

Ramses and Moses embraced warmly.

'I lacked confidence in you, Ramses. I didn't think you'd come.'

'Man of little faith! Why did you run away?'

'I thought at first that panic could explain my behaviour. But in the land of Midian where I hid, I had time to reflect. I wasn't running away; I had been called.'

Moses' cell was clean and airy, with a floor of beaten earth. The king sat down on a three-legged stool, facing his friend.

'Who did this call come from?'

'From the God of Abraham, Isaac and Jacob. From Yahveh.'

'Yahveh is the name of a mountain in the Sinai desert. It's not surprising that it's been made the symbol of a deity. After all, the Peak of the West, in Thebes, is the home of the goddess of silence.'

'Yahveh is the One God. He can't be reduced to part of the scenery.'

'What happened during your exile?'

'In the mountains I came face to face with God, in the form of a burning bush. He revealed His name to me: "I am".'

'Why does he restrict himself to one aspect of reality? Aton, the creator, is both "The one who is" and "The one who is not".'

'Yahveh has entrusted me with a mission, Ramses, a sacred mission which may well displease you. I must lead the Hebrew people out of Egypt to a holy land.'

'Did you really hear the voice of God?'

'It was as clear and deep as your own.'

'The desert is full of mirages, of course . . .'

'You won't make me doubt. I know what I saw and heard. My mission has been determined by God and I shall carry it out.'

'Do you mean *all* the Hebrews?'

'An entire people will leave Egypt in freedom.'

'But no one stops a Hebrew moving about freely.'

'I demand official recognition of the Hebrews' faith and permission to undertake an exodus.'

'First of all, we must get you out of prison. I've had a search for Abner instituted. His evidence will be decisive in favour of your acquittal.'

'He may have left Egypt.'

'You have my word that no effort will be spared to bring him before the court.'

'My friendship for you is as strong as ever, Ramses, and I wished for your victory in your struggle against the Hittites; but you are Pharaoh, and I am the future leader of the Hebrew people. If you do not bow to my will, I shall become the most implacable of your enemies.'

'Don't friends always find an area of agreement?'

'Our friendship will count for less than my mission. Even if it breaks my heart I must obey the voice of Yahveh.'

'We shall have time to discuss this again. First, though,

113

you must regain your freedom.'

'Imprisonment is no burden to me. Solitude helps me prepare myself for future trials.'

'The first of those could be a heavy sentence.'

'Yahveh protects me.'

'I hope it may be so, Moses. By digging into your memory, can't you find one fact which would help your defence?'

'I have spoken the truth and the truth will shine forth.'

'You're not helping me very much.'

'When one is Pharaoh's friend, why should one worry about injustice? You would never allow it to invade the kingdom and the hearts of the judges.'

'Have you ever met someone called Ofir?'

'I can't remember.'

'Try to remember. Ofir was a bogus architect who got in touch with you in Pi-Ramses, when you were building my capital. He probably extolled the merits of the religion of Akhenaton.'

'That's right, he did.'

'Did he make you any concrete proposals?'

'No, but he seemed aware of the affliction of the Hebrews.'

'Affliction? Isn't that a bit of an exaggeration?'

'You are an Egyptian; you wouldn't understand.'

'This Ofir is a Hittite spy and is plotting against Egypt; he's also a murderer. The slightest cooperation with him would lay you open to suspicion of high treason.'

'Whoever helps my people deserves my gratitude.'

'Do you hate the land of your birth?'

'My childhood and adolescence, our studies in Memphis, my career in your service – all that is dead and forgotten, Ramses. I love only one land: the land God has promised to my people.'

Nedjem was unusually irritable. Normally affable and jolly, he had snapped at his secretary for no reason. Unable to concentrate on his dossiers, he left his office and made his way to the laboratory of Setau and Lotus.

Lotus was crouching down, restraining a crimson-headed viper, which was thrashing its tail about wildly.

'Hold this copper bowl,' she told the minister.

'I don't know if . . .'

'Hurry up.'

Nedjem reluctantly took the vessel which contained a sticky brown liquid.

'Don't spill any of it. It's very corrosive.'

Nedjem was trembling. 'Where can I put it?'

'On the shelf.' Lotus pushed the viper into a basket and closed the lid. 'What can I do for you, Nedjem?'

'You and Setau . . .'

'What does anyone want with Setau?' the snake-charmer asked gruffly.

Disturbing fumes rose from filters of various sizes; on shelves pots stood next to sieves, flasks next to test tubes, decoctions next to potions.

'I want to say—' A fit of coughing prevented the minister from continuing.

'Well, say it!' insisted Setau. Unshaven, square-shouldered and irrascible, he was scarcely visible in the fumes that filled the part of the laboratory where he was decanting diluted venom.

'It's about little Kha.'

'What's that matter with him?'

'It's you who . . . Well, I mean . . . up till now I've been responsible for the child's education. He likes to read and write, and shows exceptional maturity for his age. He already knows much that would be the envy of many scribes, and doesn't hesitate to study the secrets of heaven and earth, and wants—'

'I know all that, Nedjem, and I've got work to do. Get to the point.'

'You . . . you aren't an easy man.'

'Life isn't easy. When you live every day in the company of reptiles, you haven't time to waste on frivolities.'

Nedjem was shocked. 'But my visit isn't a frivolity!'

'Well then, tell me what you have to say.'

'All right, I'll be more direct. Why are you leading Kha into bad ways?'

Setau put down on a shelf the flask he was working with and wiped his brow with a cloth. 'You come into my laboratory, Nedjem, you disturb me in my work and, what is more, you insult me! You may well be a minister, but I feel like shoving my fist in your face.'

Nedjem backed away, bumping into Lotus. 'Forgive me. I didn't think. But the child . . .'

'Does Kha's initiation into magic seem premature to you?' asked Lotus, with an engaging smile.

'Yes! Yes, that's it,' Nedjem replied.

'These scruples are a credit to you, but your fears are unfounded.'

'Such a young child, faced with such a complex, such a dangerous science . . .'

'Pharaoh has ordered us to protect his son. To do so, we need Kha's cooperation.'

The minister blanched. 'Protect him? Against what threat?'

'Do you like beef marinade?' asked Lotus.

'I . . . Of course.'

'It's one of my specialities. Will you share our meal?'

'To intrude on you like this, at the last moment—'

'Done!' retorted Setau. 'Kha is no fragile little object but Ramses' first-born son. By attacking him, someone wants to weaken the royal couple and the whole country. We shall construct a magic wall around Kha so as to ward off the harmful influences launched against him. The enterprise demands precision, and it will be difficult and risky, so any positive help will be welcome.'

116

20

Over the alleyway of the Hebrew district there were beams covered with criss-crossed reeds to protect the passers-by from the heat of the sun. Housewives sat chatting in the doorways of their houses. When the water-carrier went past, they quenched their thirst before resuming their interminable conversations – artisans taking a moment's rest and brick-makers returning from the building sites joined in.

One subject occupied all their minds: the trial of Moses. According to some, he would be condemned to death; others thought he'd get a light prison sentence. Some extremists advocated rebellion, but the majority were fatalists: who'd dare oppose the army and Pharaoh's police? Anyway, Moses was only getting what he deserved, because he had, after all, killed a man. No one was shocked that the law should be applied in all its rigour, even though Moses remained very popular and no one had forgotten his dedication to the brickmakers' cause and the material advantages he had gained for them. Many workers wished he could become an architect again and take an interest in their fate again.

Aaron shared the general pessimism. True, Moses' destiny was in the hands of Yahveh, but Egyptian justice was tough on criminals. If Abner had agreed to appear, the accusation would have been dropped. But the brickmaker maintained firmly that Moses was lying, and so had refused to leave his hiding-place before the end of the trial. As Aaron couldn't find anything specific to blame Abner for, he couldn't ask the chief of his tribe to insist that he give evidence.

As he walked down the alleyway, Aaron noticed a beggar whose head was covered with a hood. He was slumped against a wall, his legs bent under him, and gnawing pieces of bread which passers-by threw to him. On the first day, Aaron tried to forget the wretched creature; on the second day, he gave him some food; on the third day, he sat down beside him.

'Have you no family?'

'Not any longer.'

'Were you married?'

'My wife's dead, and my children have left.'

'What unhappy fate has brought you so low?'

'I was a grain merchant. I had a fine house. I led a peaceful existence. And then I made a bad mistake by deceiving my wife.'

'God has punished you.'

'You're right, but He's not the one responsible for my downfall. A man found out about my affair, blackmailed me and destroyed my marriage. My wife died of grief.'

'That man must be a monster!'

'A monster who continues in his evil ways, spreading misery. I'm not the only one to have suffered from his cruelty.'

'What's his name?'

'I'm ashamed to utter it.'

'Why?'

'Because he's a Hebrew, like you and me.'

'My name's Aaron and I have some influence in our community. You have no right to remain silent, because one bad apple can contaminate the whole barrel.'

'What does it matter now? I'm alone and in despair.'

'In spite of your distress, you must think of others. This

man must be punished.'

'His name is Abner,' whispered the beggar.

Now Aaron had a serious motive for complaining about Abner's behaviour. That same evening, he called a meeting of the council of elders and heads of tribes and told them of the grain merchant's tribulations.

'Some time ago,' one elder agreed, 'Abner is said to have blackmailed some brickmakers, but they didn't complain and only rumours reached our ears. Now we understand why Abner doesn't want to appear before a court. He prefers to let this trouble die down.'

'Meanwhile, Moses is in prison and only Abner's evidence can save him!'

The elders were embarrassed and were not inclined to take sides. The head of one of the tribes summed up their opinion.

'Let's be frank: Moses has committed a crime which has cast suspicion on all the Hebrews. It's not unjust for him to be punished. What's more, he's returned to sow trouble among us with his crazy ideas. The wisest thing would be to let things take their course.'

Aaron was furious. 'You're a lot of cowards! So, you choose to help a scoundrel like Abner, and you send Moses, who fought for you, to his death ! May Yahveh plunge you into misery and distress!'

The head of the assembly, a retired brickmaker, intervened firmly. 'Aaron is right, our behavour is contemptible.'

'We've protected Abner,' the head of one tribe reminded them. 'We've no right to force him to risk punishment, on the strength of vague accusations.'

Aaron struck the ground with his staff. 'Could Abner by any chance have helped you to get rich on the backs of your brothers?'

'How dare you!'

'We must confront Abner with this beggar.'

'Agreed,' declared the head of the assembly.

Abner was hiding in the heart of the brickmakers' district, in a two-storey house which he would not leave until Moses had been sentenced. Grown rich and respected, he gorged on cakes and spent most of his time sleeping.

When the council of elders and the heads of tribes insisted on the confrontation, he laughed. In the first place, a beggar carried very little weight with him; besides which Abner would accuse the Hebrew people of letting a man starve, which was against Egyptian law. If, by some extraordinary chance, the affair turned nasty, his allies would see to it that his wretched accuser disappeared.

The interview took place on the ground floor of Abner's house, in the reception hall, whose benches were covered with cushions. There were present the head of the elders; the head of one of the tribes, delegated by his peers; and Aaron, supporting the bent old beggar, who seemed barely able to walk.

Abner jeered at the beggar. 'So this is the miserable wretch who's rambling on about me. Is he even capable of speaking? The wisest thing would be to give him some food and send him off to end his days on a farm in the Delta.'

Aaron helped the man to a seat.

'We can avoid a confrontation,' declared the head of the elders, 'if you agree to give evidence in favour of Moses and to confirm his version of the facts, as it appears in the document you signed.'

'Moses is a disturbed, dangerous man. For my part, I've made the fortune of a great number of our brothers! Why should I take unnecessary risks?'

'Out of concern for the truth,' Aaron put in.

'Truth can fluctuate so much. And will it be sufficient to set Moses free? After all, he did commit a murder! We've nothing to gain by getting mixed up in this affair.'

'Moses saved your life. You must save his.'

'That's old history, and my memory's not very clear. Isn't it better to think about the future? Besides, my written testimony will act in favour of Moses. With the benefit of doubt in his favour, he won't be sentenced to death.'

'A long prison sentence isn't exactly an enviable lot.'

'Moses should have restrained himself and not killed Sary.'

Aaron again struck the ground with his staff in his exasperation.

'No violence,' insisted the head of the elders.

'This fellow is a scoundrel! He betrayed his own people and he'll betray them again!'

'Calm down,' advised Abner. 'I'm a generous man and I promise to provide for your needs. For me, respect for the elders is a major virtue.'

Had it not been for the presence of the elders, Aaron would have broken Abner's head.

'Let's leave it there, friends,' said Abner, 'and celebrate our reconciliation with a good meal which I'll be pleased to offer you.'

'Aren't you forgetting the beggar?'

'Ah yes, the beggar. What's he got to say?'

Aaron addressed the miserable fellow. 'Don't be afraid. You can speak freely.'

The man remained prostrate.

Abner guffawed. 'So that's your great accuser! Let's have done with this. Hand him over to my servants, and they'll give him some food in the kitchen.'

Aaron was mortified. 'Speak, please.'

Slowly the beggar unfolded his huge body, lowered his hood and uncovered his face.

Abner was stunned, scarcely able to utter the name of his unexpected and dreaded guest. 'Serramanna!'

'You're under arrest,' declared the Sardinian, with a pirate's grin.

*

All through Abner's hearing, Serramanna was prey to conflicting emotions. On the one hand, he had hoped not to find Abner, so that the plotter Moses would not be cleared; on the other hand, he had succeeded in his mission. Ramses must be an extraordinary person to have inspired him with such obedience while he was convinced of the Hebrew's capacity to do harm. The king was wrong to trust Moses, but how could you criticize a monarch for whom friendship was one of the sacred virtues?

The whole of Pi-Ramses was awaiting the vizier's judgment, to be given at the end of the jury's deliberations. The trial had greatly increased Moses' prestige. Moreover, the humble folk and nearly all the brickmakers were now on his side: he had always been the defender of those unfortunates whom life had treated harshly.

Serramanna hoped Moses would be exiled so that he would not disturb the harmony built up, day after day, by the royal couple.

When Ahmeni left the courtroom, the Sardinian went to meet him. Ahmeni said happily, 'Moses has been acquitted.'

21

The court was convened in the palace in Pi-Ramses, in the audience chamber, which was approached by a monumental staircase adorned with the figures of fallen enemies. No one knew why Pharaoh had summoned the whole government and the principal administrators, but everyone expected an announcement of decisions crucial to the country's future.

As he passed through the monumental door, which was surrounded by cartouches containing Ramses' coronation titles painted in blue on a white background, Ahmeni found it difficult to hide his dissatisfaction. Why had the king not confided in him? At the sight of Ahsha's tight-lipped expression, he guessed that his friend was as much in the dark as himself.

The courtiers were so numerous that it was impossible to see the decoration of glazed terracotta tiles, depicting flower gardens and lakes in which fish leaped. People were squeezed between pillars and against walls painted with enchanted scenes in pale green, deep red, light blue, brilliant yellow and off-white. But in these anxious moments, who could stop to admire the impressive sight of birds flitting around in marshes planted with papyrus?

However, Setau's gaze did linger on a painting of a young woman whose features resembled those of the queen, sunk in meditation before a clump of hollyhocks. Friezes of water-lilies, poppies, daisies and cornflowers symbolized smiling nature at her most peaceful.

Ministers, senior officials, royal scribes, ritualists, guardians of secrets, priests and priestesses, great ladies and other important personalities, all fell silent when Ramses and Nefertari took their seats on their thrones. The power of the monarch was dazzling, his presence imposing beyond compare. Ramses was wearing the double crown, marking his sovereignty over Upper and Lower Egypt, a white robe and a golden kilt; in his right hand he held the 'magic' sceptre, the shepherd's crook which served to muster his people in the invisible world and maintain their link with the visible. Nefertari was grace, Ramses power. Everyone in the assembly was aware of the deep love which united them and made them both redolent of eternity.

The ritualist read a hymn to Amon, celebrating the presence of the god hidden in all forms of life. Then Ramses spoke.

'I am going to let you know of a certain number of decisions in order to dispel rumours and explain the policies I intend to follow for the time being. These choices are the fruit of long thought and deliberation with the Great Royal Wife.'

Several royal scribes prepared to note down the monarch's words, which would immediately have the force of decrees.

'I have decided to reinforce the north-east border of Egypt, build new fortresses there, strengthen the old walls, double the garrisons and improve the men's pay. The King's Wall must become impenetrable and protect the Delta from any attempt at invasion. Teams of stone-cutters and brickmakers will start leaving tomorrow to undertake the necessary work.'

An elderly courtier asked permission to speak. 'Majesty, will the King's Wall be sufficient to stop the Hittite hordes?'

'By itself, no. It is only the last element in our defence system. Thanks to our army's recent campaign, which shattered the Hittite counter-offensive, we have reconquered our protectorates. Canaan, Amurru and southern Syria now stand between us and the invader.'

'But haven't the princes governing these provinces often betrayed us?'

'They have indeed. That is why I am entrusting the administrative and military government of this buffer zone to Ahsha, to whom I am granting exceptional powers in the region. I am making him responsible for maintaining our supremacy, keeping control over the local rulers, setting up an efficient intelligence service and preparing an elite army, capable of containing any Hittite attack.'

Ahsha remained impassive, although all eyes were upon him, some admiring, others envious. The minister for foreign affairs was becoming a leading figure in the state.

'I have also decided to undertake a long journey with the queen,' Ramses continued. 'During my absence, Ahmeni will be responsible for day-to-day administration and he will consult my mother, Tuya, every day. We shall remain in contact by courier; no decree will be issued without my agreement.'

The court was dumbfounded. Ahmeni's role as power behind the throne was not a revelation, but why was the royal couple going so far from Pi-Ramses at such a crucial time?

The head of protocol ventured to ask the question on everyone's lips: 'Majesty, would you agree to let us know the purpose of your voyage?'

'To reinforce the sacred foundation of Egypt. The queen and I will first go to Thebes, to check the progress of my Temple of a Million Years, then we shall leave for the Far South.'

'As far as Nubia?'

'Yes.'

'Forgive me, Majesty, but is this long journey necessary?'

'Imperative.'

The court understood that Pharaoh would say no more. And everyone started imagining the secret reasons for this astonishing decision.

Wideawake, the king's golden-yellow dog, licked Tuya's hand, while the lion lay at her feet.

'These two faithful companions wanted to pay tribute to you,' Ramses pointed out.

Tuya was preparing a great floral arrangement to be placed on the table intended for the offerings to the goddess Sekhmet. The Mother of Pharaoh wore a long linen gown, bordered with gold, a short cape draping her shoulders, and round her waist a scarlet girdle with striped ends reaching nearly to the ground. She was most noble, but also rather forbidding, with her piercing eyes and her fine, severe countenance: she looked every inch a powerful woman, exacting and inflexible.

'What do you think of my decisions, mother?'

'Nefertari had spoken of them to me at length, and I'm afraid I was even to some extent responsible for suggesting them. The only efficient protection of our north-eastern border is to maintain a firm hand over our protectorates, to prevent a Hittite invasion. That was your father's policy, and it must be yours too. Nine years of reigning, my son. How are you bearing that burden?'

'I've scarcely had time to think about it.'

'All the better. Continue to advance and to plot a straight course. Do you feel that the crew of the ship of state obey your orders as they should?'

'My immediate entourage is very much reduced, and I've no intention of increasing it.'

'Ahmeni is an outstanding individual,' said Tuya thoughtfully, 'even if his vision is too narrow. He has two very rare virtues, honesty and loyalty.'

'Do you think equally highly of Ahsha?'

126

'He possesses an exceptional quality too: courage, a particular form of courage based on a deep analysis of situations. He's by far the best person to watch over our northern protectorates.'

'And Setau? Does he find favour in your eyes?'

'He hates convention and he's sincere. How could I not look with favour on such a valuable ally?'

'That only leaves Moses . . .'

'I know your friendship for him.'

'But you don't approve of him.'

'No, Ramses. This Hebrew is pursuing aims which you will be forced to disapprove of. Whatever the circumstances, always put your country before your feelings.'

'Moses is not yet a troublemaker.'

'If he becomes one, the Rule of Ma'at, and that alone, must inspire your conduct. The ordeal may be terrible, even for you, Ramses.' Tuya straightened the stem of a lily; the arrangement had the splendour of a hundred flowers.

'Are you willing to rule over the Two Lands during my absence?'

'Have I any choice? The burden of age is beginning to wear me down, though.'

Ramses smiled. 'I don't believe that.'

'You have too much inner strength to be able to imagine what the weight of old age can be. And now, will you tell me the real reason for this long journey?'

'My love for Egypt and for Nefertari. I want to revive the hidden fires of the temples, so that they can produce more energy.'

'Do you mean that the Hittites are not our only enemies?'

'A Libyan magus, Ofir, is using the forces of darkness against us. Perhaps I'm wrong to attach such importance to his deeds, but I shall take no chances. Nefertari has already suffered too much from his evil spells.'

'The gods have favoured you, my son. They could have

granted you no greater happiness than such a brilliant wife.'

'It would be a grave error not to offer her suitable veneration. So I have conceived a grand project to let her name shine forth for millions of years and for the royal couple to appear as the tangible foundation on which Egypt is built.'

'Since you are conscious of this requirement, your reign will be a great reign. Nefertari is the magic without which no deed can last. Violence and darkness will not vanish as long as one generation follows another, but this land will know harmony as long as the royal couple reigns. Strengthen this couple, Ramses, make it the foundation stone of the edifice. When love shines over a people, it offers them more happiness than any amount of wealth.'

The flower arrangement was completed; the goddess would be satisfied.

'Do you ever think about Shanaar?' asked Ramses.

Sadness clouded Tuya's eyes. 'How could a mother ever forget her son?'

'Shanaar is no longer your son.'

'The king is right and I should listen to him. Will he forgive my weakness?'

Ramses clasped Tuya lovingly to him.

'By depriving him of burial,' she explained, 'the gods have inflicted a terrible punishment on him.'

'I confronted death at Kadesh. Shanaar met his death in the desert. Perhaps death purified his soul.'

'And what if he is still alive?'

'That thought has occurred to me, too. If he were in hiding, in the shadows, with the same intentions as before, would you be lenient?'

'You are Egypt, Ramses, and anyone who attacks you will first have to deal with me.'

22

Ramses meditated before the statue of Thoth that stood at the entrance to the Foreign Affairs secretariat, and laid a bunch of lilies on the altar as an offering. Thoth was represented as a great stone ape, the master of hieroglyphs, the 'words of the gods', and his eyes were raised to the sky.

Pharaoh's visit was an honour which delighted the secretariat's officials. Ahsha welcomed the monarch and bowed to him. When Ramses embraced him, the young minister's subordinates felt proud to work under a dignitary to whom the king granted such a mark of trust.

The two men shut themselves up in Ahsha's sumptuous office, which was in exquisite taste. There were roses imported from Syria, floral arrangements of narcissi and marigolds, cedar chests, chairs whose panels were decorated with water-lilies, brocaded cushions and pedestal tables with bronze feet. On the walls were painted scenes depicting the shooting of marsh birds.

'You've not opted for austerity,' noted Ramses. 'The only things missing are Shanaar's exotic vases.'

'Too unpleasant a memory! I had them sold in aid of my secretariat's finances.'

With his neat little moustache and his light, perfumed wig, Ahsha was an elegant figure. He looked as though he were about to attend some fashionable banquet.

'When I've the good fortune to enjoy a few peaceful weeks in Egypt,' he admitted, 'I make the most of the countless pleasures this land has to offer. But let the king be reassured: I'm not forgetting the mission he has entrusted me with.'

Such was Ahsha: cynical, apparently frivolous, a womanizer, going from conquest to conquest, but a statesman familiar with the requirements of international politics, a perfect judge of any territory and an adventurer capable of running the wildest risks.

'What do you think of my decisions?'

'I'm overwhelmed and delighted, Majesty.'

'Do you find them . . . adequate?'

'There's one essential item missing, isn't there? And that's precisely the reason for this visit, which has nothing to do with protocol. Let me guess: could it by any chance be Kadesh?'

'I made the right choice of minister for foreign affairs and head of my intelligence service.'

'Are you still thinking of seizing that stronghold?'

'We won a victory at Kadesh, but the Hittite fortress is intact and continues to defy us.'

Ahsha was not pleased. He went to pour a fine red wine, of a brilliant colour, into two silver goblets with handles shaped like gazelles.

'I suspected you'd return to the subject of Kadesh. Ramses cannot live in the shadow of failure. Yes, this fortress still defies us; and yes, it is as strong as ever.'

'That's why I consider it a permanent threat to our southern Syrian protectorate. It's from Kadesh that attacks will come.'

'At first glance, the reasoning seems perfect.'

'But you don't agree?'

'A pot-bellied, peace-loving minister, comfortably ensconced in his position with its privileges and dignities, would bow low before you and speak to you more or less as

130

follows: "Ramses the Great, O King, with your piercing eyes and your victorious arm, do set off to conquer Kadesh!" and this courtier would be a dangerous imbecile.'

'And why should I give up this conquest?'

'Thanks to you, the Hittites discovered that they are not invincible. True, their army is still powerful, but they are disturbed. Muwatallis promised an easy invasion and a crushing victory, and he has had great difficulty in justifying his troops' retreat from their usual positions. And there is another dispute in process: the struggle for the succession between his son, Uri-Teshup, and his brother, Hattusilis.'

'Who looks likely to win?'

'It's impossible to say; both possess adequate weapons.'

'Is Muwatallis's downfall imminent?'

'In my opinion, yes. Killing is common at the Hittite court. In a war-based society, any leader who doesn't win victories must be eliminated.'

'Then surely this is the ideal moment to attack Kadesh and seize it?'

'True, if our only interest were to undermine the foundations of the Hittite Empire.'

Ramses usually appreciated Ahsha's keen intelligence and quick wit, but this time he was taken aback. 'Isn't that the main aim of our foreign policy?'

'I'm no longer very sure.'

'You must be joking!'

'When a decision involves the life or death of thousands of human beings, I have no taste for joking.'

'Well then, you have some piece of information which will radically change my judgment.'

'Simple intuition, based on information gleaned by our informers. Have you heard of the Assyrians?'

'They're a warlike tribe, like the Hittites.'

'Up till now, Assyria has been under Hittite influence. But when Hattusilis formed his coalition, he gave the Assyrians large quantities of precious metal, to persuade them to maintain a friendly neutrality, and this unexpected wealth has been transformed into weapons. At present there are more soldiers in Assyria than diplomats. The next great power in the region between Canaan and Asia could well be Assyria – even more keen on conquest and even more destructive than Hatti.'

Ramses thought for a moment. 'Would Assyria be prepared to attack Hatti?'

'Not yet, but in due course war between them seems to me inevitable.'

'Why doesn't Muwatallis cut off the evil at the roots?'

'Because of the internal dissension threatening his throne and because he fears our army will advance on Kadesh. For him, we remain the principal enemy.'

'And what about those who covet his power?'

'His son, Uri-Teshup, is blind; he thinks of nothing but gaining possession of the Two Lands and killing as many Egyptians as possible. Hattusilis is more far-sighted and must be more aware of the growing peril at the very gates of the Hittite Empire.'

'So you don't advise me to launch a vast offensive against Kadesh.'

'We'd lose a great many men, and so would the Hittites. The real winner might well be Assyria.'

'You haven't only been thinking, of course. What is your plan?'

'I'm afraid it may not please you, inasmuch as it contradicts the policy you feel to be correct.'

'Take the risk.'

'Let us give the Hittites the impression that we're preparing the attack on Kadesh. Rumours, false information, bogus confidential documents, manoeuvres in southern Syria . . . I'll see to it.'

'So far, I'm not shocked.'

'What follows is rather more delicate. When this part of the plan has proved effective, I shall leave for Hatti.'

'On what pretext?'

'A secret mission, with full powers to negotiate.'

'But . . . to negotiate what?'

'Peace, Majesty.'

'Peace? With the *Hittites*?'

'It's the best way to prevent Assyria becoming a much more dangerous monster than Hatti.'

'The Hittites will never accept.'

'If I have your support, I'm quite sure I can convince them.'

'If anyone but you had suggested this to me, I'd have accused him of high treason.'

Ahsha smiled. 'I rather suspected that. But Ramses can see far ahead, far, far beyond the present moment.'

'Don't the sages teach us that to flatter a friend is an unforgivable fault?'

'I am addressing not my friend but Pharaoh. Taking a short-sighted view, with our eyes fixed only on the present, would mean using our present strength to confront the Hittites – and there's a real possibility that we'd defeat them. But the irruption of the Assyrians on to the international scene must modify our strategy.'

'It's only intuition, Ahsha. You said so yourself.'

'In my job, it's essential to foresee the future and to be the first to be forewarned. And intuition often leads to the right decision.'

'I've no right to let you run such a risk.'

'Do you mean my stay with the Hittites? It won't be the first.'

'You want more experience of their prisons, do you?'

'There are pleasanter resorts for a restful stay, but one must be able to tempt fate.'

'I'll never find such a good minister for foreign affairs.'

'I fully intend to return, Ramses. And besides, leading an easy, social life would eventually weaken my mind. Spending my time going the round of several mistresses, dressing them, taking them about and eventually tiring of them . . . I need a new adventure to keep my mind sharp and ready for new conquests. I'm not afraid of this experiment. It's up to me to exploit the Hittites' weaknesses and persuade them to end hostilities.'

'You do know, don't you, Ahsha, that this plan is completely mad?'

'It has the freshness of novelty and the appeal of the unknown. What more could one want?'

'All the same, you can't really believe I'll give my consent.'

'Yes, I believe you will, because you aren't an over-cautious old monarch incapable of changing the world. Give me the order to negotiate with the barbarians who want to destroy us and I'll make them our vassals.'

'I'm about to undertake a long journey to the Far South, and you'll be isolated in the north.'

'Since you are busy with the next world, leave the Hittites to me.'

23

The 'Royal Sons' were aged between fifteen and twenty-five. Their heads were shaven, leaving only one lock, consisting of a series of parallel plaits held in place by a wide bar just above one ear, to fall over the right cheek. They wore earrings, wide collars, bracelets and pleated kilts, and proudly carried long staffs tipped with ostrich feathers.

Ramses had charged these young men, all chosen for their physical and intellectual ability, with representing him in the different army corps. He had not forgotten the soldiers' cowardice at Kadesh, when faced with the coalition assembled by the Hittites; so the Royal Sons' task on the battlefield was to rekindle the troops' efforts if these should fail.

These young men were about to leave for the north to take charge of the administration of the protectorates. They had received strict orders from Ahsha which they would scrupulously obey.

Already the legend was spreading that Ramses the Great, a tireless procreator and prolific father, had sired a hundred children, whose existence was clear proof of the monarch's divine power. There was thus built up a fabulous genealogy, which the sculptors were expressing in stone and the scribes would delight in handing down.

In the shade of his lemon tree, old Homer was dabbing

perfume on his white beard. Hector, the fat black and white cat, purred as soon as Ramses stroked him.

'Forgive my indiscretion, Majesty, but I get the impression you are vexed.'

'Let's say . . . worried.'

'Bad news?'

'No, but I'm about to go on a long journey which presents some dangers.'

The poet stuffed some sage leaves into the snail-shell bowl of his pipe. 'Ramses the Great, that's what the people call you now. I have just written: "The magnificent gifts of the gods are not to be despised. The gods alone can grant these to us, for no man could acquire them by himself."'

'I didn't know you were such a fatalist.'

'It's the privilege of age, Majesty. My *Iliad* and my *Odyssey* are completed, and I've put the finishing touches to my poem celebrating your victory at Kadesh. There's nothing left for me to do except smoke sage leaves, drink wine flavoured with aniseed and be rubbed down with olive oil.'

'Don't you want to reread your works?'

'Only second-rate authors gaze at themselves in the mirror of their words,' said Homer. Then, 'Why this journey, Majesty?'

'"Return often to Abydos," my father insisted, "and watch over the temple there." I've neglected his orders, and I must attend to that sanctuary.'

'But there's something else, isn't there?'

'To the question "What is a pharaoh?" Seti used to reply, "He who makes his people happy." How is that to be achieved? By actions which are beneficial to the Principle and to the gods, so that they are reflected on to mankind.'

'Did the queen suggest you do this?'

'I wish to build something with her and for her, something which will be the source of that luminous force we so much need, and which will protect Egypt and Nubia from misfortune.'

'Have you chosen the site?'

'In the heart of Nubia, Hathor has marked with her presence a place called Abu Simbel. By becoming embodied in the stone, the Lady of the Stars has revealed the secret of her love. It is that love which I wish to offer to Nefertari, so that she will be known for ever as the Lady of Abu Simbel.'

The bearded, unkempt cook squatted down on his heels, his knees bent under him, to fan with a palm leaf the flame of a brazier over which he was roasting a trussed goose. He had stuffed a skewer through the beak and neck of the fowl and held it upright above the fire. When he'd finished he was going to pluck a duck, gut it, cut off the head, the tips of the wings and the claws, and put it on a spit to roast over a slow heat.

A noble lady called out to him, 'Has all your poultry been reserved by customers?'

'Nearly all.'

'If I order a duck from you, can you prepare it for me straight away?'

'The thing is . . . I'm very busy.'

Dolora adjusted the left shoulder-strap of her gown, which tended to slip down, then placed a pot of honey at the cook's feet. 'Your disguise is perfect, Shanaar. If you hadn't asked me to meet you right here, I wouldn't have recognized you.'

'Have you learned anything important?'

'I think so. I was present at the royal couple's grand audience.'

'Come back in two hours' time and I'll give you your duck and shut my shop. Then follow me and I'll take you to Ofir.'

The cooks' and butchers' district was alongside the warehouses, and didn't become quiet until nightfall. A few heavily laden apprentices were making their way to the homes of the wealthy to deliver the fine cuts of meat which would be served at their banquets.

137

Shanaar entered a deserted alleyway, stopped in front of a low door painted blue, and gave four spaced knocks. As soon as the door opened he gestured to Dolora to hurry inside. The tall brunette forced herself to obey. She found herself in a low-ceilinged place, cluttered up with baskets. Shanaar lifted a trap-door and he and his sister descended wooden stairs leading to a cellar.

When she saw the magus, Dolora fell at his feet and kissed the hem of his gown. 'I was afraid I'd never see you again!'

'I promised you I'd return. Days meditating in the City of the Sun have strengthened my faith in Aton, the One God, who tomorrow will rule over this land.'

Dolora gazed in ecstasy at the hawk-faced magus. She was bewitched by this prophet of the true faith. Tomorrow people would be guided by his strength; tomorrow he would overthrow Ramses.

'Your help is very valuable to me,' Ofir said gently in his deep voice. 'Without you, how could we struggle against this impious and detested tyrant?'

'Ramses no longer suspects me. I'm even convinced he trusts me again, because of my intervention on behalf of his friend Moses.'

'What are the king's intentions?'

'He has entrusted the administration of the northern protectorates to the Royal Sons, who'll act under Ahsha's orders.'

'That damned diplomat!' roared Shanaar. 'He deceived me and made a fool of me. I'll get my revenge, I'll trample on him, I'll—'

'We've got more urgent business,' Ofir interrupted him curtly. 'Let's hear what Dolora has to say.'

She was proud to be playing a major role. 'The royal couple are going on a long journey.'

'What's their destination?'

'Upper Egypt and Nubia.'

'Do you know why they're going?'

'Ramses wants to offer the queen an extraordinary gift. A temple, it seems.'

'Is that the only reason for this journey?'

'Pharaoh wants to revive the divine powers, gather them together, rekindle their energy and weave a protective net which he'll stretch over Egypt.'

Shanaar sniggered. 'Has my beloved brother gone out of his mind?'

'No,' protested Dolora. 'He knows he's threatened by mysterious enemies. He has no solution but to appeal to the gods and muster an invisible army to fight against the enemies he fears.'

'He *is* going mad,' sneered Shanaar, 'and he's sinking deeper and deeper into his lunacy. An army of deities? It's ridiculous!'

He felt Ofir's icy glance upon him.

'Ramses has become aware of the danger,' Ofir said.

'All the same, you don't think—' Shanaar broke off. A terrifying violence emanated from the magus. For one moment Shanaar no longer doubted the Libyan's occult powers.

'Who is protecting Kha?' Ofir asked Dolora.

'Setau, the snake-charmer. He's passing on his knowledge to Kha and has surrounded him with forces which protect him from any attack, no matter what its source.'

'Snakes do possess the earth's magic,' Ofir conceded. 'Anyone who keeps company with them knows this magic. Nevertheless, with the help of the child's writing-brush I shall manage to destroy those defences. But I shall need more time than I thought.'

Dolora's heart rebelled at the thought that Kha would have to suffer from the war of the spirits; but her mind accepted the magus's strategy. This attack would weaken Ramses, lessen his *ka* and perhaps even make him abdicate. However cruel the assault, she would not oppose it.

'We must separate,' decided Ofir.

Dolora clutched the magus's gown. 'When shall I see you again?'

'Shanaar and I will be leaving the capital for some time. We can't stay long in the same place. You'll be the first to know of our return. In the meantime, continue to gather information.'

'I shall continue to spread the true faith,' she declared.

'Nothing could be more important,' murmured Ofir with a knowing smile.

24

To celebrate Moses' acquittal, the Hebrew brickmakers had organized an enormous banquet in the workers' district where they lived. Triangular loaves, pigeon stew, stuffed quails, stewed figs, strong wine and cool beer were offered to the guests, who sang throughout the night, now and then chanting the name of Moses, who had become the most popular of all Hebrews.

Wearied by the din, Moses slipped away from the celebration when his supporters were too drunk to notice his absence. He needed to be alone, to ponder on the struggles which lay ahead. It wouldn't be easy to persuade Ramses to let the entire Hebrew people leave Egypt. And yet, whatever the cost, he had to carry out the mission Yahveh had entrusted to him. To achieve it, he would move mountains.

Moses sat down on the edge of the local millstone. Two Bedouin, bald, bearded Amos and lean Baduch, came up to him.

'What are you doing here?' he asked.

'We're sharing in the rejoicing,' declared Amos. 'Isn't this a wonderful moment?'

'You aren't Hebrews.'

'We could be your allies.'

'I don't need you.'

'Aren't you overestimating your people's strength? Without weapons, you'll never realize your dreams.'

'I shall use certain weapons, but not yours.'

'If the Hebrews ally themselves with the Bedouin,' said Baduch, 'they'll form a real army.'

'What purpose would that serve?'

'To fight the Egyptians and defeat them.'

'That's a dangerous dream.'

'You, Moses, are in no position to criticize it. To lead your people out of Egypt, to defy Ramses, to place yourself above the laws of this country – isn't that dream just as bad and just as dangerous?'

'Who told you about my plans?'

'There's not a single brickmaker who doesn't know about them! They even say you intend to seize the Two Lands, fighting under the banner of Yahveh, the warrior god.'

'Men are quick to talk wildly when a grand plan upsets their routine.'

An unwholesome gleam shone in Baduch's cunning eyes. 'The fact remains that you intend to stir up the Hebrews against the Egyptian government.'

'Get out of my way, both of you!'

'You're wrong, Moses,' Amos insisted. 'Your people will have to fight, and they have no experience of this. We could be their teachers.'

'Go away, and leave me to think.'

'As you wish. We shall meet again.'

The two Bedouin, armed with a travel permit from Meba, travelled with donkeys, like simple peasants. They halted in a field to the south of Pi-Ramses, and were just sampling some sweet onions, fresh bread and dried fish when two men came and sat down beside them.

'How did the interview go?' asked Ofir.

'That Moses is stubborn,' admitted Amos.

'Threaten him,' demanded Shanaar.

'That wouldn't help. We must let him get more and more

committed to his crazy plans. Sooner or later, he'll need us.'

'Have the Hebrews accepted him?'

'His acquittal has raised him to the rank of a hero, and the brickmakers are convinced he'll defend their rights, as before.'

'What do they think of his plan?'

'It's much disputed but some young ones, who dream of independence, are enthusiastic about it.'

'We must encourage them,' said Shanaar. 'By stirring up unrest, they'll weaken Ramses' power. If he starts suppressing them, he'll make himself unpopular.'

Amos and Baduch were the only two survivors of the Hittite spy ring in Egypt. They moved outside the traders' closed world, and so had not been detected by Serramanna. In the Delta they enjoyed considerable support.

The meeting between Ofir, Shanaar, Amos and Baduch was a veritable council of war, marking the resumption of the offensive against Ramses.

'Where are the Hittite troops?' asked Ofir.

'According to our Bedouin informants,' Baduch replied, 'they're camped out on the heights of Kadesh. The garrison has been reinforced in the expectation of an assault by the Egyptian army.'

'I know my brother,' declared Shanaar ironically. 'He won't resist the desire to forge ahead!'

At the battle of Kadesh, Amos and Baduch, pretending to be panic-stricken prisoners, had lied to Ramses to lure him into a trap from which he should not have escaped. They retained a bitter memory of their failure, which they burned to wipe out.

'What are the instructions from Hatti?' Ofir asked Baduch.

'To destabilize Ramses by all possible means.'

Ofir knew all too well the meaning of this vague order. On one hand, Egypt had reconquered her protectorates and the Hittites were in no position to recover them; on the other, the emperor's son and brother were engaged in a bitter power struggle. At present power was still in Muwatallis's hands – but how long could he survive?

The defeat at Kadesh, the failure of the counter-offensive in Canaan and Syria, and the lack of reaction when Egypt retook these territories, were signs that dissent was undermining the Hittite Empire. But this sad truth would not prevent Ofir from pursuing his mission. When Ramses was struck dead, a fresh fire would burn in Hatti.

'You two,' Ofir ordered Amos and Baduch, 'must continue to infiltrate the Hebrews. Tell your men to declare themselves supporters of Yahveh and urge the brickmakers to follow Moses. Dolora will let us know of any developments at court while the royal couple are away. For my part, I'll deal with Kha, no matter what protection surrounds him.'

'And I'll keep Ahsha for myself,' muttered Shanaar.

'You've better things to do,' judged Ofir.

'I want to kill him with my own hands, before I do away with my brother!'

'Why not begin with the latter?'

The magus's suggestion awoke in Shanaar a new burst of hatred for the tyrant who had stolen his throne.

Ofir went on, 'I'm leaving for Pi-Ramses again, to co-ordinate our efforts. You, Shanaar, must leave for the south.'

Shanaar scratched his beard. 'To hold up Ramses' advance? Is that what you mean?'

'You'll have to do more than that.'

'How?'

Ofir was obliged to reveal Muwatallis's strategy. 'The Hittites will invade the Delta, while the Nubians will cross the border and attack Elephantine. Ramses won't be able to extinguish the fires that we shall light simultaneously in different places.'

'What support will I have?'

'A troop of well-trained warriors is waiting for you near

the City of the Sun, together with some Nubian chieftains on whom we've been showering gifts for months. Ramses doesn't know it, but, by going into the heart of this region, he is rushing headlong into a trap. See to it that he does not return alive.'

Shanaar's face lit up with a broad smile. 'I believe neither in God nor in the gods, but I'm beginning to believe in my luck again. Why didn't you tell me sooner about these valuable allies?'

'I had orders,' explained Ofir.

'Which you are now disobeying.'

'I trust you, Shanaar. Now you know all the targets that have been set for me.'

Ramses' brother angrily tore up tufts of grass, which he tossed into the air; he rose to his feet and took a few steps. At last he was getting the power to act as he pleased, without the presence of the magus. Ofir made too much use of magic, of cunning and subterranean forces. He, Shanaar, would adopt a less complicated and more violent strategy.

Already a hundred ideas were jostling in his head. To interrupt Ramses' journey for good . . . That was his sole aim.

Ramses, Ramses 'the Great', whose outrageous success was eating away at his heart! Shanaar had no illusions about his own inadequacy, but he had one quality which no disappointment had weakened: obstinacy. His resentment grew daily, in proportion to the stature of his enemy, and this gave him the strength to confront the Lord of the Two Lands.

Then, for one moment, influenced by the peace of the countryside, Shanaar hesitated. What had he got to reproach Ramses with? Since the beginning of his reign, Seti's successor had done nothing wrong, either to his country or to his people. He had protected them against adversity, had been a valiant warrior, had guaranteed prosperity and justice.

What could he reproach him with – except being Ramses the Great?

25

Emperor Muwatallis summoned a meeting of the principal representatives of the military and merchant castes at which he reminded them of the words of one of his predecessors: 'Nowadays, murder has become common practice in the royal family; the queen has been assassinated, as has the king's son. To prevent similar tragedies in future, it is necessary to impose a law: no one shall kill a member of the royal family, no one shall draw a sword or dagger against such a member, and there shall be agreement over finding a successor to the sovereign.'

While declaring firmly that the question of his succession was not under discussion, the emperor expressed his pleasure that the time of murders was past, and renewed his trust in Hattusilis, his brother, and Uri-Teshup, his son. He confirmed the latter's appointment as commander-in-chief of the army and assigned to his brother responsibility for strengthening the economy and maintaining solid links with Hatti's foreign allies. In other words, he withdrew all military power from Hattusilis and rendered Uri-Teshup untouchable.

At the sight of Uri-Teshup's triumphant smile and Hattusilis's discomfiture, it was not difficult to identify the successor Muwatallis had chosen, though no name had been announced.

Weary and bent, tightly wrapped in his black and red woollen cloak, the emperor withdrew, surrounded by his personal body-guards, without adding any comment on his decisions.

In her fury the beautiful priestess Putuhepa stamped on the silver earrings that her husband, Hattusilis, had given her the previous day.

'It's incredible! Your brother treats you like dirt, and you weren't even informed!'

'Muwatallis is a secretive man, and I still retain some important functions.'

'Without the army you're nothing but a puppet dependent on Uri-Teshup's goodwill.'

'I've still got some firm friends among the generals and officers of the fortresses protecting our border.'

'But the emperor's son is already in full control of the capital!'

'Reasonable people are frightened of Uri-Teshup.'

'How much would it cost us to persuade them not to side with him?'

'A lot, but the merchants would help us.'

'Why has the emperor changed his mind? He seemed antagonistic to his son and had approved my plan to kill him.'

'Muwatallis never acts precipitately,' Hattusilis reminded her. 'He must have taken the threats from the military caste into consideration. He's appeased them by restoring Uri-Teshup's former privileges.'

'It's absolutely ridiculous! A man who's so crazy about war will take advantage of it to seize power.'

Hattusilis remained sunk in thought for a long time. Then he said, 'I wonder if the emperor hasn't tried to give us a message in some subtle way? Uri-Teshup becomes the strong-man of Hatti, so we seem a negligible quantity to him. Isn't that our best moment to do away with him? I'm convinced the emperor is using this means to suggest you hurry. We must strike and strike quickly.'

'I was hoping Uri-Teshup would come some day to pray in the Temple of Ishtar, to question the principal soothsayers. With this new appointment, it's essential for him to consult the vulture's entrails. As the new head of the Hittite army he must be anxious to know his future. I'll be the one to officiate. When I've killed him, I'll explain that he was the victim of the goddess's anger.'

Heavily laden with tin, cloth and foodstuffs, the donkeys made their slow, steady way into the Hittite capital. The leaders of the caravan led them to a counter where a merchant checked the lists and amounts of the goods, drew up the acknowledgement of debts, signed contracts and threatened bad debtors with legal action.

The principal representative of the merchant caste, a portly man in his sixties, sauntered through the trading district, keeping a sharp eye on transactions and never failing to intervene in cases of dispute. When he met Hattusilis, his professional smile faded: the emperor's brother seemed more tense than usual.

'The news is bad,' the merchant admitted.

'Trouble with your deliveries?'

'No, much worse: with Uri-Teshup.'

'But the emperor put *me* in charge of the economy!'

'That doesn't seem to worry Uri-Teshup.'

'What has he been doing?'

'He's decided to levy a new tax on every commercial transaction, in order to raise the soldiers' pay.'

'I'll protest vigorously.'

'It wouldn't be any use. It's too late.'

Hattusilis was like a man shipwrecked in a storm. For the first time, the emperor had not confided in him, and he had heard important news not from Muwatallis's own lips but from an outsider.

'I shall ask the emperor to declare this tax invalid.'

'You'll not succeed,' the merchant predicted. 'Uri-Teshup wants to restore Hatti's military power by crushing the merchants and robbing them of their wealth.'

'I shall oppose this.'

'May the gods assist you, Hattusilis.'

Hattusilis had been cooling his heels for more than three days in the cold little antechamber of the emperor's palace. Usually he entered his brother's private apartments without ceremony. This time, two members of Muwatallis's personal bodyguard had forbidden him to enter, and a chamberlain had heard his request without promising him anything.

It would soon be night. Hattusilis addressed one of the guards: 'Let the chamberlain know I shan't wait any longer.'

The soldier hesitated, looked at his companion for guidance, then left the room. The other seemed prepared to run Hattusilis through with his lance if he tried to enter by force.

A few minutes later the chamberlain reappeared, escorted by six aggressive-looking guards, who Hattusilis thought were going to arrest him and throw him into prison, from where he would never be freed.

'What do you want?' the chamberlain asked.

'To see the emperor.'

'Didn't I tell you he wasn't seeing anyone today? It's useless to wait any longer.'

The guards didn't move as Hattusilis stormed out.

As he was leaving the palace he passed Uri-Teshup, who was bursting with vitality. The commander-in-chief of the army did not even greet his uncle, and his lips were twisted in a contemptuous sneer.

Muwatallis gazed down on his capital from the top terrace of his palace. An enormous fortified rock, in the heart of the arid plains, Hattusa had been built to testify to the Hittite Empire's invincibility. At the very sight of it, any invader would turn round and go home. No one could seize its towers, no one could reach the imperial citadel overlooking the temples of the gods.

No one except Ramses. Since this pharaoh had mounted the throne of Egypt, he had made the huge fortress totter on its foundations and struck severe blows at the empire. The hideous possibility of defeat occasionally crossed Muwatallis's mind; at Kadesh he had avoided disaster, but would fortune continue to favour him? Ramses was young, masterful, beloved of the gods, and would not give up until he had eliminated the Hittite menace.

He, Muwatallis, the head of a warlike people, must think of a new and different strategy.

The chamberlain announced Uri-Teshup's arrival.

'Let him approach.'

The warrior's martial tread on the terrace made the paving stones tremble.

'May the God of Storms watch over you, father. The army will soon be ready to win back the lost ground.'

'Haven't you just levied a new tax which has angered the merchants?'

'They are cowards and profiteers. Their wealth will serve to strengthen our army.'

'You are trespassing on territory I entrusted to Hattusilis.'

'What does Hattusilis matter to me? Anyway, didn't you refuse to receive him?'

'I don't have to justify my decisions.'

'You've chosen me as your successor, father, and you were right to do so. The army is enthusiastic, the people reassured. You can count on me to impose our rule again and to massacre the Egyptians.'

'I know your courage, Uri-Teshup, but you have much to learn. Hatti's foreign policy can't be reduced to a perpetual war with Egypt.'

'There are only two kinds of men, the victors and the vanquished. The Hittites can only belong to the first category. Thanks to me, we shall triumph.'

'You must be content to obey my orders.'

'When are we going to attack?'

'I have other plans, my son.'

'Why delay a war that the empire demands?'

'Because we must negotiate with Ramses.'

'We, the Hittites, negotiate with the enemy? Have you gone out of your mind, father?'

'I forbid you to speak to me in that tone!' Muwatallis shouted angrily. 'Kneel before your emperor and beg his forgiveness.'

Uri-Teshup crossed his arms, but otherwise did not move.

'Obey, or else—' Muwatallis gasped for breath. Lips twisted in a grimace, eyes staring into space, he clutched his chest and collapsed.

Uri-Teshup just gazed at him.

'My heart . . . my heart is like a stone. Call the palace physician!'

'I insist on full powers. I must be the one to give orders to the army in future.'

'A physician, quickly!'

'Relinquish the throne.'

'I'm your father. Are you going . . . to let me . . . die?'

'Relinquish the throne!'

'I . . . do . . . You have . . . my word.'

26

The chiefs of the Hebrew tribes met in council to hear Moses, and listened attentively to what he had to say. His acquittal had increased his popularity so much that the voice of the one they called 'the prophet' could not be ignored.

'God has protected you,' Libni declared gruffly. 'Offer up praises to Him and spend the rest of your life in prayer.'

'You know my real intentions.'

'Your luck may run out, Moses. Don't tempt fate.'

'God has ordered me to lead the Hebrew people out of Egypt, and I shall obey Him.'

Aaron thumped his staff on the floor. 'Moses is right: we must obtain our independence. When we live in our own land we shall know happiness and prosperity at last. We must all leave Egypt together, and do the will of Yahveh!'

'Why should we drag our people along the path of misery?' argued Libni. 'The army will massacre the rebels, and the police will arrest the insurgents.'

'Let us drive out fear,' urged Moses. 'Our faith will give us the strength to defeat Pharaoh and avoid his anger.'

'Isn't it enough to serve Yahveh here, in this land of our birth?'

'God appeared to me, and He spoke to me,' Moses reminded them. 'He is the architect of our destiny. To refuse it would bring about our ruin.'

*

Kha was fascinated. Setau was telling him about the energy that flows through the universe and gives life to all things, from grains of sand to stars, an energy concentrated in the statues of the gods. When Setau took him into the temple, he could not tear himself away from the sight of the stone figures.

The child was filled with wonder. A priest purified his hands and feet, then asked him to purify his mouth with natron and dressed him in a white kilt. As soon as he entered the fragrant silent world of the sanctuary, Kha sensed the presence of a strange force, the 'magic' that linked all the elements of life, the magic that sustained Pharaoh and enabled him to sustain his people.

In the Temple of Amon, Setau showed Kha the laboratory, whose walls were covered with inscriptions revealing the secrets of the manufacture of the ritual salves and remedies that the gods used to treat the eye of Horus, to prevent the world being deprived of light.

Kha eagerly read the inscriptions and memorized as many of the hieroglyphs as possible. He would have liked to remain in the sanctuary, so as to be able to study them in detail. It was by means of these life-giving symbols that the wisdom of the ancients was conveyed.

'Here the real magic is revealed,' Setau explained. 'It's the weapon the gods gave men to fend off misfortune and disaster.'

'Can one escape from one's destiny?'

'No, but one can live in awareness of it. That's how to ward off the blows of fate. If you know how to turn everyday life into magic, you'll possess a power which will enable you to learn the secrets of heaven and earth, day and night, mountains and rivers; you'll understand the language of birds and fish, you'll be reborn at dawn with the sun and you'll see the divine power hover over the waters.'

'Will you teach me the formulas of knowledge?'

'Perhaps, if you persevere, and if you overcome vanity and laziness.'

'I'll fight them with all my might!'

'Your father and I are leaving for the Far South and shall be away for several months.'

Kha looked sulky. 'I'd like you to stay and teach me the true magic.'

'Turn this trial into a victory. Come here every day and absorb the sacred symbols that inhabit the stone; that way you'll be protected against all external attacks. For extra security, I'm going to arm you with an amulet and a protective cloth.'

Setau raised the lid of a gilded wooden chest and took out an amulet in the form of a papyrus stem, symbolic of vitality and flowering. He strung it on a cord and hung it round Kha's neck. Then he unrolled a little strip of cloth and, with fresh ink, drew on it a flawless open eye. As soon as the ink was dry, he tied the cloth round the child's left wrist.

'Be careful not to lose this amulet or this papyrus; they will prevent negative forces from infiltrating your blood. They've been charged with fluid by the hypnotizer-priests and act as prevention.'

'Are the snakes the ones who possess the formulas?'

'They know more than we do about life and death, the two aspects of reality. To understand their message is the beginning of all knowledge.'

'I should like to be your apprentice and prepare remedies.'

'Your destiny is not to heal but to reign.'

'I don't want to reign! I like hieroglyphs and the precepts for learning. A pharaoh has to meet too many people and solve too many problems. I prefer silence.'

'Our lives don't conform to our wishes.'

'Yes they do, if we have the magic!'

*

Moses was dining with Aaron and two tribal chiefs who were attracted by the idea of the exodus.

There was a knock at the door. Aaron opened it and Serramanna entered.

'Is Moses here?'

The two chiefs placed themselves in front of the prophet.

'Come with me, Moses.'

'Where are you taking him?' asked Aaron.

'That's not your business. Don't oblige me to use force.'

Moses stepped forward. 'I'm coming, Serramanna.'

The Sardinian made the Hebrew get into his chariot. Escorted by two other vehicles belonging to the guard, he drove swiftly out of Pi-Ramses, through cultivated fields and then branched off towards the desert.

Serramanna halted at the foot of a low hill which overlooked a stretch of sand and loose stones.

'Climb to the top, Moses.'

The climb presented no difficulties. Ramses was waiting for him, seated on a rock eroded by the winds.

'I love the desert as much as you do, Moses. Didn't we live through some unforgettable times in Sinai?'

The prophet sat down next to the pharaoh, and they gazed in the same direction.

'Which is the god you're so obsessed with, Moses?'

'The only God, the true God.'

'You were educated in the wisdom of Egypt. Consequently your mind has been opened to the many facets of the Divine.'

'Don't count on taking me back to the past. My people has a future, and that future will be realized outside Egypt. Allow the Hebrews to journey into the desert, three days' march away, to sacrifice to Yahveh.'

'You know very well that's impossible. Such a journey would necessitate heavy protection from the army. Under present conditions we can't rule out a raid by the Bedouin, who would claim many victims among an unarmed population.'

'Yahveh will protect us.'

'The Hebrews are my subjects, and I'm responsible for their safety.'

'We are your prisoners.'

'The Hebrews are free to come and go at will, as long as they respect the law. What you're asking me, in time of war, is unreasonable. What's more, many wouldn't follow you.'

'I shall lead my people to the Promised Land.'

'Where is that?'

'Yahveh will reveal it to us.'

'Are the Hebrews so unhappy in Egypt?'

'That's not important. The only thing that counts is the will of Yahveh.'

'Why are you so inflexible? There are sanctuaries in Pi-Ramses where foreign gods are welcome. The Hebrews can practise their beliefs as they wish.'

'That's not enough. Yahveh cannot tolerate the presence of false gods.'

'Aren't you missing the point, Moses? In our country, the sages have always respected the unity of the Divine in its Principle and its multiplicity in the way it manifests itself. When Akhenaton tried to impose Aton to the detriment of the other creative powers, he made a mistake.'

'His doctrine has been revived today, purged of its impurities.'

'The promotion of one, exclusive god would prevent the exchange of deities between countries and would extinguish the hope of kinship between peoples.'

'Yahveh is the protector and the succour of the just.'

'Aren't you forgetting Amon? He drives out evil, listens to the prayer of anyone who entreats him with a loving heart, and rushes instantly to help anyone who calls on him. Amon is the physician who can restore the sight of the blind without the use of remedies. No one can escape from his gaze. He is both one and multiple.'

156

'The Hebrews worship not Amon but Yahveh, and it is Yahveh who will lead them to their destiny.'

'An inflexible doctrine leads to death, Moses.'

'My decision is taken and I shall abide by it. Such is the will of God.'

'Isn't it vanity to believe that you are the sole agent of this will?'

'I'm not interested in what you think.'

'So, it's the end of our friendship.'

'The Hebrews have chosen me for their leader. You are the master of the land that keeps us prisoner. Whatever the friendship and esteem I have for you, these feelings count for nothing in the face of my mission.'

'In your obstinacy, you flout the Rule of Ma'at.'

'That doesn't matter to me!'

'Do you believe yourself better than the eternal norm of the universe, which existed before mankind and will endure after they are extinct?'

'The only law the Hebrews respect is that of Yahveh. Will you grant us permission to journey into the desert and make sacrifices in His honour?'

'No, Moses. During the war with the Hittites I haven't the right to take such a risk. No unrest must disorganize our defences.'

'If you persist in your refusal, Yahveh will strengthen my arm, and I shall perform miracles which will plunge your land into despair.'

The king rose. 'My friend, to the list of things you are sure about, add this: Ramses will never give in to blackmail.'

27

The caravan was moving through an arid region. The Egyptian delegation, made up of some thirty scribes and soldiers on horseback, accompanied by a hundred donkeys laden with gifts, made its way between two rock faces carved with gigantic figures of Hittite warriors marching towards the south, towards Egypt. Ahsha read the inscription: 'The God of Storms shows warriors the way and bestows victory on them.'

Time and again, Ahsha had had to reprimand the little troop, when they were overcome with panic at the sight of the terrifying landscape and the thought of obscure forces which circulated in the forests, passes and mountain ranges. Although he himself was ill at ease, he pressed on, glad to have avoided the bands of pillagers that were active in the region.

The delegation emerged from the narrow gorge, proceeded along the banks of a river, past more rocks decorated with Anatolians in warlike poses, then marched across a wind-swept plain. In the distance, on a height, stood an enormous, menacing fortress, marking the border of the empire.

Even the donkeys were reluctant to continue; it took all their herdsman's powers of persuasion to make them advance towards the sinister stronghold. On its battlements, archers were ready to shoot.

Ahsha ordered the members of the delegation to dismount and to lay down their weapons.

The herald took a few steps towards the gate of the fortress, waving a multicoloured standard. An arrow broke the shaft of the standard, a second fell at his feet, and a third grazed his shoulder. He turned back, wincing with pain,

The Egyptian soldiers immediately picked up their weapons.

'No!' shouted Ahsha. 'Don't touch them!'

'We're not going to let ourselves be massacred!' protested one of the officers.

'This behaviour isn't normal. For the Hittites to be so touchy and defensive, something serious must have happened in the heart of the empire – but what? I shall only know when I've met the commander of the fortress.'

'After such a welcome, you can't really mean to—'

'Take ten men and gallop back to our advance positions. See that the troops in our protectorates are put on the alert, prepared for a possible Hittite attack. And see that messengers inform Pharaoh of the situation so that our north-eastern line of defences is put on a war footing. I'll send fuller information as soon as possible.'

Only too happy to return to a more welcoming land, the officer didn't have to be given his orders twice. He picked the ten men, took the wounded herald and galloped off with the squad.

Those who remained with Ahsha had their hearts in their boots. Ahsha himself wrote his name and titles in Hittite script on a papyrus which he fixed to an arrowhead, and got an archer to shoot it to land beside the gate of the fortress.

'Now we must wait,' recommended Ahsha. 'Either they'll receive us to discuss matters, or they'll massacre us.'

'But . . . we're a delegation!' one of the scribes reminded him.

'If the Hittites wipe out diplomats who ask to talk, a new

phase of the war will have begun. Now that's an important piece of information.'

The scribe gulped. 'Couldn't we retreat?'

'That would not be proper. We represent Pharaoh's diplomatic service.'

Unconvinced by the force of the argument, the scribe and his colleagues shivered.

The gate of the fortress opened, letting several Hittite horsemen through. An officer, wearing a helmet and a thick breastplate, picked up the message and read it. Then he bade his men surround the Egyptians.

'Follow us,' he ordered.

The interior of the fortress was as sinister as the outside. Cold walls, freezing rooms, an armoury, dormitories, footsoldiers exercising . . . this stifling atmosphere gripped Ahsha by the throat but he reassured his delegation, who already saw themselves as prisoners.

After a short wait, the officer in the helmet reappeared. 'Which of you is the ambassador, Ahsha?'

Ahsha came forward.

'The commander of the fortress wishes to see you.'

Ahsha was shown into a square room with a fire burning in a hearth, near which stood a short man wearing a thick woollen cloak.

'Welcome to Hatti. I'm pleased to see you again, Ahsha.'

'I confess I am surprised to find you here, Hattusilis.'

'What mission brings Pharaoh's minister for foreign affairs here?'

'To offer the emperor a great quantity of gifts.'

'We are at war. This step is rather . . . unusual.'

'Must the conflict between our two countries last for ever?'

Hattusilis did not hide his surprise. 'What am I to understand by that?'

'That I'd like an audience with the emperor to discuss

160

Ramses' intentions.'

Hattusilis turned to warm his hands at the fire. 'That will be difficult, very difficult.'

'Do you mean it's impossible?'

'Go back to Egypt, Ahsha . . . No, I can't let you leave . . .'

Faced with his host's confusion, Ahsha disclosed his mission. 'I have come to propose peace to Muwatallis.'

Hattusilis spun round. 'Is this a trap or a joke?'

'Pharaoh is convinced that this is the best way for Egypt and for Hatti.'

'Ramses wants peace? Incredible!'

'It's my task to convince you and to lead the negotiations.'

'Give it up.'

'Why?'

Hattusilis gauged Ahsha's sincerity. At the point they had reached, how risky would it be to tell the truth? 'The emperor has had a heart attack. He's paralysed, can't speak and is incapable of ruling.'

'Who's exercising power?'

'His son, Uri-Teshup, supreme commander of the armed forces.'

'Didn't Muwatallis trust you?'

'He put me in charge of the economy and of diplomacy.'

'Then you are authorized to conduct negotiations.'

'I'm nothing any longer, Ahsha. My own brother slammed the door in my face. As soon as I learned of the state of his health, I took refuge here in this fortress, whose garrison is loyal to me.'

'Will Uri-Teshup proclaim himself emperor?'

'As soon as Muwatallis dies.'

'Why give up the struggle, Hattusilis?'

'I've no longer anything to fight with.'

'Is the whole army under Uri-Teshup's thumb?'

'Some officers fear him as an extremist, but they daren't say anything.'

'I'm ready to go to your capital and make proposals for peace.'

'Uri-Teshup doesn't know the meaning of the word "peace"! You've no chance of succeeding.'

'Where is your wife, Putuhepa?'

'She's still in Hattusa.'

'Isn't that unwise?'

Hattusilis turned back to the fire. 'She has a plan to halt the rise of Uri-Teshup.'

The noble, proud Putuhepa wore a silver diadem on her head, and was draped in a long deep-red gown. She had been meditating for three days in the Temple of Ishtar.

When the chief diviner laid on the altar a dead vulture, shot down by an archer, she knew her hour had come. She grasped the handle of the dagger she would plant in Uri-Teshup's back when, at the invitation of the soothsayer, he stooped over the vulture's entrails.

The beautiful priestess had dreamed of an impossible peace, of a reconciliation between all the sharply divided forces of Hatti, and of a truce with Egypt. But the very existence of Uri-Teshup reduced such plans to nothing. She alone could prevent this devil from succeeding in his work of destruction. She alone could hand over power to her husband, Hattusilis, who would lead the empire back on to the path of reason. She concealed herself behind a massive pillar, near the altar.

Uri-Teshup entered the sanctuary. He had not come alone: four soldiers ensured his protection.

Putuhepa was irked and wanted to give up and leave the temple without being seen. But would she ever have a better opportunity? In future, Uri-Teshup would never take the slightest risk. If she was quick enough, she would succeed in killing the future despot, though she would then be killed by his bodyguard. It would be cowardly to shirk this sacrifice.

She must think of the future of her country, not of her own life.

The soothsayer opened the vulture's belly, which gave off a terrible stench. He plunged his hands into the entrails, and spread them on the altar.

Uri-Teshup approached, leaving his bodyguards several paces behind. Putuhepa gripped the handle of the dagger tightly and prepared to leap forward; she must be as swift as a wild cat and use every bit of her strength in her murderous blow.

The soothsayer's cry rooted her to the spot. Uri-Teshup recoiled.

'My lord, this is horrible!'

'What do you see in the entrails?'

'You must postpone your plans. Fate is unfavourable to you.'

Uri-Teshup felt like cutting the augur's throat, but the members of the guard, who had come close, would spread the unfavourable prediction everywhere. In Hatti, no one ignored the soothsayers' predictions.

'How long must I wait?'

'Until the omens are favourable, my lord.'

Uri-Teshup stormed out of the temple.

28

The court hummed with contradictory rumours about the royal couple's departure for the Far South. Some declared it was imminent, others that it had been postponed indefinitely on account of the unsettled situation in the protectorates. There were even those who thought that the king would be obliged to set out for war again, in spite of the presence of the Royal Sons at the head of the regiments.

Light flooded into Ramses' office, where he was meditating before the statue of his father. Dispatches from Canaan and southern Syria lay on the large table. Wideawake, the golden-yellow dog, was asleep on his master's chair.

Ahmeni burst into the office. 'A message from Ahsha!'

'Have you authenticated it?'

'It's certainly his handwriting and he has mentioned my name in cipher.'

'How did it get here?'

'One of the members of his network brought it from Hatti. No one else has handled it.'

Ramses read Ahsha's message, which revealed the extent of the unrest that threatened to tear the Hittite Empire apart. He now understood why the previous dispatches had urged him to put the forts on the north-eastern border in a state of alert.

'The Hittites are unable to attack us, Ahmeni. The queen and I can leave.'

*

Armed with his amulet and his magic inscription, Kha was copying out a mathematical problem which consisted of calculating the ideal angle of a slope in order to hoist stones to the top of a building under construction, surrounded by mounds of earth. His sister, Meritamon, was becoming daily more proficient on the harp, and delighted her baby brother, Meneptah, who was beginning to take his first steps, under the watchful eyes of Iset the Fair and Invincible. The enormous Nubian lion liked watching the little boy toddle awkwardly about.

The great cat raised his head when Serramanna appeared at the entrance to the garden. Aware of the Sardinian's peaceful intentions, he simply gave a growl and resumed his sphinx-like posture.

'I'd like to talk to Kha,' Serramanna said to Iset.

'Has he done something wrong?'

'No, of course not; but he might be able to help me in my investigation.'

'I'll send him to you as soon as he's solved his problem.'

Serramanna had made progress. He knew that a Libyan magus named Ofir had killed the unfortunate Lita, who had died because she believed in an impossible dream. Ofir had presented himself as the mouthpiece for Akhenaton's heresy and had hidden behind this doctrine the better to deceive people and disguise his role as a spy in the service of the Hittites. It was no longer a question of assumptions but one of certainties, obtained from questioning a travelling merchant who had fallen into the hands of Serramanna's men when he turned up at Shanaar's former home, where Ofir had hidden for a long time. True, this person was only a minor agent in the Hittite network; but as he only occasionally worked for the Syrian merchant Raia, his immediate superior, who had returned to Hatti, he had not been warned that the underground organization had been dismantled and its members dispersed. Fearing torture when questioned, he had told all he knew, thus allowing Serramanna to throw light on some dark areas.

But Ofir could still not be found and Serramanna was not convinced that Shanaar had died in the desert. Had the magus found his way to Hatti, accompanied by Ramses' brother? In the Sardinian's experience, evil beings continued to do harm indefinitely, and there was no limit to what they could dream up.

Kha approached the giant and looked up at him. 'You're very big and very strong.'

'Will you answer some questions?'

'Do you know mathematics?'

'I can count my men and the weapons I hand over to them.'

'Do you know how to build a temple or a pyramid?'

'Pharaoh has given me a different job: to arrest criminals.'

'I like to write and read hieroglyphs.'

'Exactly: I want to talk to you about the brush someone stole from you.'

'It was my favourite. I miss it very much.'

'Since that incident, you must have thought about it. I'm sure you have some suspicions and you'll help me identify the guilty person.'

'Yes, I've thought about it, but I'm not sure of anything. To accuse someone of theft is too serious to do lightly.'

The boy's maturity astonished Serramanna; if there really were a clue, Kha would not have missed it. 'Among the people around you,' he went on, 'did you notice any unusual behaviour?'

'For a few weeks, I had a new friend.'

'Who was that?'

'The diplomat Meba. Suddenly he was interested in my work and he disappeared just as suddenly.'

A broad smile lit up the Sardinian's craggy face. 'Thank you, Prince Kha.'

*

In Pi-Ramses, as in all the other Egyptian cities, the feast of flowers was a day of popular rejoicing. As the head of all the priestesses, Nefertari did not forget that, since the first dynasty, the government of the land had rested on a calendar of feasts celebrating the marriage of heaven and earth. The rites practised by the royal couple allowed the entire population to share in the life of the gods.

Floral art was displayed in all its splendour on the altars of the temples, and in front of every house: here huge arrangements of palm branches and bundles of reeds; there, water-lilies, cornflowers, mandrakes with their stems.

The servants of the goddess Hathor, carrying round or square tambourines, waving acacia branches and wearing garlands of cornflowers and poppies, danced through the main streets of the capital, treading thousands of petals underfoot.

Dolora was anxious to appear near the queen, whose beauty dazzled all who had the good fortune to set eyes on her. Nefertari thought of her youth, when she had wished to become a recluse in the service of a goddess, far from the world. How could she ever have imagined the duties of a Great Royal Wife, whose burden was becoming more overwhelming by the day?

The procession made its way to the Temple of Amon, where it was greeted by joyful chanting.

'Has the date for your departure been fixed, Majesty?' asked Dolora.

'Our boat will set off tomorrow,' replied Nefertari.

'The court is anxious. There are rumours that you will be away for several months.'

'That's possible.'

'Will you really travel as far as Nubia?'

'That is Pharaoh's decision.'

'Egypt has such need of you!'

'Nubia is part of Egypt, Dolora.'

'But that region is sometimes dangerous.'

'It's not a question of a pleasure trip.'

'What work must you do that is urgent enough to take you so far from the capital?'

Nefertari smiled dreamily. 'Love, Dolora. Simply love.'

'I don't understand, Majesty.'

'I was thinking aloud,' said the queen, seeming far away.

'I would so like to help you. What task can I undertake while you are away?'

'Help Iset, if she wishes. My only regret is that I do not have enough time to see to the education of Kha and Meritamon.'

'May the gods protect you, as they protect them.'

As soon as the celebrations were over, Dolora passed on to Ofir the information she had gleaned. By leaving the capital for a long period, Ramses and Nefertari were making a mistake which their enemies would know how to make the most of.

Meba intended to undertake a long boat trip on the lake of Pi-Ramses, accompanied by his sandal-bearer. The diplomat felt the need to reflect, while gazing on the calm waters.

Meba's mind was in turmoil; he was not himself. What did he want except a quiet life of luxury, an important post in the higher ranks of public service where he could conduct some complicated intrigues to consolidate his position? But he was a member of a Hittite spy ring, working for the destruction of Egypt . . . No, he hadn't wanted that.

Meba was afraid. Afraid of Ofir, of his icy gaze, of his barely controlled violence. No, he could no longer escape from the trap. His future was tied up with the downfall of Ramses.

His sandal-bearer called to a man sleeping on the bank, who hired out boats.

Serramanna intervened. 'Can I help you, my lord Meba?'

The diplomat started. 'No, I don't think so.'

'But I do. I would very much enjoy an outing on this wonderful lake. Will you allow me to row you?'

The Sardinian's physical strength frightened Meba. 'As you wish.'

Serramanna quickly pushed the boat out from the bank. 'What a delightful spot. Alas, you and I are so overloaded with work that we seldom have time to appreciate it.'

'What's the reason for this interview?'

'Be reassured, I've no intention of questioning you.'

'Questioning *me*!'

'I simply need your advice on a delicate matter.'

'I'm not sure I can help you.'

'Have you been informed about a strange theft? Someone stole one of Kha's brushes.'

Meba avoided the Sardinian's eyes. 'Stolen? Are you sure?'

'Kha's evidence is definite.'

'He's only a child.'

'I wonder if you haven't some idea, however vague, about the identity of the thief?'

'That question is insulting. Row me back to the bank immediately.'

Serramanna grinned like a carnivore in sight of his prey. 'That was a very instructive outing, my lord Meba.'

29

Ramses stood at the prow of the royal ship, clasping Nefertari fondly in his arms; she wore a simple white gown, and her hair was blowing in the wind. The royal couple were enjoying a moment of intense happiness, in communion with the spirit of the river, the great nourisher which rose at the ends of the universe and came down to earth to pass on the benefit of its life-giving floodwaters.

The water level was high; they sailed swiftly, helped by a favourable north wind. The captain remained permanently on the alert, for the current created dangerous whirlpools; a faulty manoeuvre could lead to shipwreck.

Every day Ramses marvelled more at Nefertari's beauty. She combined grace and supreme authority; in her was found the miraculous alliance of a brilliant mind and a perfect body. This long journey to the South would be a journey of love, the love the king felt for a sublime woman, whose very presence was for Pharaoh, as for his people, the embodiment of serenity. Ever since he had lived with Nefertari, Pharaoh could understand why the sages had insisted that Egypt be governed by a royal couple, who saw as one person.

After nine years of reigning, Ramses and Nefertari, strengthened by the ordeals they had undergone, were as much in love as at the moment when they had first sensed that they were to travel together along the road of life and death.

Nefertari delighted in the landscapes of Middle Egypt, which filled her with wonder: palm groves, cultivated fields on the banks of the river, villages with white houses built on hillocks, all embodied the pleasures of a paradise such as the just would discover on the other side of death, and which it was the royal couple's duty to try to build on earth.

'Aren't you afraid,' she asked, 'that in our absence . . . ?'

'I have devoted the greater part of my reign to the North; the time has come to concern myself with the South. Without the union of the Two Lands, Egypt would not survive. And this war with Hatti has kept me too long away from you.'

'It isn't over yet.'

'There will be great upheavals in Asia; if even one chance of peace exists, we must seize it.'

'That's the reason for Ahsha's secret mission, isn't it?'

'The risks he's running are enormous. But no one except him could possibly succeed in such a delicate mission.'

'We are together, in joy as in sorrow, in hope as in fear. May the magic of this journey protect Ahsha.'

They heard footsteps on the deck.

'May I intrude?' asked Setau.

'Yes, of course, Setau.'

'I'd have liked to stay near Kha. That boy will become a great magician. As far as his protection is concerned, you can set your mind at rest: no one could get through the defences I've set up for him.'

'Aren't you and Lotus eager to see your beloved Nubia again?' asked Nefertari.

'That land is home to some of the finest snakes in creation!' said Setau. Then, 'I came to tell you that the captain is anxious about the drift of the water. He thinks we're approaching a dangerous area and intends to make for the bank as soon as we've passed that little grassy island in the middle of the river.'

After a series of meanders they passed a steep cliff with a

sheer drop down to the Nile; vultures nested there. Then the countryside opened up and soon a semicircular mountain range, stretching right across the horizon, came into view.

Nefertari put her hand to her throat.

'What is it?' asked Ramses anxiously.

'Some difficulty in breathing. It's nothing.'

A violent shock made the ship pitch and toss. Then the distant roar of a whirlpool resounded. On the bank stood the ruined buildings of Akhenaton's abandoned capital.

'Take the queen back to our cabin,' Ramses told Setau, 'and keep an eye on her.'

Some of the sailors lost their heads in their panic. One of them fell from the mainmast when he was trying to lower a sail, and crashed into the captain, half stunning him. The latter stared dazedly into space, unable to give clear instructions. From all sides came a stream of contradictory orders.

'Silence!' ordered Ramses. 'Every man to his post. I shall direct the manoeuvre.'

In a few minutes the danger was apparent. The escorting boats, not understanding the reasons for the royal ship's convulsive movements, and suddenly caught up in an adverse current which swept them some way away, were unable to come to her assistance.

While his vessel was righting her course, the king perceived the double obstacle.

It was impassable.

In the middle of the river was a huge whirlpool; towards the landing-stage of the City of the Sun, where the river should have been navigable, there was a barrage of rafts on which braziers had been placed. The king had the choice between shipwreck and the fire, which would not fail to destroy his vessel if she struck the rafts at full speed.

Who had left such a trap, on a level with the deserted city? Ramses now understood Nefertari's unease; she had the gift of clairvoyance and had had a premonition of danger.

The king had only a few seconds to reflect. This time his lion could do nothing for him.

'There he is!' yelled the lookout.

Shanaar threw away the roast leg of goose he was gnawing, and seized his bow and his sword. He, the great dignitary, lover of his comfort, had forged for himself the heart of a warrior.

'Is Pharaoh's ship isolated?'

'Exactly as you predicted. The following boats are some distance away.'

The mercenary's mouth watered. Shanaar had promised rich booty to him and his companions, who made up the little group assembled by Ofir. The king's brother made a fine speech, showing rare eloquence, and fired them with the hatred that was eating away at his heart.

No mercenary would dare strike Ramses, for fear of being struck down by the divine energy with which the pharaoh was imbued. Since his victory at Kadesh, everyone dreaded the supernatural powers of the Lord of the Two Lands. Shanaar had shrugged his shoulders and promised to kill the tyrant himself.

'Half the men to the rafts, the others with me.'

Ramses was going to perish near the City of the Sun, as if Akhenaton's heresy were finally overcoming Amon and the other deities worshipped by the King of Egypt. His death would cause an enormous breach, into which his brother would rush without wasting a moment.

Several mercenaries leaped from the landing-stage on to the rafts and prepared to shoot blazing arrows at the royal ship, which their companions, commanded by Shanaar, were attacking from the rear.

Victory was in sight.

*

'All the oarsmen to the starboard side!' ordered Ramses.

The first blazing arrow stuck in the wooden bulkhead of the central cabin. Lotus swiftly seized a piece of coarse cloth, with which she prevented the fire from spreading.

Ramses climbed on to the roof of the cabin, bent his bow, aimed at one of his adversaries, held his breath and shot. The arrow pierced the mercenary's throat; his comrades crouched down behind the braziers to protect themselves from the monarch's deadly aim. Their own arrows, less accurate, fell uselessly into the swirling waters – to which the ship was now dangerously near.

The desperate manoeuvre ordered by Ramses had altered her course. Her prow had reared up like a maddened horse and she had turned sideways, battered on the port side by the raging waters. There was a chance that she would drift towards the bank, provided she was not caught in the whirlpool and overtaken by the swift boats of Shanaar's men, who had already shot down two sailors standing in the bows; the poor wretches had toppled over into the river, with arrows through their chests.

Setau ran to the bows, carrying an egg fashioned from clay, which he handled with care. The talisman, covered with hieroglyphs, was a replica of the 'egg of the world', which was kept in the inner shrine of the great Temple of Thoth in Khmun. Only state magicians like Setau were allowed to use such a symbol, charged as it was with waves of fearsome power.

Setau was angry. He had foreseen having to use the talisman in Nubia, if an unexpected danger threatened the royal couple. He was furious at having to deprive himself of such a weapon, but it was essential to subdue this cursed whirlpool.

The snake-charmer swung his arm wide and cast the egg of the world into the water. It seethed and boiled, giving way to a swirling hollow; then a wave broke over the rafts, washing away several of the braziers and drowning two mercenaries.

For the moment the royal ship was safe from being wrecked or set on fire, but in the bows the situation had deteriorated. Shanaar's men had thrown up grapnels and were beginning to climb up the rigging. Their leader furiously shot arrow after arrow, preventing the Egyptian sailors from taking a hand in the fight.

Two blazing arrows caught in the sail and started a fire, which Lotus again extinguished. Although exposed to the enemy arrows, Ramses did not change his position and continued to shoot down the mercenaries. Alerted by shouts from the stern of the ship, he turned and saw a pirate raising his battle-axe above the head of an unarmed sailor. The sovereign's arrow pierced the wrist of the attacker, who fell back, crying out in pain. Invincible sank his fangs into the head of another mercenary who had managed to climb on to the deck.

For one moment Pharaoh's eyes met those of the leader of the band, a bearded, frenzied man who stared at him. With an almost imperceptible movement, the monarch swayed to his left; the attacker's arrow skimmed past his cheek. Furiously, the attacker ordered the survivors of his band to retreat.

A new burst of flame took Lotus by surprise, and her gown caught fire. She dived overboard, and had the ill luck to be caught in the last swirl of the whirlpool. Unable to swim, she raised her arm to call for help.

Ramses dived straight in.

Emerging from the central cabin, Nefertari saw the king disappear into the Nile.

30

Minutes passed.

The royal ship and the escorting vessels had dropped anchor abreast of the City of the Sun, where the water was calm again. Three or four mercenaries had managed to flee, but neither Nefertari nor Setau was concerned with their fate. Like Invincible, they kept their eyes glued to the spot where Ramses and Lotus had vanished.

The queen had burned incense to Hathor, the goddess of navigation. Nefertari's calm and dignity, as she awaited the report of the men who had been sent to search for the missing two, won the hearts of the sailors. Some of them rowed back and forth across the river; others took to the towpaths the better to scan the high grass lining the banks. The current had probably dragged the king and Lotus far to the south.

Setau stayed close to the queen.

'Pharaoh will return,' she murmured.

'Majesty, the river is sometimes ruthless.'

'He will return, and he has saved Lotus.'

'Majesty . . .'

'Ramses has not completed his work. A pharaoh who has not completed his work cannot die.'

Setau realized that he could not shake the queen's heart-rending certainty. But how would she react when she was obliged to accept the inescapable truth? He forgot his own sorrow to share that of Nefertari. He imagined the terrible return to Pi-Ramses, and the announcement to the court of Ramses' disappearance.

Shanaar and his companions waited until they had sailed a good distance to the north, helped by a strong current, before they breathed freely again. Then they sank their boat and plunged into the grassy countryside, where they exchanged some amethysts for donkeys.

'Where are we going?' asked a Cretan mercenary.

'You are going to Pi-Ramses to warn Ofir.'

'He won't be pleased to see me.'

'We've nothing to be ashamed of,' said Shanaar.

'Ofir doesn't appreciate failure.'

'He knows we're dealing with a tough opponent, and I'm sparing no efforts. And you'll give him two pieces of good news. First, I saw Setau on board the royal vessel, so Kha no longer has the benefit of his protection. Secondly, I'm going to Nubia, where I shall kill Ramses.'

'I'd rather go with you,' said the Cretan. 'My comrade will be an excellent messenger. For my part, I can fight and track game.'

'Very well.'

Shanaar was not discouraged. The violent action had transformed him into a war leader; at last he could freely express his rage, which had been pent up for too many years. With only a few men and by an ingenious strategy, he had taken Ramses the Great by surprise – and had almost triumphed. Fate would eventually reward his perseverance with a favourable outcome.

Silence reigned on all the vessels of the royal flotilla. No one dared talk, for fear of disturbing the queen's sorrowful meditation. As evening approached, she remained motionless at the prow of Pharaoh's ship.

Setau, too, kept silent, in order to preserve the ultimate hope which linked her to Ramses' shade. But with the setting of the sun, Nefertari would be forced to admit the terrible reality.

'I knew it,' she said softly, to his astonishment.

'Majesty?'

'Ramses is over there, on the roof of the white palace.'

'Majesty, night is falling and—'

'Look carefully.'

Setau stared in the direction in which Nefertari pointed. 'No, it's just an illusion.'

'I can see him, we must get nearer.'

Setau dared not oppose the queen's request. The royal vessel weighed anchor and moved towards the City of the Sun, which would soon be shrouded in darkness.

The snake-charmer again stared at the roof of the white palace which had been the home of Akhenaton and Nefertiti. For one moment he thought he could make out a man standing there; he rubbed his eyes to see better. The mirage had not vanished.

'Ramses is alive,' repeated Nefertari.

'Row faster!' ordered Setau.

And the figure of Ramses approached, growing bigger by the minute, silhouetted against the last rays of the sun.

Setau was still angry. 'Why didn't the Lord of the Two Lands make every effort to let us know he was there and call to us for help? After all, that wouldn't have demeaned him!'

'I had more important things to do,' replied the king. 'Lotus and I swam under water, but she lost consciousness and I thought she had drowned. We reached the bank at the southern extremity of the deserted city, and I spent a long time hynotizing her back to life. Then we walked towards the middle of the town and I looked for the highest point, so as to signal our presence. I knew that Nefertari's spirit was following us step by step and that she would look in the right direction.'

Nefertari radiated serenity as she discreetly showed her emotion by clinging to Ramses' right arm, while he patted his lion.

'I thought the egg of the world hadn't been able to save us,' muttered Setau. 'If you'd disappeared, my reputation would have been tarnished.'

'How is Lotus?' inquired the queen.

'I've given her a soothing draught; after a good night's sleep she'll forget this misadventure.'

A cup-bearer filled their goblets with cool white wine.

'About time!' said Setau. 'I was wondering if we were still in a civilized country.'

'During the fight,' asked Ramses, 'did you notice the leader of the men who attacked us?'

'They all seemed equally fierce to me. I didn't even notice that they had a leader.'

'He was bearded, frantic, with eyes filled with fury . . . For one moment I thought I recognized Shanaar.'

'Shanaar died in the desert, on the way to the prison settlement. Even scorpions die eventually.'

'But what if he survived?'

'If he had, he'd think only of staying in hiding and wouldn't have launched a party of mercenaries against you.'

'That trap wasn't improvised, and it nearly succeeded.'

'Can hatred eat away at someone so much that it transforms a functionary into a warrior, ready to go to any lengths to kill his own brother and attack Pharaoh's sacred person?'

'If it really was Shanaar, he's just given you the answer.'

Setau glowered. 'If that monster's still alive, we mustn't just do nothing. The demons of the desert are the source of the madness that drives him.'

'This attack was not perpetrated by chance,' was Ramses'

opinion. 'Summon the stone-cutters from the nearest towns urgently.'

Some stone-cutters came from Khmun, the city of Thoth, others from Asyut, the city of Anubis; several dozen of them encamped in tents. A few hours after arriving, they heard a brief, determined speech by Ramses and then they began work under the orders of two overseers.

Standing in front of the white palace, Pharaoh had set out his demands: the City of the Sun, dedicated to the god Aton, must disappear. One of Ramses' predecessors, Horemheb, had dismantled some of the temples and had used the stones as filling for his pylons in Karnak. Once Ramses saw that there was no more trace of the palaces, houses, workshops, wharfs and other buildings of the deserted city, he would have completed Horemheb's work. Stones and bricks would be re-used in other towns. The tombs, which sheltered no mummies, would remain intact.

The royal ship rode at anchor until only the foundations of the buildings remained. Soon wind and sand would cover them, casting into oblivion the lost capital, which had become the home of evil forces.

Labourers carried the materials to cargo boats; they would be divided according to the needs of neighbouring towns. Additional supplies of meat, oil, beer and clothing encouraged the workmen to finish their task fast.

Ramses and Nefertari paid a last visit to the palace of the City of the Sun before it was demolished; its decorated pavement would be re-used in the royal palace at Khmun.

'Akhenaton was mistaken,' decided Ramses. 'The religion he advocated led to dogmatism and intolerance. He betrayed the very spirit of Egypt. Unfortunately, Moses has taken the same path.'

'Akhenaton and Nefertiti were a royal couple,' Nefertari reminded him. 'They respected our laws and were wise enough to limit their experiment in time and place. By setting up boundary stones, they confined the worship of Aton within his city.'

'But the poison spread – and I'm not sure that its effects will be dispelled with the disappearance of this city, where darkness had replaced light. Still, at least the site is being returned to the mountains and the desert, and no future rebellion will use it as a base.'

When the city had been razed to the ground, to be henceforth buried in silence and oblivion, and the last stone-cutter had left, Ramses gave the order to set sail for Abydos.

31

As they approached Abydos, Ramses felt his heart wrung with emotion. He knew how much his father had loved this site and what importance he had attached to the construction of the great Temple of Osiris, and he reproached himself for not having returned here for so long. True, the war against the Hittites and the need to ensure Egypt's safety had occupied his mind and his hands, but no excuse would meet with mercy before the god of resurrection at the time of judgment.

Setau had imagined that a crowd – of shaven-headed 'pure priests', perfumed and dressed in immaculate white gowns, peasants loaded with offerings, priestesses playing the lyre and the lute – would have gathered to welcome the king. But the landing-stage was deserted.

'This isn't normal,' he declared. 'We mustn't disembark.'

'What are you afraid of?' asked Ramses.

'Other outlaws might have seized the temple and laid an ambush for you.'

'Here, on the sacred soil of Abydos?'

'We mustn't take any risks. Let's go on to the South and send the army.'

'I will never admit that a single cubit of ground in my own land is inaccessible to me. Especially not when it's Abydos!'

Ramses' anger was as violent as a storm whipped up by the god Set. Nefertari herself did not attempt to appease him.

The flotilla drew alongside. Pharaoh in person led out a detachment of chariots, whose separate parts had been transported by boat and hurriedly assembled.

The processional way, leading from the landing-stage to the square in front of the temple, was also deserted, as if the holy city had been abandoned. In front of the great gateway, there were blocks of limestone bearing the marks of the stone-cutters' tools, and boxes containing those tools. Under the tamarisk trees shading the square were huge wooden sledges laden with blocks of granite from the Aswan quarries.

Unable to believe his eyes, Ramses made his way to the palace adjoining the temple. On the steps leading to the main entrance, an old man was spreading goat's cheese on slices of bread. The appearance of this army took his appetite away. In his panic he abandoned his meal and tried to run, but he was caught by a footsoldier, who led him to the monarch.

'Who are you?' asked Ramses.

The old man's voice trembled. 'I'm one of the palace launderers.'

'Why aren't you at work?'

'Well . . . er . . . there's nothing to do, because everyone's left. That is, nearly everyone – there are still a few priests, as old as me, near the sacred lake.'

In spite of Ramses' energetic efforts at the beginning of his reign, the temple was still unfinished. The king and some of the soldiers passed through the gateway, crossed the administrative enclave, consisting of offices, workshops, a butchery, a bakery and a brewery, empty of all employees, and hurried towards the homes of the resident priests.

Seated on a stone bench, grasping the knob of his acacia-wood staff, an old shaven-headed man tried to rise as the king approached.

'Don't bother to get up, servant of god.'

'You are Pharaoh! I've been told so much about the Son of the Light, who radiates power like a sun! My eyes are weak, but I'm not mistaken. How happy I am to see you before I die. Now I'm ninety-two, the gods offer me immense joy.'

'What's happening here?'

'It's the two weeks of the requisition.'

'The requisition? Who has taken this liberty?'

'The mayor of the neighbouring town. He thought there were too many staff in the temple and they'd be more use repairing canals than celebrating rites.'

The mayor was a jovial fellow, with plump cheeks and fleshy lips; his large paunch hampered his walking, so he always moved around on a litter. But it was in a chariot, driven at full speed by an officer, that he arrived at the palace of Abydos.

With a painful effort the mayor prostrated himself before the king, who was seated on a gilded wooden throne with feet shaped like a lion's paws.

'Forgive me, Majesty! I wasn't warned of your arrival. If I'd known, I'd have organized a reception worthy of you, and I'd have—'

'Are you responsible for requisitioning the Abydos staff?'

'Yes, but—'

'Have you forgotten that that is formally forbidden?'

'No, Majesty, but I thought that all these people had nothing to do and it would be better to give them some work which would be useful to the province.'

'You took them away from tasks which my father had assigned to them and which I myself confirmed.'

'All the same, I thought—'

'You are guilty of a serious offence, for which the punishment is laid down by decree: a hundred strokes, and nose and ears to be cut off.'

The mayor went white as a sheet and stammered, 'That's not possible, Majesty! It's inhuman!'

'You were aware of doing wrong and you knew the punishment; there is no need for a trial.'

184

Certain that the tribunal would pronounce the same sentence, and perhaps even increase it, the mayor poured out a stream of excuses. 'I acted wrongly, it's true, but it wasn't for my personal benefit. Thanks to the staff from Abydos, the dykes have been repaired quickly and the canals thoroughly cleaned out.'

'In that case, I give you the choice of another punishment: you and your officials will work as labourers on the temple building site until it's completed.'

All the priests and priestesses carried out their ritual duties, making the Temple of Osiris resemble the horizon of the heavens, lighting up all faces. Ramses had consecrated a golden statue to the effigy of his father and, accompanied by Nefertari, had made the ceremonial offering to the Rule of Ma'at. With its gates of cedar from Canaan, covered with an alloy of gold and silver, its granite doorsteps and multi-coloured bas-reliefs, the temple was like a place from the Otherworld, where the divine powers delighted to dwell. On the altars were flowers, vases of perfume and food intended for the Invisible.

The treasure-house was filled with gold, silver, royal linen, oils for the celebrations, incense, wine, honey, myrrh and salves. The stables housed fat oxen, sturdy cows and calves; the granaries stored vast quantities of the finest grain. As an inscription in hieroglyphs proclaimed, 'Pharaoh increases all kinds for the god.'

Ramses made a speech to all the notables of the province, gathered in the audience chamber of the palace of Abydos, decreeing that the boats, fields, lands, cattle, donkeys and all other goods that belonged to the temple could not be removed from it, under any pretext. As for the men guarding the fields, the bird-catchers, fishermen, farmers, beekeepers, gardeners, wine-growers, hunters and other staff belonging to the domain of Osiris to ensure its prosperity, not one of them could be requisitioned to carry out any task in any other place. Anyone transgressing the directives of the royal decree would suffer corporal punishment, be relieved of all his offices and be sentenced to several years' hard labour.

With Ramses as the driving force, the work advanced rapidly. The rites lit up the figures of the gods installed in the shrines, evil was banished and the temple was filled with Ma'at's nourishment.

These were happy days for Nefertari. This stay in Abydos offered her an unexpected opportunity to realize the dream of her adolescence: to live in close proximity to the deities, to meditate before their beauty and to sense their secrets while practising the rites.

As the moment approached to close the gates of the innermost shrine for the night, Ramses was not at her side. She went to look for him and found him in the Corridor of the Ancestors, where he was gazing at the list of all the pharaohs who had preceded him since the First Dynasty. Through the power of the hieroglyphs, their names would be present for ever in men's memory; the name of Ramses the Great would follow that of his father, Seti.

'How can I show myself worthy of these exceptional beings?' the king wondered aloud. 'Disloyalty, cowardice, lies . . . what pharaoh will ever succeed in rooting out these evils from men's hearts?'

'None,' replied Nefertari. 'But they have all waged this fight, thought lost in advance, and have sometimes been victorious.'

'If even the sacred territory of Abydos is not respected, what is the use of issuing decrees?'

'This momentary dejection isn't like you.'

'That's why I came here to consult my ancestors.'

'They could only have given you one piece of advice: to

continue, to profit from tribulation in order to increase your power.'

'We are so happy in this temple; here reigns the peace that I have not succeeded in bringing to the secular world.'

'It is my duty to rescue you from this temptation, even if I speak against my dearest wish.'

Ramses took the queen in his arms. 'Without you, my actions would be nothing but pathetic gestures. In two weeks' time, the mysteries of Osiris will be celebrated. We shall take part in them and I shall have a suggestion to make to you. It will be up to you to decide.'

Armed with sticks, shouting and screaming, a band of scoundrels attacked the front of the procession. Wearing the mask of the jackal-god, 'the Opener of the Ways', the priest of Abydos drove off the assailants by uttering the ritual curses, in order to ward off the creatures of darkness from the ship of Osiris. The initiates to the mysteries came to the assistance of the Opener of the Ways, and dispersed those who had rebelled against the light.

The procession resumed its way towards the island of the first morning, where Ramses, identified with Osiris, who had been murdered by his brother Set, rested on a bed with the head of a lion. The waters of the Nile surrounded this primordial mound, which the two divine sisters, Isis and Nephthys, reached by means of a footbridge.

The island lay in the middle of a colossal structure formed from ten monolithic pillars supporting a ceiling worthy of the builders of the pyramids. The secret sanctuary of Osiris ended in a transversal chamber about forty cubits by twelve. There the sarcophagus of the god was kept.

Nefertari enacted the part of Isis, wife of Osiris, and Iset the Fair enacted the part of Nephthys, whose name meant 'the Sovereign of the Temple'. The sister of Isis, she witnessed the rites that brought Osiris back from the domain of death.

Nefertari had accepted Ramses' suggestion: Iset's ritual presence had seemed desirable to her.

The two women knelt down, Nefertari at the head of the bed, Iset at the foot; each held a ewer of fresh water in her right hand and a round loaf of bread in her left, and recited long, moving litanies, needed to make fresh energy flow in the veins of the inert being.

Their voices were united in melody, under the protection of the goddess of the sky, whose enormous body, covered with stars and astrological texts, stretched over the ceiling above the bed of the resurrection.

At the end of a long night, Ramses–Osiris awoke and uttered the words his predecessors had uttered when taking part in the same mysteries: 'May light be granted me in the sky, life-giving power on earth, a just voice in the realm of the Otherworld, and the ability to travel at the head of the stars; may I grasp the cord in the bows of the ship of night, and the cord in the stern of the ship of day.'

32

Uri Teshup was furious. Consultation with another soothsayer, in the Temple of the God of Storms, had given the same result: pessimistic forecasts, a ban on launching an offensive. The majority of the soldiers were so superstitious that Uri-Teshup could not disregard these prognostications and no soothsayer could give a date when the omens would be propitious.

Although the court physicians were unable to improve Muwatallis's condition, the emperor just would not die. To tell the truth, this slow death pleased Uri-Teshup: no one could accuse him of assassination. The doctors had certified a heart attack and praised the devotion of the son who visited the patient every day. Uri-Teshup criticized Hattusilis for being away: didn't he care about his brother's health?

When he met the noble, proud Putuhepa, the prince couldn't resist asking ironically, 'Is your husband in hiding?'

'Hattusilis is on a mission by order of the emperor.'

'My father has not spoken to me about it.'

'According to the physicians, Muwatallis cannot utter a single word.'

'You seem well informed.'

'Yet you have forbidden everyone to enter the emperor's chamber, and you claim to be the only one who has the right to enter it.'

'Muwatallis needs rest.'

'We all hope that he'll soon be able to carry out his duties fully.'

'Naturally. But suppose his incapacity lasts a long time? It will be necessary to make a decision.'

'Without the presence of Hattusilis, that is impossible.'

'Send for him. Tell him to return to the palace.'

'Are you ordering or advising me?'

'Believe whatever you like, Putuhepa.'

Putuhepa left the capital at night, with only a small escort, and checked several times that Uri-Teshup had not had her followed.

At the sight of the sinister fortress where Hattusilis had taken refuge, she shuddered. Perhaps the garrison had imprisoned her husband to please the commander-in-chief? If so, her life, like that of Hattusilis, would come to a violent end behind those grey walls.

Putuhepa had no wish to die. She felt able to serve her country and she wished to live for many more hot summers, to travel a thousand more times along the wild paths of Anatolia, and to see Hattusilis rule over Hatti. If there was even one chance, however slight, of defeating Uri-Teshup, she would seize it with both hands.

The welcome by the soldiers of the fortress reassured the priestess. She was immediately led to the central tower, to the commander's apartments.

Hattusilis ran to greet her and they embraced.

'Putuhepa, at last! You managed to escape . . .'

'Uri-Teshup is already in command of the capital.'

'Here we are safe. All the men of this garrison detest him. Too many soldiers have suffered from his injustice and his acts of brutality.'

Putuhepa noticed a man seated in front of the fire. 'Who is that?' she asked softly.

190

'Ahsha, Pharaoh's minister for foreign affairs and ambassador extraordinary.'

'Whatever is he doing here?'

'He may be our best chance of success.'

'But . . . what is he proposing?'

'Peace.'

Hattusilis witnessed an extraordinary phenomenon: his wife's dark brown eyes grew lighter, as if lit up by an inner fire.

'Peace?' she repeated, unable to believe her ears. 'With Egypt? We know that that's impossible!'

'All the same, this unexpected ally may help to further our interests.'

Putuhepa detached herself from Hattusilis's embrace and went over to Ahsha, who rose and bowed to her.

'Forgive me, Ahsha. I should have greeted you sooner.'

'Not at all. I am glad to see you and your husband reunited.'

'You're taking a huge risk by staying here.'

'I had intended to go to the capital, but Hattusilis persuaded me to await your arrival.'

'You must know about the emperor's illness,' said Putuhepa.

'Nevertheless, I shall try to speak to him.'

'It would be no use. He's dying, and the empire is already in Uri-Teshup's hands.'

'I came to propose peace and I shall obtain it.'

'Aren't you forgetting that Uri-Teshup's sole aim is the destruction of Egypt? I don't approve of his obstinacy, but I'm aware that the unity of our empire is founded on war.'

'Have you thought about the real danger that threatens you?' asked Ahsha.

'An attack by the entire Egyptian army, with Ramses at its head!'

'Don't overlook another possibility: the irresistible rise of the Assyrian power.'

Hattusilis and Putuhepa had difficulty in hiding their astonishment. Ahsha's intelligence service was more efficient than they had realized.

'Assyria will eventually attack you,' he went on, 'and you will be caught between two fires, unable to hold out on two fronts. It's an illusion to think that the Hittite army will destroy Egypt. Strengthened by the lessons we learned in the last war, we have set up a defensive barrier in our protectorates. It will be difficult for you to break through this and its resistance will allow the bulk of our troops to counterattack rapidly. And you have learned, to your cost, that Amon protects Ramses and makes his arm more effective than thousands of soldiers.'

'So you are predicting the downfall of the Hittite Empire!'

'No, Lady Putuhepa. Egypt is not interested in seeing her old enemy disappear. We are just beginning to get to know each other better. Contrary to his reputation, Ramses loves peace, and the Great Royal Wife, Nefertari, will not dissuade him from following that path.'

'What does Queen Tuya think?'

'She shares my view, namely that Assyria will soon represent a formidable danger. The Hittites will be affected first, then it will be Egypt's turn.'

'An alliance against Assyria . . . is that what you are really proposing?'

'Peace and the alliance, in order to protect our peoples from invasion. The next Emperor of Hatti will have to make a decision fraught with consequences.'

'Uri-Teshup will never give up fighting Ramses!'

'And where does Hattusilis stand?'

'Hattusilis and I no longer have any power.'

'Please answer my question,' Ahsha insisted.

'We would agree to enter into negotiations,' declared Hattusilis, 'but is there any point in having this discussion?'

192

'Only the unachievable amuses me,' the Egyptian said with a smile. 'Today you are powerless, but it is with you that I wish to negotiate in order to offer my country a brighter future. Let Hattusilis become emperor, and our words will take on an incalculable value.'

'That's just a dream,' objected Putuhepa.

'You can either fight or run away.'

The fair Hittite's pride was stirred. 'We shall not run away.'

'Hattusilis and you must win or buy the trust of as many senior officers as possible. The commanders of the fortresses will probably come over to your side, because Uri-Teshup despises them and blocks their promotion on the pretext that they play only a defensive role. Use the merchants, who are nearly all favourable to you, to spread the rumour that the Hittite economy will not stand a new war effort, and that war against Egypt will bring ruin and misery. Create divisions among Uri-Teshup's supporters, and widen those divisions until he is seen as a troublemaker, incapable of reigning.'

'That's a long and demanding job.'

'That's the price you must pay for your success and to obtain peace.'

'For your part, what do you intend to do?' asked Putuhepa.

'It will be a bit risky, but I fully intend to win over Uri-Teshup.'

Ahsha gazed at the ramparts of Hattusa and amused himself by imagining the Hittite capital painted in bright colours, adorned with banners and filled with magnificent young women dancing on the battlements. But this fine vision faded, to give way to a sinister fortified city, clinging to the mountainside. He was accompanied by only two compatriots, an attendant and a sandal-bearer; the other members of the expedition had returned to Egypt.

When Ahsha showed his seal at the first guardroom in the

lower town, the officer couldn't believe his eyes.

Ahsha said, 'Be so good as to let the emperor know of my presence.'

'But . . . you're an Egyptian!'

'A special ambassador. Hurry up, please.'

Completely at a loss, the officer kept a close watch on Ahsha and sent one of his subordinates to the palace.

Ahsha was not surprised to see the arrival, marching in quick time, of a squad of footsoldiers armed with lances and commanded by a big bully who was incapable of thinking for himself and merely obeyed orders implicitly.

'The general-in-chief wishes to see the ambassador.'

Ahsha greeted Uri-Teshup and stated his credentials.

'Ramses' most brilliant minister in Hattusa! What a surprise!'

'And you at the head of an enormous army. Please accept my congratulations.'

'Egypt should fear me.'

'Egypt knows your bravery and your warlike qualities, and we fear those. That is why I have massed soldiers in our protectorates.'

'I shall annihilate them.'

'They are prepared for the fight, however fierce it promises to be.'

'Enough of this idle chatter. Why have you come here?'

'I heard that Emperor Muwatallis was ill.'

'Content yourself with rumours. The health of our leader is a state secret.'

'The Lord of Hatti is our enemy, but we respect his greatness. That is why I am here.'

'What do you mean by that, Ahsha?'

'I have access to the remedies needed to treat the emperor.'

33

The seven-year-old boy was putting into practice the precept that his father, who had learned it from his own father, had himself practised: giving a fish to someone who's hungry is less useful than teaching him to fish.

So he was trying to prove his skill by striking the water with a stick, to drive his prey towards the net which his comrade, as hungry as himself, had stretched near some tall papyrus reeds.

Suddenly the lad saw them: a fleet of ships arriving from the north, headed by a vessel bearing a golden sphinx on its prow. Yes, it really was Pharaoh's vessel!

Forgetting fish and net, the apprentice fisherman dived into the Nile and swam towards the bank, in order to warn the village. For several days there would be celebrations.

The immense Hall of Pillars of Karnak was revealed in all its splendour; in the body of the temple, the twelve pillars, each fifty cubits high, symbolized the power of creation rising out of the primeval ocean.

It was there that Nebu, the High Priest of Amon, walking with the help of a stick gilded with fine gold, came to meet the royal couple. In spite of his rheumatism, he managed to bow to Ramses, who helped him to straighten up again.

'I'm happy to see you again, Majesty, and delighted to

admire the queen's beauty.'

'Can it be that you're becoming a perfect courtier, Nebu?'

'No hope of that, Majesty. I shall continue to say what I think, as I have just done.'

'How are you?'

'One must put up with old age, although it makes my joints ache. But the temple doctor gives me a willow-based remedy that brings some relief. I admit that I haven't really time to think about my health. You've charged me with such demanding work!'

'Judging by the results, I've good reason to be pleased with my choice.'

Eighty thousand employees, among whom the high priest shared out duties, nearly a million head of cattle, a hundred cargo boats, fifty building sites kept permanently busy, an enormous area of land under cultivation, gardens, woodland, orchards and vineyards: such was the world of Karnak, the rich domain of Amon.

'The most difficult thing, Majesty, is to maintain harmony among the scribes of the domains, those of the granaries, those of the accounts office, and their other colleagues. Without a higher authority this little society would soon become chaotic, with everyone thinking only of his own interests.'

'Your good sense and tact work wonders.'

'I know only two virtues: obedience and service. The rest is idle chatter – and at my age, one hasn't time for that.'

Ramses and Nefertari studied admiringly each of the hundred and thirty-four pillars decorated with the names of the deities and the figure of Pharaoh endlessly making offerings to them. The plant-like pillars, which the stone would make endure for eternity, linked the ground, the symbol of the primeval swamps, to the blue-painted ceiling, where golden stars shone.

As Seti had wished, the great Hall of Pillars of Karnak

would embody for ever the glory of the hidden god, while revealing his mysteries.

'Will the royal couple be merely making a brief stay in Thebes,' asked Nebu, 'or will they grace us with a long visit?'

'To guide Egypt to peace,' Ramses replied, 'I must satisfy the gods by offering them temples where they will be happy to dwell, and by completing my own House of Eternity and that of Nefertari. The gods will take back, when the time comes, the life they have planted in my heart. We must be ready to appear before them, so that the people of Egypt do not suffer by our deaths.'

Ramses awoke the divine force secreted in the innermost shrine of the temple of Karnak, and hailed its presence: 'Greetings to thee, the source of life, the begetter of gods and humans, the creator of my land and of distant lands, thou who dost fashion green meadows and the flooding. Every creature is filled with thy perfection.'

Karnak awoke.

The light of day replaced that of oil lamps, the ritualists filled the purification vases with water from the sacred lake, renewed the blocks of incense which filled the shrines with fragrance, and decorated the altars with flowers, fruit, vegetables and fresh bread; processions formed to carry round the offerings which would be raised up to Ma'at. She alone could quicken the various forms of life; she alone brought new life with the scent of her dew which flooded the land at sunrise.

Accompanied by Nefertari, Ramses took the ceremonial avenue lined with sphinxes, which led to the temple of Luxor. A man was waiting for the royal couple in front of the great gateway, a square-faced, sturdy man, the former inspector of the royal stables.

'We met and fought when I was still very young,' the king told his wife, 'and I was very proud to have stood up to him.'

Since abandoning the career of arms, Bakhen had changed a lot from his uncouth former self. Now in the fourth rank of the priestly hierarchy of Karnak, he was moved to tears. He could find no words to express his great joy at seeing Pharaoh again. Preferring to let his work speak for him, he left the royal couple to admire the impressive façade of Luxor, in front of which stood two slender obelisks and several colossi representing Ramses. On the fine sandstone were depicted scenes from the battle of Kadesh and the King of Egypt's victory.

'Majesty,' declared Bakhen with pride, 'the building is finished!'

'But work must go on.'

'I am ready.'

The royal couple and Bakhen entered the great temple court situated behind the gateway. It was lined with pillared porticos, between which there had been raised statues of Ramses containing his *ka*, the immortal energy that made him capable of reigning.

'The work of the stone-cutters and the sculptors is admirable, Bakhen, but I cannot let them rest, and I intend to take them to a more difficult, even dangerous site.'

'May I know what your plan is, Majesty?'

'To build several sanctuaries in Nubia, including one huge temple. Call your artisans together and consult them. I shall accept only volunteers.'

The House of Ramses, Ramses the Great's Temple of a Million Years, built to plans drawn up by the king himself, was already an imposing monument, the most enormous on the west bank. Granite, sandstone and basalt had been used to create gateways, courtyards and shrines; several gates of gilded bronze marked off the separate areas of the monument, which was protected by a surrounding brick wall.

Shanaar had succeeded in getting into an empty warehouse

at dusk. Armed with a weapon which Ofir had entrusted to him, and which he hoped would strike the decisive blow, he waited until it was much darker before venturing into the sacred space.

He kept close to the wall of the palace, which was still under construction, and crossed a courtyard. A few yards away from the shrine dedicated to Seti, he faltered.

Seti, his father . . .

But a father who had betrayed him by choosing Ramses as pharaoh! A father who had despised and rejected him, by favouring the rise of a tyrant.

When he had carried out his plan, Shanaar would no longer be the son of Seti. But what did that matter? Contrary to what the initiates to the mysteries claimed, no one could cross over the barrier of death. Seti had been swallowed up by oblivion, and in just the same way it would swallow up Ramses. Life had only one meaning: to obtain as much power as possible, by any possible means, and exercise it without restraint, trampling underfoot all second-raters and useless people.

To think that thousands of fools were beginning to consider Ramses a god! When Shanaar had overturned the idol, the way would be open for a new regime. He would suppress the antiquated rites and would rule according to the only two main principles worthy of interest: territorial conquest and economic development.

As soon as he was on the throne he would have the House of Ramses razed to the ground and all the representations of Ramses destroyed. Although still unfinished, the Temple of a Million Years already produced energy which Shanaar himself had difficulty in resisting. Hieroglyphs, carved and painted scenes were alive, asserting the presence and power of Ramses in every stone. No! It was only an illusion engendered by the night.

Shanaar forced himself out of the lethargy that was threatening to overcome him. He put in place the device prepared by Ofir and left the enclosure of the House of Ramses.

It was taking shape, it was growing like a creature full of vigour, this Temple of a Million Years, and was helping to shape the reign of Ramses. The king paid homage to the building where he would come in future to draw the strength which nourished his thoughts and actions.

As at Karnak and Luxor, planners, stone-cutters, sculptors, painters and designers had worked wonders. The sanctuary, several shrines and their annexes, and a small hall of pillars, were all completed, as well as the building reserved for the worship of Seti. And all the other parts of the sacred domain were under construction, not counting brick warehouses, the library and the priests' homes.

Planted in the second year of his reign, the acacia tree of the House of Ramses had also grown with astonishing speed. Although still a slender young tree, its foliage already gave refreshing shade. Nefertari stroked its trunk.

The royal couple crossed the great temple court, under the respectful and wondering eyes of the stone-cutters, who had put down their mallets and chisels.

After exchanging a few words with their overseer, Ramses questioned each man on the difficulties he had encountered. The king had not forgotten the exciting hours spent in the quarries of Geb el-Silsila, at the time when he had wanted to become a stone-cutter himself. The monarch promised the artisans a special bonus: wine and fine-quality clothing.

As the royal couple were making their way to the shrine of Seti, Nefertari caught her hand to her heart and stood still. 'Danger . . . danger, close by.'

'Here, in the temple?' cried Ramses in astonishment.

The feeling of disquiet wore off. The royal couple approached the sanctuary where the soul of Seti would be for ever venerated.

'Don't open the door of this sanctuary, Ramses. The danger is there, behind the door. Leave it to me.'

Nefertari pushed open the gilded wooden door.

On the threshold lay a cornelian eye broken into several fragments; in front of the statue of Seti, in the depths of the shrine, was a red ball made of hairs from desert animals.

Invested with the power of Isis, the great magician, the queen pieced the eye together. If the king's foot had touched the fragments of the desecrated symbol, he would have been paralysed. Then Nefertari scooped up the red ball in the bottom of her gown, without touching it with her hands, and took it outside to be burned.

The evil eye, the couple noted, that was what creatures from the world of darkness had dared to use, in their desire to break the link uniting Seti to his son and to reduce the Lord of the Two Lands to a mere despot, deprived of the supernatural teachings of his predecessor.

Who but Shanaar, thought Ramses, would have gone so far on the path of evil, with the help of the magus in the pay of the Hittites? Who but Shanaar would be so eager to destroy what his heart was too small to contain?

34

Moses hesitated. True, it was his duty to carry out the mission God had laid down for him, but was it beyond his power to overcome this obstacle? He no longer harboured any illusions: Ramses would not give way. Moses knew the King of Egypt well enough to accept that he had not spoken lightly and that he considered the Hebrews an integral part of the Egyptian people.

Nevertheless, the idea of the exodus was taking root in his people's minds and opposition to the prophet grew weaker by the day. Many thought that Moses' privileged relationship with Pharaoh would make it easy to reach an agreement. One by one, the tribal chiefs had backed down; at the last council of elders, Aaron had not been contradicted when he presented Moses as the leader of a Hebrew people linked by one belief and one will. With the old divisions forgotten, the prophet had only one enemy left to defeat: Ramses the Great.

Aaron disturbed Moses' reflections. 'A brickmaker is asking to see you.'

'You deal with him.'

'He wants to see you, no one else.'

'What about?'

'Promises he says you made to him in the past. He trusts you.'

'Bring him to me.'

Wearing a short black wig, tied with a white bandeau which hid his forehead and left his ears free, with a sunburnt face, a little beard and a ragged moustache, the supplicant looked like any other Hebrew brickmaker. However, his build aroused Moses' suspicions; this man was somehow familiar.

'What do you want of me?' asked Moses.

'Our ideals led in the same direction once.'

'Ofir!'

'That is indeed who I am.'

'You are much changed.'

'Ramses' police are looking for me.'

'And with good reason. If I'm not mistaken, you are a Hittite spy.'

'I used to work for them, it's true, but my network was destroyed, and anyway the Hittites are no longer in a position to destroy Egypt.'

'So you lied to me, and you tried to use me against Ramses!'

'No, Moses. You and I believe in one all-powerful God and my contact with the Hebrews has convinced me that this God is Yahveh and none other.'

'Do you think me stupid enough to be seduced by these fine words?'

'Even if you refuse to accept that I am sincere, I shall serve your cause, because it is the only one which deserves to be served. You must know that I expect no personal benefit, except the salvation of my soul.'

Moses was troubled. 'Have you renounced your belief in Aton?'

'I've realized that Aton was only a prefiguration of the true God. Since I became aware of the truth, I have renounced my errors.'

'What has become of the young woman you wanted to put in power?'

'She died a violent death; I've grieved greatly for her. Yet the Egyptian police accuse me of a horrible crime which I didn't commit. In this tragedy I saw the sign of destiny. You are the only one, today, who can oppose Ramses. That is why I shall give you all my support.'

'What do you want, Ofir?'

'To help you impose the belief in Yahveh, nothing more.'

'Do you know that Yahveh demands the exodus of my people?'

'I approve this grand project. If it is accompanied by the downfall of Ramses and the advent of the true religion in Egypt, I shall want nothing more.'

'Isn't a spy always a spy?'

'I no longer have any contact with the Hittites, who are riven by quarrels over the succession. That episode of my life is over. You, Moses, are the future and the hope.'

'How do you intend to help me?'

'The struggle against Ramses will not be easy. My experience of underground struggles will be useful to you.'

'My people want to leave Egypt, not to rebel against Ramses.'

'What is the difference, Moses? Your attitude is rebellious in Ramses' eyes, and he will repress it as such.'

In his innermost heart, Moses had to admit that the Libyan was right. 'I must think about it, Ofir.'

'You are the master, Moses. Allow me to give you just one piece of advice: don't undertake anything in Ramses' absence. With him you might possibly be able to negotiate. But his henchmen Ahmeni and Serramanna, not to mention Queen Tuya, will show no indulgence to your people. In order to maintain public order, they will order brutal repression. Let us take advantage of the royal couple's travels to develop our solidarity, to convince those who are undecided and to prepare ourselves for the inevitable conflict.'

Ofir's determination impressed Moses. Although he hadn't decided whether to ally himself with the magus, it was difficult to deny the significance of his words.

*

The head of the Theban police confirmed that his men had spared no effort to find Shanaar and his possible accomplices. Ramses had given them a description of the man who had attacked him on the Nile and tried to shoot an arrow through him, but the police investigation had been fruitless.

'He has left Thebes,' Nefertari confirmed.

'Like me, you are convinced he is alive.'

'I sense a dangerous presence, a dark force . . . but is it Shanaar, the magus or one of their co-plotters?'

'It's Shanaar,' decided Ramses. 'He has tried to cut for ever the link that united me to Seti and to deprive me of my father's protection.'

'The evil eye will not be effective; the fire prevented it from doing any harm. With the help of a resin-based glue, we have pieced together the good eye, which was stolen from the Temple of Set in Pi-Ramses.'

'The desert animals whose hair formed the red eye are creatures of Set. Shanaar intended to wreak destruction by making use of his formidable energy.'

'He underestimated the strength of your links with Set.'

'That union has to be recreated every day. At the slightest error through inattention, Set's fire destroys the one who thought he had mastered him.'

'When do we leave for the Far South?'

'After we have been to see our deaths.'

The royal couple made their way to the southernmost valley of the Theban mountains, which bore the names 'the Place of Regeneration' and 'the Place of the Lotus'. This was the Valley of the Queens where Tuya, the Mother of Pharaoh, and Nefertari, the Great Royal Wife, would rest for eternity. Their tombs had been dug out of the rock under the summit of the mountain, the domain of the goddess of silence. Here Hathor, the smiling Lady of Heaven, who caused the stars to shine and the hearts of the faithful to dance, reigned over a desert burned up by the sun's oppressive heat.

Nefertari found Hathor's image on the walls of her own tomb, in the attitude of the healer, transmitting her energy to resuscitate an eternally young Great Royal Wife, who wore a golden headdress in the shape of a vulture, symbolizing the divine mother. The artists had succeeded in reproducing the beauty of the 'sweet beloved' in incredibly perfect forms.

'Does this dwelling suit you, Nefertari?'

'Such splendour . . . I'm not worthy of it.'

'There never was such a House of Eternity, nor will there ever be another such as this. You, whose love is the breath of my life, you will reign for ever in the hearts of gods and men.'

Green-faced Osiris, draped in a white mantle; luminous Ra, crowned with an enormous sun; Khepri, the principle of metamorphoses, with the head of a scarab; Ma'at, the universal Rule, a slender, beautiful young woman, whose emblem was an ostrich feather, light as the truth. The divine powers had gathered together to regenerate Nefertari, in time and beyond all times. Soon, on the pillars that were not yet decorated a scribe of the House of Life would trace the hieroglyphs from the *Book of Exit into the Light* and the *Book of the Doors* that would allow the queen to journey along the splendid paths of the Otherworld and to avoid its dangers.

It was no longer death, but the smile of mystery.

Nefertari spent several days studying the divine figures which dwelt in the House of Eternity, whose privileged guest she would become at the moment of the great crossing. She familiarized herself with what lay beyond her own existence, and shared in the silence which, in the bowels of the earth, had the flavour of heaven.

When she decided to leave the Place of the Lotus, Ramses took her to the 'Great Meadow', the Valley of the Kings, where pharaohs had rested since the beginning of the eighteenth dynasty. The royal couple spent long hours in the tomb of Ramses, the first of that name, and that of Seti. Each painting was a masterpiece and the queen read, column by column, the *Book of the Hidden Chamber*, which revealed the phases of the transmutation of the dying sun into the young sun, the model for Pharaoh's resurrection.

Nefertari was most moved to see the House of Eternity of Ramses the Great. The painters were blending finely crushed mineral pigments in little pots, in preparation for enlivening the walls with symbolic figures which would safeguard the monarch's survival. The coloured powders, mixed with water and acacia resin, allowed them extraordinary precision of execution. 'The House of Gold', the eight-pillared hall of the sarcophagus, was almost finished.

Ramses called for the overseer. 'As in the tombs of certain of my ancestors, you will dig out a corridor deep into the rock and you will leave the rough stone there. It will suggest the ultimate secret, which no human mind can know.'

Nefertari and Ramses had the impression that they had just passed a decisive stage. To their love was now added the consciousness of their own deaths, an awakening and not a demise.

35

Serramanna had to exercise patience.

Meba had left his house more than an hour ago, to attend a banquet organized by Tuya, who was concerned to hold the court together in the absence of the royal couple. She kept in regular contact with Ramses by courier, and she was satisfied with Ahmeni's scrupulous work and knew Serramanna could be relied on to maintain strict and constant order.

The unrest among the Hebrews seemed to have died down, but the former pirate, trusting to his intuition, was convinced that this was just the calm before the storm. True, Moses was doing nothing more than holding discussions with the notables among his people, but he had become the Hebrews' uncontested leader. What is more, a number of Egyptian dignitaries, knowing Ramses' loyalty to his friends, thought it as well to keep on the right side of Moses. One day, they believed, he would obtain an important post again and would abandon his woolly ideas.

One of Serramanna's chief worries was Meba. The Sardinian was convinced that the diplomat had stolen Kha's brush, but for what purpose? The former pirate detested diplomats in general, and Meba in particular: too worldly, too elegant and too eager to please. Lying came naturally to a fellow like him.

What if Kha's brush were hidden in Meba's house?

Serramanna could then have this aristocrat accused of theft, and he would have to explain in a court of law the reasons for his action.

Meba's gardener went off to bed, and the servants retired to their quarters. Serramanna climbed up the back of the house and reached the roof terrace. Walking as lightly as a cat, he raised a trapdoor which opened on to an attic. From here he could easily get down to the main rooms. He had a good part of the night to complete his exploration.

'Nothing,' grumbled the unshaven Sardinian.

'That search was completely illegal,' Ahmeni reminded him.

'If it had been successful, Meba wouldn't have been able to do any more damage.'

'Why have you got it in for him?'

'Because he's dangerous.'

'Dangerous? Meba? He's only concerned with his career, and worrying constantly about that doesn't give him time for anything else.'

Serramanna tucked into some dried fish dipped in a spicy sauce. 'Perhaps you're right,' he said with his mouth full, 'but my instinct tells me he's a bad lot. I'd like to put him under constant surveillance; he'll make a mistake eventually.'

'As you wish. But no blunders!'

'Moses ought also to have been placed under surveillance.'

'He was my friend in our student days,' Ahmeni reminded him, 'and Ramses' friend too.'

'That Hebrew is an agitator, and one to be feared. You're the servant of Pharaoh and Moses will rebel against Pharaoh.'

'He won't go to those lengths.'

'Of course he will! In the crews I commanded, I could spot types like him straight away. They're the worst trouble-makers. But you and Pharaoh refuse to listen to me.'

'We know Moses and we're less pessimistic than you.'

'One day, you'll be sorry you were so blind.'

'Go to bed and be careful not to upset the Hebrews. Our job is to keep order, not to sow unrest.'

Ahsha had been lodged in the palace, and provided with plain but adequate fare and medium-quality wine; he also enjoyed the professional amorous attentions of a fair-haired Hittite woman, whom the chamberlain had had the excellent idea of providing for him. Lacking even the slightest sense of modesty, she wanted to verify personally the reputation attributed to Egyptians of being wonderful lovers. Ahsha had been only too ready to cooperate in the experiment, sometimes actively, sometimes passively, but always with enthusiasm. Was there a pleasanter way of passing the time?

Uri-Teshup was astonished by Ahsha's move, but nevertheless flattered by the presence of Pharaoh's minister for foreign affairs. After all, this must mean that Ramses acknowledged him, the son of Muwatallis, as the future emperor.

Uri-Teshup burst into Ahsha's chamber just as the blonde Hittite was embracing the Egyptian most ardently.

'I'll come back,' said Uri-Teshup.

'No, stay,' Ahsha said. 'This young person will understand that affairs of state take precedence over pleasure.'

The delightful young Hittite slipped away. Ahsha donned an elegant tunic.

'How is the emperor?' he asked.

'His condition is unchanged.'

'I renew my offer: let me treat him.'

'Why come to the assistance of your worst enemy?'

'Your question embarrasses me.'

'I want an answer, at once,' Uri-Teshup demanded curtly.

'Diplomats don't like revealing their secrets so directly. Doesn't the humanitarian character of my mission satisfy you?'

'I demand a real reply.'

Ahsha looked uncomfortable. 'Well, Ramses has got to know Muwatallis. He feels great respect for him, and even a certain admiration. His illness distresses him.'

'Are you mocking me?'

'I think I know you wouldn't like to be accused of assassinating your father,' Ahsha suggested.

In spite of his growing anger, Uri-Teshup did not protest.

Ahsha followed up his advantage. 'Everything that happens at the Hittite court concerns us. We know that the army wants the transfer of power to take place peacefully and wants the emperor himself to appoint his successor. That is why I want to use the resources of our medicine to help him recover his health.'

Uri-Teshup could not agree to that request. If Muwatallis recovered his powers of speech, he would have his son thrown into prison and entrust the empire to Hattusilis.

'How is it that you are so well informed?' he asked Ahsha.

'It's difficult for me to—'

'Answer me.'

'I'm sorry, I must keep silent.'

'You're not in Egypt, Ahsha, but in my capital!'

'In my capacity as an ambassador on an official mission, what do I have to fear?'

'I'm a soldier, not a diplomat. And we are at war.'

'Is that a threat?'

'I'm not famed for my patience, Ahsha. Hurry up and speak.'

'Would you go so far as to use . . . torture?'

'I wouldn't hesitate for a moment.'

Ahsha was shivering. He wrapped himself in a woollen blanket. 'If I speak, will you spare me?'

'We shall remain good friends.'

Ahsha looked down. 'I have to confess that my real mission is to propose a truce to Emperor Muwatallis.'

'A truce? For how long?'

'As long as possible.'

Uri-Teshup rejoiced. So, Pharaoh's army was at the end of
its tether! As soon as those accursed auspices were
favourable again, the new master of Hatti would rush to
attack the Delta.

'And then . . .' Ahsha went on hesitantly.

'Then?'

'We know that the emperor is hesitating between you and
Hattusilis for his successor.'

'Where do you get your information from, Ahsha?'

'Would you grant us this truce, if you had the power?'

Why not use the strategy so dear to my father? thought Uri-
Teshup.

'I'm a man of war, but I don't rule out the possibility,
providing it doesn't weaken Hatti.'

Ahsha relaxed. 'I told Ramses that you were a statesman,
and I wasn't wrong. If you wish for it, we shall have peace.'

'Peace, certainly. But you haven't answered my question:
what is the source of your information?'

'Senior officers who pretend to support you. In reality,
they are betraying you for the benefit of Hattusilis.'

This revelation hit Uri-Teshup like a thunderbolt.

'With Hattusilis,' Ahsha continued, 'we shall obtain
neither peace nor a truce. His sole aim is to be at the head of
a vast coalition, as at Kadesh, and crush our army.'

'I want names, Ahsha.'

'Are we to be allies against Hattusilis?'

Uri-Teshup suddenly felt his muscles stiffen as at the
approach of battle. To use this Egyptian to get rid of his rival,
what a strange twist of fate! But he would not let such an
opportunity pass.

'Help me to get rid of the traitors, Ahsha, and you'll get
your truce – and perhaps more besides.'

The diplomat began to speak. Each name he gave felt to
Uri-Teshup like a stab from a dagger. In the list were some of

212

his keenest supporters, at least as far as words went. And there were even senior officers who had fought at his side and who asserted that they already considered him the new Lord of Hatti.

Enraged, Uri-Teshup strode to the door of the room.

'One more detail,' Ahsha called to him. 'Would you ask my young friend to return?'

36

As he walked through the Aswan granite quarries with Bakhen, Ramses could still see his father, Seti, choosing the right stone to be transformed into obelisks and statues. At the age of seventeen, he had been happy to discover this magical site, searching under Pharaoh's guidance for perfect veins of granite. Today, it was he himself, Ramses, who was leading this exploration and he had to demonstrate the same qualities of perception.

Ramses used Seti's divining-rod, which allowed his hands to feel the earth's hidden currents. The world of men was but one form that emerged at 'the First Time' from the primordial ocean of energy, into which it would return when the gods created a new life cycle. Under the earth, as in the sky, metamorphoses were endlessly taking place; an acute mind could detect their echo.

In appearance, the quarries were a motionless universe, enclosed and hostile, where the heat was unbearable for a good part of the year. But the bowels of the earth proved extraordinarily generous, causing granite of incomparable splendour to appear on its surface. It was, above all, a hard-wearing material, one which would allow the 'Houses of Eternity' to endure for ever.

Ramses stood still.

'You must dig here,' he ordered Bakhen 'and you will

extricate a monolith from which you will fashion a colossus for the House of Ramses. Have you consulted the artisans?'

'They all volunteered for Nubia. I had to select a limited number for your team. Majesty . . . this isn't something I'm used to doing, but I have a request to make to you.'

'I'm listening, Bakhen.'

'Would you permit me to come on this expedition?'

'I must refuse, for a good reason: your appointment to the rank of Third Prophet of Amon at Karnak obliges you to remain in Thebes.'

'I . . . I did not wish for this promotion.'

'I know, Bakhen, but the High Priest and I judged that we could place a heavier burden on your shoulders. You will help Nebu to preserve the prosperity of his domains and supervise the construction of my Temple of a Million Years. Thanks to you, Nebu will be able to face day-to-day difficulties with a light heart.'

With his clenched fist on his heart, Bakhen swore that he would assume the duties of his new post.

The rise in the water level was great, not so excessive as to damage the dykes, the canals and the cultivated lands, but sufficient to facilitate the voyage of the royal couple, their escort and the stone-cutters. The jumble of rocks around the First Cataract was invisible under the turbulent waters of currents and whirlpools, which made navigation dangerous. In particular, it was necessary to beware of sudden differences in level, visible only at the last minute, and violent waves, capable of wrecking any boats whose cargoes were unstable. So a wealth of precautions were taken to prepare a channel through which the royal flotilla could negotiate the cataract without risk.

Normally placid and indifferent to human agitation, Invincible seemed tense. The huge lion was in a hurry to leave for his native Nubia. Ramses stroked his mane to calm him.

Two men asked to come aboard and speak with the monarch.

The first, a scribe responsible for overseeing the river-gauge, presented his report. 'Majesty, the rise in the water level has reached twenty-one cubits, three and a third hands.'

'That seems excellent.'

'Quite satisfactory, Majesty. This year Egypt will have no difficulty with irrigation.'

The second person was the head of the Elephantine police. What he had to say was much less reassuring. 'Majesty, the customs office has noted the passage of a man corresponding to the description you gave.'

'Why was he not intercepted?'

'The senior customs officer was away, and no one wanted to take the responsibility, especially as no offence had been committed.'

Ramses controlled his anger. 'What else?'

'The man chartered a fast boat for the South; he said he was a trader.'

'What was his cargo?'

'Jars containing dried beef for the forts at the Second Cataract.'

'When did he leave?'

'A week ago.'

'Send his description to the commanders of the forts and order them to arrest him if he turns up at their gates.'

Relieved to have escaped punishment, the policeman hurried to carry out his orders.

'Shanaar has preceded us on the way to Nubia,' stated Nefertari. 'Do you think it wise to continue our journey?'

'What have we got to fear from a fugitive?'

'He's prepared for anything. Won't his hatred lead him into acts of madness?'

'We won't let Shanaar prevent our journey. I don't underestimate his capacity to do harm, Nefertari, but I'm not

216

afraid of it. One day we shall come face to face and he will bow down to his king before being punished by the gods.'

They embraced and this moment of communion strengthened Ramses' determination.

Setau didn't trust anyone; he leaped from the bow of one boat to that of another, crossed over this one, jumped on to the next one, examined the cargoes, checked the ropes, fingered the sails, tested the soundness of the rudders. Sailing was not his favourite occupation, and he didn't trust sailors who were overconfident. Fortunately, the river administration had had a channel cleared, away from the reefs, and navigable even in the high-water season. But the snake-charmer would not feel really safe until he had his feet on dry ground again.

Back on the royal ship, where a cabin had been reserved for him, Setau checked that nothing had been forgotten: filtering jars, little bottles filled with solid and liquid remedies, baskets for snakes of various sizes, grinders, mortars, pestles, bronze razors, little packets of rust from lead, copper filings, red ochre, medicinal clay, bags of onions, compresses, jars of honey, flasks . . . Everything was there.

Singing an old Nubian song, Lotus was folding loincloths and tunics and putting them away in wooden chests. Because of the heat, she was naked and her catlike movements delighted Setau.

'These boats seem sturdy enough to me,' he said clasping her round the waist.

'Did you do a thorough inspection?'

'I'm reliable, aren't I?'

'Go and check the masts more closely; I haven't finished putting things away.'

'That's not so urgent.'

'I can't stand a mess.'

Setau's loincloth fell to the floor of the cabin. 'Would you be cruel enough to abandon a lover in this state?'

His caresses became so intimate that Lotus couldn't carry on with her methodical work.

'You're taking advantage of my weakness, just when I'm going to see Nubia again,' she said.

'What better way to celebrate this wonderful moment than by making love?'

The fleet of boats leaving for the South was seen off by a large crowd. A few intrepid lads, floating on makeshift reed rafts, followed the fleet as far as the entrance to the channel. Who could ever forget the open-air banquet that the royal couple had given the people, in the course of which the beer had flowed freely?

The boats built for the voyage to Nubia were veritable floating houses, both solid and comfortable. They had one central mast and one large sail, held by a quantity of rigging, and were provided with double rudders, one to port, the other to starboard. The entrances to the cabins, which were spacious and well furnished, had been calculated to ensure good ventilation.

Once past the cataract, the flotilla adopted its cruising formation.

Nefertari wanted to invite Setau and Lotus to share some carob juice, but the sighs of pleasure coming from the couple's cabin dissuaded her from knocking at their door. Amused, the queen leaned in the prow, beside Invincible, whose nostrils quivered in anticipation of the air of Nubia.

The Great Royal Wife thanked the gods for having granted her so much happiness, happiness which it was her duty to let shine forth over her people. This modest, shy lute-player, promised to an obscure yet peaceful career, was living an incredible life at Ramses' side.

Every morning she discovered him afresh, and her love grew, with the untroubled strength of a magic link which

218

nothing would ever break. Even if Ramses had been a farmer or a man who hollowed vases out of hard stone, Nefertari would have loved him with the same passion. But the part that destiny had called on the royal couple to play forbade them to enjoy their bliss selfishly. They must never cease to think of this civilization which their predecessors had entrusted to them and which they had to bequeath, even finer, to their successors.

The Egypt of the pharaohs was just that, a succession of creatures of love, faith and duty, who had rejected mediocrity, baseness and vanity, in order to form a chain of human lights in the service of the divine light.

When Ramses put his arm round the Great Royal Wife and clasped her to him, with that strength tinged with gentleness which had made Nefertari fall in love with him at their first meeting, she relived immediately their past years together, a mixture of joys and trials, joys and trials overcome, thanks to the certainty of being as one in all circumstances.

And merely through the touch of his body, she knew that the same impulses burned in his heart and transported them both along the paths of the Invisible, where the goddess of love played the music of the stars.

37

Sometimes it raced straight ahead, impetuous and proud, sometimes it flowed languidly in seductive curves, pausing to caress in its passage a village enlived with children's laughter: such was the Nile of the Far South, always retaining the majesty of the celestial river of which it was the earthly continuation. Passing between barren hills and granite islets, it nurtured a narrow strip of grassland, with a scattering of dom-palms. Crested cranes, ibis, pink flamingoes, and pelicans flew over the royal flotilla. Those aboard were fascinated by the purity of the sky and the desert.

Whenever they stopped, local tribes came to dance round the royal tent. Ramses conversed with the chiefs while Setau and Lotus recorded their complaints and requirements. At nightfall, round the fire, there was talk of the mystery of the creative floodwater, the beneficial rise in the water level and they extolled the name of Ramses the Great, the Spouse of Egypt and of Nubia.

Nefertari realized that the pharaoh's fame was growing and that some thought him the equal of a god. Since his victory at Kadesh, the story of the battle was on everyone's lips, even in the most remote villages. It was considered a divine favour to see Ramses and Nefertari, for had not Amon entered into the spirit of the king to strengthen his arm, and Hathor into that of the queen to spread love like a shower of sparkling precious stones?

As the north wind blew softly, their progress was slow. Nefertari and Ramses enjoyed these hours of quietness and spent most of their time on deck, sheltered by a sunshade. Invincible had recovered his serenity and slept on the deck.

The golden sand and the purity of the desert echoed the Otherworld. The further the ship progressed towards the domain of Hathor, that deserted region where the goddess had fashioned a miraculous stone, the more Nefertari felt she was performing an important act which linked her to the origin of all things.

The nights were bliss. In the royal couple's cabin, Ramses' favourite bed had a mattress made of skeins of hemp closely intertwined and fixed to the framework; two straps gave it great flexibility. The frame, assembled with mortice-and-tenon joints, had a double base for extra solidity. On the toe-clips, papyrus and water-lilies were depicted, surrounded by papyrus plants, cornflowers and mandrakes, symbolizing the goddesses of the North and the South. Even during his sleep, Pharaoh remained the mediator.

The nights were bliss, for in the heat of the Nubian summer, Ramses' love was as boundless as the starry heaven.

With the pieces of silver given him by Ofir, which amounted to a veritable fortune, Shanaar had procured the services of some fifty Nubian fishermen, who were delighted to improve their everyday lot, even if what the Egyptian demanded was crazy and dangerous. Most of them believed this was the passing folly of a rich and capricious man who wanted to witness an unusual spectacle and who paid well, thus ensuring a comfortable life for them and their families for many years.

Shanaar did not like Nubia. He detested the sun and the heat, he perspired the whole day and was obliged to drink great quantities of water, and there was only mediocre food to eat; he nevertheless rejoiced at having drawn up a plan to get rid of Ramses.

However, this abhorred Nubia was providing him with a cohort of ruthless killers which Ramses' soldiers would be unable to repel. An undisciplined cohort, but of incomparable violence and aptitude for battle.

It only remained to wait for Ramses' boat.

The Viceroy of Nubia spent his days peacefully in his comfortable palace at Buhen, near the Second Cataract, which was overlooked by several forts built to prevent any attempt at aggression by the Nubians. In the past, the chiefs of some tribes had tried to invade Egypt, and it had been decided to suppress this danger by building impressive strongholds whose garrisons were regularly provided with fresh supplies and enjoyed good rates of pay.

The Viceroy of Nubia, who also bore the title of 'Royal Son of Kush' (Kush was one of the Nubian provinces), had only one major worry: ensuring the extraction of gold and its transport to Thebes, Memphis and Pi-Ramses. The goldsmiths used the precious metal, 'the flesh of the gods', to adorn doors, temple walls and statues, and Ramses used it in his diplomatic relations with several countries whose benevolent neutrality he had purchased in this way.

The post of Viceroy of Nubia was a very enviable one, even if its incumbent did have to live far from Egypt for months on end. This high official administered a vast country and relied on an experienced military clan, whose ranks included many natives. As he no longer feared the slightest rebellion on the part of the subdued tribes, the viceroy devoted himself to the pleasures of good food, music and poetry. His wife, who had borne him four children, was ferociously jealous, which precluded him from casting admiring glances at the tempting figures of the young Nubian women, who were expert in amorous play. Divorce would have brought about the viceroy's ruin, as his wife would have obtained enormous compensation and the cost of supporting her would have prevented him from living in grand style.

He had a horror of incidents likely to upset his peaceful existence. And here was an official dispatch announcing the arrival of the royal couple! But the document did not give the exact aim of the journey, nor the date of their arrival at Buhen. And another dispatch ordered the arrest of Shanaar, Ramses' elder brother, thought dead long ago, and whose appearance would now be greatly changed! The viceroy hesitated to send a vessel to meet the monarch. Since Pharaoh ran no risk, it was better to concentrate on the quality of the welcome and on organizing receptions in honour of the royal couple.

The commander of the Buhen fortress brought his daily report to the viceroy. 'No trace of the suspect in the area, but there is one strange fact.'

'I detest incidents, Commander!'

'I ought to mention this, nevertheless.'

'Oh, very well, if you must.'

'Several fishermen left their village for two days,' the officer informed him. 'When they returned, they got drunk and fought. One of them died during the brawl and I found a little bar of silver in his hut.'

'That's a fortune to a fisherman!'

'True, but our questioning was fruitless. No one told us where the bar came from. I'm convinced someone paid the men to steal fish intended for the army.'

If the viceroy embarked on a futile investigation, Pharaoh would accuse him of inefficiency; so the best solution was to do nothing, hoping that His Majesty would never know about it.

The wind was so slack that the sailors, who had nothing to do, slept or played dice. They were enjoying this peaceful voyage

223

and the merry stopovers, occasions for pleasant encounters with welcoming Nubian women.

The captain of the rearmost vessel did not like seeing his crew idle. He was just about to order them to swab down the decks when there was a violent shock, which made the vessel reel. Several sailors fell heavily to the deck.

'A rock! We've struck a rock!'

Standing in the bows of the royal ship, Ramses had heard the hull crack. All the boats immediately shortened sail and hove to in the middle of the river, which here was not very wide.

Lotus was the first to realize the truth of the situation. Several dozen grey rocks were scarcely visible above the surface of the muddy water, but a keen eye could make out eyes and tiny ears.

'Herds of hippos,' she told Ramses.

She climbed to the top of the mast and noted that the flotilla was trapped among them. She climbed down agilely and didn't disguise the truth.

'I've never seen so many, Majesty! We can go neither forward nor back. It's strange . . . you'd swear they'd been herded together here by force.'

Pharaoh knew the danger. Adult hippopotami weighed as much as a block of granite and were equipped with formidable weapons: yellow teeth, nearly a cubit long and capable of biting through the hull of a boat. These lords of the river were very much at ease in the water and could swim with surprising agility; they were also very irascible. When their anger was aroused, they would open their enormous jaws in a threatening yawn.

'If the leading males have decided to fight over the females,' Lotus told them, 'they will destroy everything in their way and sink our boats. Many of us will be either mauled to death or drowned.'

Dozens of ears quivered, half-closed eyes opened, nostrils

appeared on the surface of the water, jaws opened and sinister grunts scattered the egrets perched on the acacia trees. The bodies of the males were marked with scars, traces of furious fights, many of which had ended in the death of one of the combatants.

At the sight of those horrible yellow teeth the sailors' jaws dropped. It didn't take them long to spot several enormous males at the head of a score of individuals getting more and more agitated. If they attacked, they would begin by crushing the rudders in their jaws, which would make it impossible to manoeuvre, and then they would hurl their weight against the boats until they sank. To leap into the water and try to swim to the bank was risky, for how could anyone force a way through all these furious monsters?

'We must harpoon them,' suggested Setau.

'There are too many of them,' judged Ramses. 'We'd only kill a few and provoke the fury of the rest.'

'Surely we're not going to let ourselves be massacred without reacting!'

'Is that how I acted at Kadesh? My father Amon is the lord of the winds. We must keep silent so that his voice can be heard.'

Ramses and Nefertari raised their hands, with their palms turned up towards the sky, as a sign of offering. Planted firmly on his paws, gazing into the distance, the enormous lion adopted a dignified pose on his master's right.

The order was transmitted from boat to boat, and silence reigned over the flotilla.

The jaws of several of the hippopotami closed slowly. The lords of the Nile, whose skin was fragile, submerged and let only the tips of their nostrils and their ears appear. With their half-closed eyes, they looked as though they were almost asleep.

For several interminable minutes nothing stirred.

Then the north wind cooled Lotus's cheeks, this breeze

which embodied the breath of life. The royal ship advanced slowly, soon followed by the other craft, and passed between the hippos, which had suddenly become subdued.

From the top of a dom-palm, where he had taken up his position to watch the shipwreck, Shanaar witnessed another miracle performed by Ramses. A miracle? No, a crazy coincidence, an unexpected wind which had risen in the middle of the day, in the heart of the midsummer heat!

Shanaar's hand furiously closed over dates saturated with sunshine and crushed them.

38

During the hot season, the Hebrew brickmakers were laid off. Some of them took advantage of this to rest with their families, others earned a wage by taking work as gardeners on the large estates. The fruit crop promised to be remarkable; the celebrated Pi-Ramses apples would have pride of place on the banquet tables.

Beautiful girls dozed in the shelter of wooden summer-houses covered with climbing plants, or bathed in the pleasure lakes; young men swam in front of them, performing a multiplicity of feats to dazzle them; the older men enjoyed the shade of the espalier vines, and talked of Ramses' latest exploit: subduing an immense herd of angry hippopotami by magic. And time and again could be heard the song 'What joy it is to reside in Pi-Ramses; the palaces are replendent in gold and turquoise; the wind is gentle; the birds frolic around the ponds,' a song that even the Hebrew brickmakers hummed.

The planned exodus seemed forgotten. Yet when Ahmeni saw Moses enter his office, he feared that this peace would be disrupted.

'Don't you ever rest, Ahmeni?'

'As soon as I finish one dossier, there's another to tackle; with Ramses away, it's even worse. The king can make a decision in just a few minutes; I have to worry over every detail.'

'Have you ever thought of getting married?'

'That'd be a calamity! A wife would reproach me for working too hard, and she'd upset all my arrangements and prevent me serving Pharaoh correctly.'

'Pharaoh, our friend . . .'

'Is he really still your friend, Moses?'

'Do you doubt it, Ahmeni?'

'Your attitude does make one wonder.'

'The Hebrews' cause is just.'

'But the exodus! What madness!'

'If your people were in captivity, wouldn't you want to free them?'

'What captivity, Moses? Everyone is free in Egypt, you the same as everyone else.'

'Our real liberty is to assert our belief in Yahveh, the true God, the only God.'

'I'm concerned with administration, not theology.'

'Will you tell me the date of Ramses' return?'

'I don't know it.'

'If you knew it, would you tell me?'

Ahmeni fiddled with a tablet of writing. 'I don't approve of your plans, Moses. Because I'm your friend I have to tell you that Serramanna considers you a dangerous man. Don't become a troublemaker, otherwise he'll clamp down and you might suffer.'

'Thanks to Yahveh, I fear no man.'

'All the same you should fear Serramanna. If you disturb public order, he will strike.'

'Won't you help me, Ahmeni?'

'My religion is Egypt. If you betray your country, you'll pass into the realm of darkness.'

'I'm afraid we no longer have anything in common.'

'Whose fault is that, Moses?'

As he left Ahmeni's office, the Hebrew was prey to gloomy thoughts. Ofir was right: he had to wait for Ramses' return and try to persuade him, hoping that words would be an adequate weapon.

Ofir was lodged in a house in the Hebrew quarter, where he had just finished setting up his laboratory. He had already begun experimenting with spells, using Kha's brush, but with no success. The object remained inert, with no vibrations, as if no human hand had ever touched it.

The magic protection from which Kha benefited was totally effective, so much so that the magus was worried. Had he sufficient means to overcome this obstacle? One man could help him: the diplomat Meba.

However, the man who turned up to see him bore no resemblance to a confident, flamboyant personality: trembling, shrouded in a hooded cloak which hid his face, Meba looked more like a man on the run.

'It's already dark,' Ofir remarked.

'All the same, someone might recognize me. It's very dangerous for me to come here. Shouldn't we avoid this type of interview?'

'It was essential.'

Meba was sorry he'd got involved with the Hittite spy, but how could he break out of the net? 'What have you got to tell me, Ofir?'

'Great changes may well be taking place in the Hittite Empire.'

'To what effect?'

'In our favour. What information have you got?'

'Ahsha is a cautious man. Only Ahmeni has any knowledge of the diplomatic messages – they're sent to him and he then passes the essential details on to Ramses. The messages are in code, and I don't know the key. If I showed too much interest, I'd become suspect.'

'I want to know the contents of those messages.'

'The risks . . .'

Ofir's icy glance dissuaded Meba from looking for more excuses.

'I'll do my best.'

'Are you sure that the writing-brush you stole really belonged to Kha?'

'Absolutely sure.'

'Setau has given him the benefit of some magical protection, hasn't he?'

'Yes indeed.'

'Setau has gone to Nubia with Ramses, but his device is proving more effective than I expected. Exactly what precautions did he take?'

'Talismans, I think. But I can't get near Kha!'

'Why?'

'Serramanna suspects me of stealing the brush. If I make another false move, he'll throw me into prison.'

'Don't lose your head, Meba. In Egypt, justice is not an empty word. The Sardinian has no proof against you, so you risk nothing.'

'I'm sure Kha suspects me too.'

'Does he confide in anyone?'

The diplomat reflected. 'Probably his tutor, Nedjem, the minister for agriculture.'

'Question him and try to find out the nature of the talismans.'

'That's extremely dangerous.'

'You are in the service of the Hittite Empire, Meba.'

The dignitary looked down. 'I'll do my best, I promise you.'

Serramanna gave the twenty-year-old Libyan girl who had come to entertain him a hearty slap on the backside. She made up in enthusiasm what she lacked in experience. She had breasts which his hands found unforgettable and most impressive thighs, whose appeal could be refused by no decent man. And the former pirate boasted now of belonging to that category.

'I'd like to begin again,' she murmured.

'Clear off. I've work to do!'

The young woman was scared and didn't insist.

Serramanna jumped on his horse and galloped off to the guardroom, where the squad on duty was being relieved. Usually they played dice or the game of snakes, and had lively discussions about their pay or their promotion. During the absence of the royal couple, Serramanna had doubled their stints of duty in order to protect the Mother of Pharaoh and the other members of the royal family.

Deep silence reigned in the guardroom.

'Have you all lost your tongues?' asked Serramanna, sensing something amiss.

The head of the guard stood up. 'First of all, chief, we carried out your orders.'

'What was the result?'

'We carried out your orders, but the man watching the Hebrew district had no luck. He didn't see Meba go by.'

'That means he was asleep!'

'It could mean that, chief.'

'And you call that "carrying out orders"?'

'It's so hot today.'

'I told you to put a tail on a suspect, not to let him out of your sight for a moment, especially if he enters the Hebrew brickmakers' district, and you bungled it and lost him!'

'It won't happen again, chief.'

'Another mistake like that, and I'll send you all home, to your Greek islands or wherever!'

Serramanna stamped furiously out of the guardroom. His intuition told him that Meba was in league with the Hebrew protesters and was ready to help Moses. Many of the court notables, who were just as stupid as Meba, had no inkling of the danger the prophet represented.

*

Ofir closed the door of his laboratory again. The two men he was receiving, Amos and Baduch, didn't need to know about his experiments. Like the magus, the two Bedouin were dressed as Hebrew brickmakers and had let their moustaches grow.

Thanks to the nomad tribes that the two men controlled, Ofir remained in contact with Hattusa, the Hittite capital. He saw to it that they were well paid, so preventing any premature betrayal.

'The emperor is still alive,' Amos told him. 'His son, Uri-Teshup, should succeed him.'

'Are the soldiers expecting an offensive?'

'Not in the immediate future.'

'Shall we have weapons?'

'Plenty, but their transport poses a problem. We shall have to make a lot of small deliveries to equip the Hebrews if we don't want to attract the attention of the Egyptian authorities. It will take a long time, but we mustn't be guilty of any incautious moves. Have you obtained Moses' agreement?'

'I shall do. You will store the weapons in the cellars of houses belonging to those Hebrews who have decided to fight against Pharaoh's army and police.'

'We'll draw up a list of reliable people.'

'When shall we begin the deliveries?'

'Next month.'

39

The officer responsible for security in Hattusa was one of Uri-Teshup's keenest supporters; like many other soldiers he was waiting impatiently for the emperor to die and for his son to take power and at last order the offensive against Egypt.

After checking for himself that his men were correctly positioned at the strategic points of the city, the officer returned to the barracks to enjoy a well-earned rest. Tomorrow he would subject the shirkers to a punitive drill session and issue orders for some arrests in order to maintain discipline.

Hattusa was rather sinister, with its fortifications and grey walls; but soon, after the victory, the Hittite army would feast in the lush Egyptian countryside and make merry on the banks of the Nile.

The officer sat down on his bed, took off his boots and massaged his feet with an inexpensive salve made from nettles. He lay back, and was beginning to doze off when the door was flung open.

Two soldiers stood over him with swords unsheathed.

'What do you think you're doing? Get out!'

'You're worse than a vulture! You betrayed our leader, Uri-Teshup!'

'What are you talking about?'

'This is your reward!'

Grunting like butchers at the slaughterhouse, the two soldiers plunged their swords into the traitor's belly.

A pale sun was rising. After a sleepless night, Uri-Teshup felt the need for some refreshment. He was breakfasting on warm milk and goat's cheese when the two killers appeared.

'Mission accomplished, sir.'

'Any difficulties?'

'None. All the traitors were taken by surprise.'

'Have a funeral pyre erected in front of the lion gate and pile up the corpses. Tomorrow I myself will light the fire to burn them. Everyone will know the fate that's in store for those who try to stab me in the back.'

Thanks to the names given by Ahsha, the purge had been swift and merciless. There were no more informers left in Hattusa among those close to Uri-Teshup.

The commander-in-chief went to his father's bedchamber. Two male nurses had propped the emperor up in an armchair on the terrace of his palace, overlooking the upper town. Muwatallis's gaze was fixed; his hands clutched the armrests of the chair.

'Can you speak, father?'

His mouth half opened, but no sound passed his lips. Uri-Teshup was reassured.

'You've nothing to fear for the empire. I'm watching over it. Hattusilis is hiding in the provinces. He's nothing now, so I don't need to get rid of him. He's a coward who will rot in dread and oblivion.'

In Muwattalis's eyes there was a gleam of hatred.

'You've no right to criticize me, father. When power isn't offered you, you must seize it by any possible means.'

Uri-Teshup unsheathed his dagger.

'Aren't you tired of suffering, father? A great emperor has no taste for anything but the art of governing. In the state you're in, what hope do you still have of practising this art again? Make an effort, let your eyes beg me to shorten this horrible torture.'

Uri-Teshup approached Muwattalis. The emperor did not lower his eyelids.

'Approve my action. Approve it and give me the throne that is mine by right.'

Muwattalis put all his strength into expressing his stubborn refusal, and stared defiantly at his assailant.

Uri-Teshup raised his arm, ready to strike. 'Will you give in, in the name of all the gods?'

Under the pressure of the emperor's fingers, one of the armrests shattered like a ripe fruit. Stunned, his son dropped the dagger, which rolled along the floor.

Inside the Yazilikaya sanctuary, built on a hillside, to the north-east of Hattusa, the priests were washing the statue of the God of Storms, to renew his power. Then they celebrated the rites intended to ward off chaos and shut evil away in the earth. They also planted seven iron nails, seven bronze and seven copper ones in the body of a young pig which was charged with obscure forces, threatening the equilibrium of the country, and finally they sacrificed the animal.

When the ceremony was over, the celebrants walked past a frieze of twelve gods, stopped in front of a stone table and drank a strong alcoholic beverage to expel all vexation from their minds. Then they descended some steps cut in the stone, leading to a shrine hollowed out of the depths of the rock, where they would pray.

A priest and a priestess left the procession and went down to a subterranean chamber lit by oil lamps; here Hattusilis and Putuhepa took off the hoods that hid their faces.

'This peaceful moment has strengthened me,' she admitted.

'We are safe here,' Hattusilis said. 'None of Uri-Teshup's soldiers will dare to venture into this sacred enclave. I've taken the precaution of posting lookouts round the sanctuary. Was your journey satisfactory?'

'Even better than I'd hoped. Many officers are less devoted to Uri-Teshup than we thought, and they are open to the idea of acquiring a fine fortune without getting killed. Some of them are also conscious of the danger that Assyria represents, and feel we should reinforce our defences instead of launching into a mad venture against Egypt.'

Hattusilis drank in his wife's words as if they were nectar.

'Am I dreaming, Putuhepa, or do you really bring genuine hope?'

'Ahsha's gold has worked wonders and loosened many tongues. Senior officers detest Uri-Teshup's arrogance, his cruelty and vanity. They no longer believe in his blustering talk or in his ability to defeat Ramses, and they can't forgive his attitude to the emperor. True, he hasn't dared assassinate him, but he openly wishes for his death. If we manoeuvre skilfully, Uri-Teshup's reign will be short.'

'My brother is dying and I can't offer him any help . . .'

'Do you want us to try to take over by force?'

'That would be a mistake, Putuhepa; Muwatallis's fate is sealed.'

The beautiful priestess gazed admiringly at her husband. 'Have you the courage to sacrifice your feelings in order to rule over Hatti?'

'Since it is necessary. But the feelings that unite me to you are indestructible.'

'We shall fight together and we shall conquer together, Hattusilis. How did the merchants receive you?'

'Their confidence has not diminished; it has even been strengthened by Uri-Teshup's mistakes. According to them he will ruin the empire. We have the provinces' support, but we still lack that of the capital.'

'Ahsha's reserve of gold is far from exhausted. I shall go to Hattusa and I shall persuade the more responsible high-ranking officers to come over to our side.'

'Suppose you fall into Uri-Teshup's hands?'

'We have friends in Hattusa. They will hide me and I shall organize short interviews in different places.'

'It's too dangerous, Putuhepa.'

'We must grant Uri-Teshup no respite and we haven't a moment to lose.'

Ahsha lay half dozing while the young blonde Hittite licked his back, slowly working her way up to the nape of his neck. When the pleasure became most sweet, the diplomat roused himself from his lethargy, turned on his side and embraced his mistress, whose beasts quivered. He was preparing to favour her with a novel caress when Uri-Teshup burst into his room.

'You think of nothing but love, Ahsha!'

'Your capital is rich in exciting discoveries.'

Uri-Teshup grabbed the blonde by the hair and threw her out of the room while the Egyptian dressed and scented himself.

'I'm in an excellent mood,' declared the Hittite, whose muscles seemed more prominent than usual. With his long hair and chest covered with a mat of red hairs, the emperor's son was the very model of a ruthless warrior.

'All my enemies have been eliminated,' he declared. 'Not a single traitor is still alive. In future the army will toe the line.'

Uri-Teshup had thought long and hard before starting the purge. If Ahsha had spoken the truth, it was an opportunity to get rid of the black sheep; if he had lied, it was a chance to suppress possible rivals. This bloody operation, decided on the suggestion of the Egyptian ambassador, presented, all things considered, nothing but advantages.

'Do you still refuse to let me treat your father?'

'The emperor is incurable, Ahsha. It's useless to torment

him with drugs which won't improve his condition and risk increasing his suffering.'

'Since he's incapable of governing, will the empire remain without a ruler?'

Uri-Teshup smiled triumphantly. 'The senior officers will soon choose me as emperor.'

'And we shall conclude a long truce, shall we not?'

'Do you doubt it?'

'I have your word.'

'There remains a major obstacle: Hattusilis, the emperor's brother.'

'But surely his influence is non-existent?'

'As long as he's alive, he'll try to harm me! With the help of the merchants, he'll plot to deprive me of the resources I need to equip the army properly.'

'Can't you catch him?'

'Hattusilis is like an eel and can hide at will.'

'Annoying,' acknowledged Ahsha. 'But there is a solution.'

Uri-Teshup's eyes lit up. 'What's that, my friend?'

'To lay a trap for him.'

'And you'd help me capture him?'

'It is part of an Egyptian ambassador's job to offer a sumptuous gift to the new Emperor of Hatti.'

40

Using her gifts as a clairvoyant, Nefertari had confirmed what Ramses had sensed: the presence of herds of hippopotami preparing to engage in a fierce battle, destroying the Egyptian flotilla as they fought, was not due to chance. Beaters and fishermen had forcibly herded the colossal beasts together.

'Shanaar! He was the one behind them,' judged Ramses. 'He'll never give up trying to destroy us; that's his sole purpose in life. Nefertari, do you agree that we should continue our journey to the south?'

'Pharaoh must not abandon his plan.'

The Nile and the Nubian countryside made them forget Shanaar and his hatred.

When they stopped, Lotus and Setau captured some remarkable cobras, including one with a black-and-red-striped head. There promised to be an abundant yield of venom. The charming, golden-skinned Nubian was lovelier than ever, there was a generous supply of palm-wine, and the pleasures of love-making, in the soft warm nights, trans-formed the voyage into a feast of desire.

When the dawn light revived the green of the palm trees and the ochre of the hills, Nefertari delighted in the joy of this rebirth, which was greeted by the songs of hundreds of birds. Every morning, wearing the traditional white gown with shoulder-straps, she offered up worship to the gods of the sky, the earth and the intermediate world, and thanked them for having given life to the people of Egypt.

On a sandbank, a trading-boat had run aground. The royal ship dropped anchor nearby. There was no sign of life on the abandoned ship.

Ramses, Setau and two sailors took to a small craft to examine the wreck more closely. Nefertari had tried to dissuade the king, but he was convinced that this was Shanaar's vessel and hoped to discover some clues.

On the deck, nothing.

'The hold,' one of the sailors pointed out. 'Its hatch is closed.' With Setau's help he smashed the wooden bolt.

Why, Ramses wondered, should this boat have run aground at a spot where the river presented no danger? Why had it been abandoned so hurriedly, not even giving the crew time to take their cargo with them?

The sailor plunged down into the hold.

A terrible scream rent the blue early-morning air. Setau shrank back. He who knew no fear in the face of the most terrifying reptiles was riveted to the spot.

Several crocodiles, which had got into the hold through a gaping hole, had seized the sailor by the legs and were eating him alive.

Ramses wanted to go to the assistance of the unfortunate victim. Setau prevented him: 'You'll get killed. No one can save him.'

In minutes, the man's screams stopped.

A new ambush, as cruel as the former one. Shanaar had foreseen the reaction of his brother, whose dauntless courage was famous.

The king turned back, fury in his heart, accompanied by Setau and the other sailor. They leaped from the wreck on to the sandbank. Between them and their boat an enormous crocodile, over ten cubits long – it must have weighed more than a dozen sacks of grain – was watching them with fixed stare and open jaws, ready to attack. Although the monster was still as a rock, it could move with extraordinary speed. In hieroglyphic script, did not the sign of the crocodile stand for lightning action against which there was no protection?

Setau looked around. Flight was impossible: they were surrounded by other crocodiles. Some of them, with closed jaws and protruding teeth sharper than daggers, seemed to be smiling at the idea of enjoying such fine prey.

From the royal ship it was impossible to see the scene. In a short while, those on board would start worrying at not seeing the little group return, but it would be too late.

'I don't want to die like this,' murmured Setau.

Ramses slowly unsheathed his dagger. He would not give in without a fight. When the monster atttacked, he would slide underneath it and try to cut its throat. A desperate struggle, from which Shanaar, without even needing to put in an appearance, would emerge victorious.

Suddenly the monster moved two paces nearer and then again came to a standstill. The sailor had fallen on his knees and covered his eyes with his hands.

'We must all yell together and hurl ourselves at the enemy,' Ramses said to Setau. 'They might hear us on the ship. You on the right, me on the left.'

Ramses' final thought was for Nefertari, so near and yet already so far. Then he emptied his mind, concentrated all his energy and stared at the enormous crocodile.

The king was about to let out his yell, when he noticed a slight movement in the thorn bushes lining the bank. And then a powerful trumpeting thundered out, striking terror into the crocodiles themselves, a trumpeting that only a gigantic bull elephant was capable of. And just such a bull rushed into the water and set foot on the sandy island. With his trunk he seized the monster by the tail and hurled it on top of its fellows. The crocodiles jostled each other as they disappeared under the water.

'You!' exclaimed Ramses. 'You, my faithful friend!'

Flapping its huge ears, the elephant, whose tusks were as thick as a man's arm, gently put its trunk round the waist of the King of Egypt, lifted him and placed him on its back.

'I saved your life once in the past. Today, you have saved mine.'

When still a young calf, the elephant had been wounded by an arrow in its trunk, and Ramses and Setau together had helped to save it; it had now become a superb adult, whose little eyes sparkled with intelligence.

When Ramses patted its head, it trumpeted again, this time for joy.

Nedjem, the minister for agriculture, put the last touches to his report. Thanks to an excellent rise in the water level, the granaries would be full and the Two Lands would live in affluence. The meticulous management by the scribes of the Treasury would even permit a reduction in taxes. On his return to the capital, Ramses would note that every official had carried out his duties zealously, under the watchful eye of Ahmeni, attentive and critical as ever.

Nedjem hurried to the palace garden where Kha should have been playing with Meritamon. But the little girl was alone there, practising the lute.

'Did your brother leave some time ago?'

'He didn't come.'

'We were supposed to meet here.'

Nedjem went to the library where, shortly after the midday meal, he had left Kha, who wanted to copy the *Wise Words* of the philosophers of the time of the pyramids. The youngster was still there, seated in the posture of a scribe, rapidly letting a very fine brush race over the papyrus, which he had unrolled on his knees.

'Aren't you tired?'

'No, Nedjem. These texts are so beautiful that the act of

copying them dispels fatigue and makes the hand more flexible.'

'You ought perhaps to have a break.'

'Oh, no, not now! I would so like to study the geometry treatise of the master craftsman who built the Unas pyramid at Saqqara.'

'What about dinner?'

'I'm not hungry, Nedjem. You will let me, won't you?'

'Well, I'll give you another few minutes, but . . .'

Kha stood up, kissed the minister on both cheeks, then resumed the scribe's posture and enthusiastically went back to his reading, writing and research.

As he left the library, Nedjem shook his head. Once more he wondered at Kha's exceptional gifts. The child prodigy had become an adolescent who confirmed the promise glimpsed earlier; if he continued to grow in wisdom the pharaoh was assured of having a worthy successor.

'Is our agriculture in good shape, my dear Nedjem?' The voice that broke into the minister's thoughts was that of smiling, elegant Meba.

'Yes, very good.'

'It's a long time since we had a chance to talk. Would you care to come to dinner?'

'I regret that I must refuse – too much work.'

'I'm so sorry.'

'I am too, Meba, but serving the kingdom must come before entertainment.'

'That's what all Pharaoh's servants firmly believe; doesn't this belief motivate every one of our actions?'

'Alas! Men are only human and they often forget their duty.'

Meba detested this naive, pontificating killjoy, but had to show him respect and consideration in order to extort from him the information he needed. The diplomat's situation was difficult. Several vain attempts had proved that he would never manage to get to know the contents of Ahsha's coded messages. Ahmeni would never do anything imprudent.

'Can I give you a lift to your home? I have a new chariot and two very docile horses.'

'I prefer to walk' was Nedjem's ungracious answer.

'Have you had the opportunity of seeing Kha?'

The minister's face lit up. 'Yes, I've had that good luck.'

'What an astonishing boy!'

'More than astonishing! He has the makings of a king.'

Meba looked grave. 'Only a man like you, Nedjem, can protect him from bad influences. Talent like his will inevitably attract jealousy and envy.'

'Don't worry. Setau has given him protection from the evil eye.'

'Are you absolutely sure he has taken every precaution?'

'He has an amulet in the form of a papyrus stem, which guarantees strength and growth, and a strip of cloth on which he's drawn a flawless eye. That should be the perfect magic equipment against harmful forces, wherever they come from, shouldn't it?'

'Impressive indeed.'

'What is more,' Nedjem added, 'every day, Kha absorbs the formulae carved on the walls of Amon's laboratory. Believe me, the child is well protected.'

'You have reassured me. When the opportunity arises, may I renew my invitation to dinner?'

'Frankly, I don't care for social occasions.'

'I do understand, dear friend! In the diplomatic service, it's unfortunately impossible to avoid them.'

When the two men parted, Meba felt like dancing for joy. Ofir would be pleased with him.

41

When the royal ship drew alongside at Abu Simbel, the huge elephant, which had followed along the desert road, trumpeted its welcome. From the top of the cliff, he would watch over Ramses, who marvelled once more at the sight of the golden sandy creek where the mountains separated and met again. The king recalled his discovery of this enchanted spot and Lotus's search, which had resulted in her finding the goddess's stone with its healing powers.

The fair Nubian could not resist the pleasure of diving naked into the waters of the river and swimming smoothly to the sun-drenched bank. Several sailors did the same, happy to have arrived safely. All were overwhelmed by the splendour of the site, over which hung a rocky spur, serving as a landmark to sailors. The Nile curved round close to a cliff, which divided into two promontories with a strip of yellow sand curling between them.

Here Lotus scrambled ashore, her body glistening with silvery drops of water, to be followed by Setau, wearing his antelope-skin soaked with medicinal solutions.

'What feelings does this place inspire in you?' Ramses asked Nefertari.

'I sense the presence of the goddess Hathor; the stones are like stars, reflecting the golden light of the sky.'

'To the north there is a sheer drop where the sandstone cliff falls steeply down to the high-water mark. To the south, the mountains part, leaving a vast open space. Most important, the two promontories form a couple. I shall commemorate our love here by building two sanctuaries, inseparable one from the other, like Pharaoh and the Great Royal Wife. Your image will be carved in the stone, for ever gazing up at the sun which will cause you to be reborn every day.'

Although such an action was hardly in keeping with a solemn occasion, Nefertari threw her arms lovingly round Ramses' neck and kissed him passionately.

When his boat came within sight of Abu Simbel, the Viceroy of Nubia rubbed his eyes, thinking he was seeing a mirage.

On the bank, dozens of stone-cutters had laid out a building site large enough for the construction of a vast edifice. Some, using wooden scaffolding, were beginning to shape the sandstone cliff, while others were cutting out blocks of stone. Cargo vessels had brought the necessary tools and the overseers, concerned about the necessity for maintaining discipline, had divided the workers into small groups, each assigned to a specific task.

The designer of this project was none other than Ramses himself. A scale model and plans of the buildings had been set out on the shore; the king made sure that his vision found perfect expression and that any errors were corrected after discussions with the architect and the head sculptor.

The viceroy wondered how to make his presence known without bothering the sovereign. He thought it wise to wait till Ramses caught sight of him, for the king was said to take offence easily and to hate being crossed.

Something brushed against his left foot, something soft and cold. He looked down and was riveted to the spot. A three-foot-long black and red snake had slithered over the sand and was lying across his foot. At the slightest movement, it would bite. Even a cry might trigger the reptile's attack.

A few paces away stood a bare-breasted young woman wearing a short kilt which the slight breeze lifted, revealing more of her charms than it hid.

'A snake,' murmured the viceroy, who had gooseflesh in spite of the heat.

Lotus was unmoved by the sight. 'What are you afraid of?'

'This snake . . .'

'Speak up. I can't hear you.'

The reptile slowly glided up his calf. The viceroy was unable to utter another word.

Lotus approached. 'Did you disturb it?'

The viceroy was nearly fainting.

She caught the red and black snake and rolled it round her left arm. Why was this overweight, flabby-muscled man afraid of the snake whose venom she had milked?

The viceroy ran till he was out of breath, stumbled over a rock and sprawled on the ground not far from the king. Ramses gazed curiously at this imposing personality, flat on his face in the sand.

'Isn't this a rather exaggerated show of respect?'

'Forgive me Majesty, but a snake . . . I've just escaped death!' The dignitary got to his feet.

'Have you arrested Shanaar?'

'You can be sure, Majesty, that I've spared no effort! Everything has been done to satisfy you.'

'You haven't answered my question.'

'Our failure is only temporary. My soldiers are in complete control of Upper and Lower Nubia. The troublemaker won't escape us.'

'Why has it taken you so long to come to meet me?'

'The demands of local security . . .'

'Does that count for more in your eyes that the security of the royal couple?'

The viceroy turned crimson. 'Of course not, Majesty! That wasn't at all what I meant, and—'

'Follow me.'

The viceroy dreaded Pharaoh's anger, but Ramses remained calm. The viceroy followed him into one of the large tents pitched at the edge of the building site. It served as Setau's field hospital and he had just finished bandaging a stone-cutter's leg, which had been grazed by a block of sandstone.

'Do you love Nubia, Setau?' asked the king.

'Do you really need to ask me that?'

'I get the impression your wife loves the country just as much as you do.'

'Here she exhausts me; you'd think she'd got double her normal amount of energy and her amorous desires are inexhaustible.'

The viceroy's jaw dropped. How could anyone address the Lord of the Two Lands in this tone?

'Do you know this high official who has given us the pleasure of his company?'

'I detest officials,' retorted Setau. 'They're gluttons for privileges, which will end by choking them.'

'I'm sorry about that for your sake.'

Setau gazed at the king in astonishment. 'What do you mean?'

'Nubia is a vast territory, and it's a heavy task to administer it. Do you agree, Viceroy?'

'Yes, oh yes, Majesty!'

'The fine province of Kush alone requires a strong hand. Do you agree with that too, Viceroy?'

'Certainly, Majesty!'

'As I set great store by your opinion, I've decided to appoint my friend Setau "Royal Son of the Province of Kush" and to entrust him with its administration.'

Setau went on folding linen as if this had nothing to do with him. The viceroy looked like a statue which the sculptor had forgotten to make look lifelike.

248

'Majesty, the problems which will arise, my relations with Setau—'

'Will be frank and cordial, I'm sure. Return to the Buhen fortress and see about arresting Shanaar.'

The viceroy withdrew, overwhelmed with shock.

Setau crossed his arms. 'I suppose, Majesty, that this is a joke.'

'There are a great many snakes in this region; you'll collect a great deal of venom. Lotus will be happy and you'll have the opportunity of living on this incomparable site. I need you, my friend, to direct the work and to watch over the growth of the two temples of Abu Simbel. Its two sanctuaries are intended to immortalize the image of the royal couple. Here, in the heart of Nubia, the central mystery of our civilization will be celebrated. But if my decision doesn't please you, I leave you free to refuse.'

Setau gave a sort of grunt. 'I'm sure you plotted this with Lotus! And who could resist the will of Pharaoh?'

The king performed the magic rite, transferring the souls of southern enemies to the north, those of northern enemies to the south, the souls of western enemies to the east and those of eastern enemies to the west. Through this reversal of the points of the compass, the site was placed outside the visible world and Abu Simbel would be protected from human upheavals. A magnetic field, created by the queen around the future buildings, would protect them from external attacks.

In the little shrine built in front of the façade of the great temple, Ramses offered up to Ma'at the love that united him to Nefertari; he linked to the light the unity of the royal couple, whose marriage, immortalized at Abu Simbel, would assemble all the divine forces, the source of nourishment for the people of Egypt.

The temples of the king and of the queen began to rise under the eyes of Ramses and Nefertari. The artisans dug into the heart of the cliff to hollow out the innermost shrine; the rock would be cut to a height of sixty-five cubits, a width of sixty-eight cubits and a depth of one hundred and twenty-four cubits.

When the names of Ramses and Nefertari were carved for the first time in the stone of Abu Simbel, Ramses gave the order to prepare for their departure.

'Are you going back to Pi-Ramses?' asked Setau.

'Not yet. I'm going to choose many other sites in Nubia to build sanctuaries. Gods and goddesses will inhabit this land of fire and you will be the one to coordinate the efforts of our builders. Abu Simbel must be the central light, surrounded by a peaceful army of sanctuaries which will help to consolidate peace. It will take many years to complete this work, but we shall win the battle against time.'

Lotus stood lost in thought at the top of the cliff. She was overcome with emotion as she watched the royal ship sail away. She gazed in admiration at Ramses and Nefertari standing at the prow of the vessel with its white sail, as it glided over the blue water, blue as the Nubian sky.

Lotus could today express what she had previously sensed: it was because he loved Nefertari and knew how to inspire her with love for him that Ramses had the stature of a great pharaoh.

Nefertari, the Lady of Abu Simbel, was opening up the paths of heaven and earth.

42

Shanaar was furious. Nothing had turned out as he had expected. After the failure of his attempts to kill Ramses and cause irreparable damage to his expedition, Shanaar had been forced to flee deeper and deeper into the Far South.

On board a boat stolen in a village whose inhabitants had had the unfortunate idea of lodging a complaint with the authorities, Shanaar had been pursued by the viceroy's soldiers. Had it not been for the skilful manoeuvring of the Nubian sailors, he would have been captured. As a precaution, he had had to abandon the vessel and venture into the desert, an attempt to cover his trail.

The Cretan mercenary, Shanaar's right hand, cursed the heat, the scorching air, the permanent threat of reptiles, lions and other wild beasts. But Shanaar pressed on stubbornly, hoping to reach the land of Irem and stir up tribes capable of attacking Abu Simbel and destroying the building site. When insecurity reigned in Nubia, the pharaoh's prestige would be impaired and his enemies would unite to bring him down.

The little band under Shanaar's command managed to get near the gold-washing region, a forbidden zone where specially skilled workers were employed under the supervision of the Egyptian army. This was the region the rebels needed to seize in order to put a stop to the delivery of the precious metal to Egypt.

From the top of a dune, Shanaar could see the Nubian workers washing the ore, separating it from the layer of mud that clung to it, even after crushing. Water, drawn from a well sunk in the middle of the desert, filled a tank which spilled over on to an incline leading to a clarification basin. The slight current was sufficient to wash away the earth and free the gold: the particles of earth remained in suspension and the heavier, denser metal sank to the bottom of the basin. For the gold to be completely purified, the operation had to be repeated several times.

The Egyptian soldiers were numerous and well armed. A mere raiding-party had no hope of overcoming them. So Shanaar had to organize a widespread rebellion which would unite hundreds of warriors from different tribes.

In the land of Irem, Shanaar, on the advice of his Nubian guide, met the chief of a tribe, a huge black man covered with scars. He received him in a spacious hut, in the centre of his village, but the reception was frosty.

'You are an Egyptian.'

'I am, but I hate Ramses.'

'I hate all the pharaohs who oppress my country. Who sent you?'

'Powerful enemies of Ramses who live to the north of Egypt. If we help them they will defeat Pharaoh and give you back your land.'

'If we rebel, Pharaoh's soldiers will massacre us.'

'Your tribe alone won't be enough, I agree. That is why it is essential to conclude alliances.'

'Alliances are difficult, very difficult. We would have to meet and parley for a long time, a very long time – for moons and moons.'

Patience was not the virtue of which Shanaar had the greatest supply. He curbed his anger and swore to himself to persevere, whatever the delays inherent in the negotiations.

'Are you prepared to help me?' he asked the chief.

252

'I have to remain here, in my village; to parley properly, I would have to travel to the neighbouring village. And that's far away.'

The Cretan mercenary handed Shanaar a piece of silver.

'With this treasure,' said the Egyptian, 'you'll be able to feed your tribe for many months. I pay anyone who helps me.'

The Nubian was openly delighted. 'If I parley, you give me that?'

'Even more if you succeed.'

'All the same, it will take a very long, long, time.'

'Let us begin at dawn.'

Iset the Fair often thought of her long-ago secret love affair with Ramses. She was still in love with him, but how could she compete with Nefertari, who had rightly become the Great Royal Wife?

Sometimes, when the pains of love were too intense, Iset ceased bothering about make-up, wore old clothes and forgot to use perfume. But her love for Kha, Meneptah and Meritamon allowed her to escape from her distress by thinking of the children's future. Meneptah, a fine sturdy boy, was already showing signs of intelligence. Meritamon was a pretty, thoughtful girl and a remarkable musician. Kha would surely become an outstanding scholar. These three children were her hope; they would be her future.

Her chamberlain brought her a necklace consisting of three rows of amethysts and cornelians, some silver earrings, and a coloured gown embroidered with gold thread. He was followed by a tall dark woman: Dolora.

'You look tired, Iset.'

'It's just a passing lassitude. But . . . who are these wonderful things intended for?'

'Will you permit me to offer you these modest gifts?'

'I'm very touched. I don't know how to thank you.'

Dolora, reassuring and protective, had decided to go on to the attack. 'Doesn't your life seem burdensome, my dear Iset?'

'No, certainly not, because I have the good fortune to bring up the children of Ramses the Great.'

'And you're satisfied with this uneventful destiny?'

'I love the king and I love his children. The gods have granted me much happiness.'

'The gods! The gods are an illusion, Iset.'

'What are you saying?'

'There is only one God, the god that Akhenaton worshipped, the one that Moses and the Hebrews pray to. It is to Him that we should turn.'

'That is the way you follow, Dolora. It is not mine.'

Dolora realized that she would not convince Iset, who was too frivolous and too timid. But there was another subject she could broach with some hope of success.

'It seems to me unjust that you should be reduced to the rank of secondary wife.'

'I don't think so, Dolora. Nefertari is cleverer and more beautiful than I am. No woman can equal her.'

'That's not true. What's more, she has one terrible defect.'

'What is that?'

'Nefertari doesn't love Ramses.'

'How dare you presume—'

'I don't presume, I know. You're aware that my favourite pastime is listening to the courtiers and receiving their confidences. So I can confirm that Nefertari is a sham and an intriguer. What was she before she met Ramses? A little priestess with no future, a second-rate musician, good only for serving the gods in a temple. And then Ramses saw her. A veritable miracle! And an upheaval which transformed the shy girl into a fanatically ambitious woman.'

'Forgive me, Dolora, but I can't accept that.'

'Do you know the real reason for the royal couple's

journey to Nubia? Nefertari insisted on a huge temple being built, in her honour and to immortalize her name! Ramses gave in and began a costly building programme which will go on for years. Nefertari's ambition is now quite clear: to take the king's place and rule the country alone. To prevent that folly, all means must be used.'

'You wouldn't dare—'

'I repeat, *all* means. Only one person can save Ramses: you, Iset.'

The young woman was shaken. True, she was suspicious of Dolora, but her arguments were disturbing. Nefertari certainly seemed sincere . . . but the exercise of power often brought with it overweening pride. Suddenly, cracks appeared in the image of a Nefertari passionately in love, worshipping Ramses. What finer destiny for an intriguer than to seduce the Lord of the Two Lands!

'What do you advise me to do, Dolora?'

'Ramses has been exploited. He should have married you: you are the mother of his first-born son, Kha, whom the court already recognizes as his successor. If you love the king, Iset, if you love Egypt and wish for Egypt's happiness, there's only one solution: get rid of Nefertari.'

Iset shut her eyes. 'Dolora, that's impossible!'

'I'll help you.'

'Crime is an abomination which leads to the destruction of the spirit, the soul and the name. To attack the Great Royal Wife would mean damnation for all eternity.'

'Who will know? When you have decided to strike, you must act in the dark and leave no trace.'

'Is that the will of your god, Dolora?'

'Nefertari is a perverted woman who defiles Ramses' heart and leads him to make grave mistakes. It is our duty to unite to prevent her from doing harm. In that way we shall be truly loyal to the king.'

'I need time to think about it.'

'That's perfectly natural. I have great respect for you, Iset, and I know that you'll make the right decision. Whatever it is, you have my love.'

Iset's smile was so faint that Dolora kissed her on both cheeks before leaving.

Iset felt unable to breathe. She took a few faltering steps to the window overlooking the palace garden and let a beam of bright light wash over her, but it did nothing to dispel her inner turmoil.

A prayer rose up within her, addressed to the forces hidden in the sky, those forces which decided the destiny of all creatures, the length of their life and the hour of their death. Had she the right to act in their place, to cut the thread of Nefertari's days because the Great Royal Wife was harming Ramses?

A rival! For the first time Iset the Fair really thought of Nefertari as a rival. Their unspoken pact was being shattered and latent conflict emerging with a violence that had been contained for too long. Iset was the mother of Ramses' two sons, the first woman he had loved, the one who should have reigned at his side. Dolora had made her see a truth which she had tried to stifle till now.

With Nefertari out of the way, Ramses would finally realize that his love for her had been nothing but a fleeting episode. Freed from that treacherous witch, he would return to Iset the Fair, to his youthful passion, to the woman he had never stopped loving.

43

Although Ofir deeply despised the Hebrews, he cynically took advantage of the fact that the brickmakers' district offered him a safe refuge, though even there he frequently had to change his lodgings in order to ensure maximum safety. Thanks to false information the magus had carefully let leak out, Serramanna had eventually come to believe that the Libyan had left Egypt, and so had resigned himself to abandoning his thorough searches, simply seeing that the usual patrols were maintained, with responsibility for preventing any nocturnal disturbance.

However, the magus was not in a mood for celebration. The situation had been unchanged for several months. Ramses was now thirty-seven and in this fifteenth year of his reign the kingdom of Egypt defiantly flaunted its prosperity.

The news from the Hittite Empire was strange and did little to encourage him. True, Uri-Teshup was advocating war to the death against Egypt, but he had launched no attacks. What was more, the protective zone formed by southern Syria and Canaan was occupied by seasoned Egyptian troops, capable of repelling a massive assault. Why was the hothead Uri-Teshup shilly-shallying like this? The all-too-brief messages that the Bedouin passed on to Ofir gave no explanations.

In the South, Shanaar was having no success in stirring up the Nubian tribes. They were parleying interminably, but with no concrete results. At court, Dolora continued to cultivate Iset's friendship in an effort to persuade her to act, but the latter seemed unable to make up her mind. As for Meba, he had failed to learn the contents of the coded messages Ahsha sent to Ahmeni, and was proving deplorably incompetent. True, he had obtained precise details of the magic protection young Kha enjoyed, but the prince was leading an ordered, studious existence in which Ofir had discovered no chink.

Ramses had returned to his capital after a long journey, during which he had founded several temples. Nefertari radiated happiness. In spite of the risks of war, the royal couple enjoyed extraordinary popularity. Everyone was convinced that they had established lasting prosperity in the country, and would be able to protect it against any attack.

After he had thus taken stock of the situation, Ofir was deeply depressed. Years were going by, and any hope of bringing Ramses down was fading. He, the master spy, who had never doubted the success of his mission, began to worry about its outcome, and to give way to discouragement.

He was sitting in the dark, at the back of his reception room, when a man came in.

'I'd like to talk to you.'

'Moses!'

'Are you busy?'

'No, I was thinking.'

'Ramses is back at last, and I've waited patiently for him, as you advised.'

Moses' firm tone restored Ofir's confidence. Had the Hebrew finally decided to take the initiative?

'The council of elders has met,' the prophet went on, 'and they've decided to appoint me their spokesman to approach the pharaoh.'

'So you are still intent on your exodus?'

'The Hebrew people will leave Egypt, since such is the

will of Yahveh. Have you done as we agreed?'

'Our Bedouin friends have delivered the weapons; they are stored in cellars.'

'We shall not use violence, but it will be as well to have the means of defending ourselves, in case we are persecuted.'

'You will be, Moses, you will be! Ramses will never permit the rebellion of a whole people.'

'We don't want to rebel. We just want to leave Egypt and reach the land promised to us.'

Ofir gloated internally. At last something to rejoice about! Moses was going to create a climate of insecurity, favourable to a military strike by Uri-Teshup.

On a stone bed facing the frieze of twelve gods in the Yazilikaya sanctuary, Putuhepa lay as if dead; her long hair was tied up in a bun and hidden under a cap. She had drunk a dangerous potion intended to plunge her into a deep sleep for three days and nights. There was no surer way of entering into communion with the powers governing man's destiny and discovering their wishes.

The usual oracles were still unfavourable to Uri-Teshup but consultation with them had not been enough to make a decision involving Hattusilis's life as well as her own. So she had decided to use this radical but dangerous method.

True, the whole of the merchant caste already favoured Hattusilis and, after intense work to win them over, a considerable portion of the army was coming over to his side. But were Putuhepa and he deluding themselves about their future? Thanks to Ahsha's gold, many senior officers were advocating the reinforcement of internal defences and border posts and abandonment of the plan to attack Egypt. But they might well change their minds if Uri-Teshup's eyes were opened and he discovered the plot being hatched against him.

To contest Uri-Teshup's seizure of power would sooner or later lead to civil war, whose outcome was uncertain. So, in spite of the amount of support at his disposal, Hattusilis was still reluctant to launch into a bloody venture in which thousands of Hittites would die.

That was why Putuhepa had wished to try to foretell the future in a dream, which could only be done during a period of drugged sleep. Sometimes, the subject did not wake up; occasionally, their mind was damaged. So Hattusilis had opposed the experiment, in spite of his wife's insistence; she had returned ten times to the attack, before finally obtaining his consent.

And so she had lain, motionless, scarcely breathing, for three days and nights. According to the books on prophecy, she should now be opening her eyes and revealing what the powers governing their destiny had told her.

Hattusilis nervously clutched his woollen cloak about him. The prescribed time was up.

'Putuhepa, wake up, I beg you!'

She gave a sudden start. No, he was mistaken. She hadn't stirred. Yes, it was really a start!

Putuhepa opened her eyes and stared at the rock with the carvings of the twelve gods. Then from her mouth came a slow, deep voice Hattusilis didn't recognize: 'I saw the God of Storms and the goddess Ishtar. They both spoke, each saying to me, "I support your husband and the whole country will be behind him, whereas his enemy will be like a pig wallowing in the mire." '

A soft hand, so soft and gentle that it made him think of honey and spring dew; caresses so insistent that they aroused in him new sensations and such intense pleasure that it totally engulfed him. Ahsha's fifth Hittite mistress had the same qualities as the preceding ones, but he was beginning to miss the Egyptian ladies, the banks of the Nile and the palm groves.

Love-making was the only thing that took his mind off the

heavy, boring atmosphere of the Hittite capital. There were many discussions with the principal representatives of the merchant caste and a few discreet high-ranking officers. Officially, Ahsha was carrying on long negotiations with Uri-Teshup, the new Lord of Hatti, the successor to Muwatallis, whose death-throes seemed interminable but whose strength was declining.

The Egyptian also had an unofficial mission: to track down Hattusilis, find his hiding-place and hand him over to Uri-Teshup. Ahsha gave the latter detailed reports at regular intervals, when he returned from his periods of training at the head of the chariot corps, the cavalry or the infantry, which were kept in a permanent state of alert. On three occasions, Uri-Teshup's soldiers had only just failed to arrest Hattusilis, who was tipped off at the last minute by his secret allies.

This time, Ahsha and his mistress had finished their amorous frolics when Uri-Teshup entered the Egyptian's bedchamber.

The general's eyes were hard, almost unblinking.

'I've got good news,' said Ahsha, rubbing his hands with scented oil.

'So have I,' announced Uri-Teshup triumphantly. 'My father, Muwattalis, has died at last and I'm the sole Lord of Hatti!'

'Congratulations! But there's still Hattusilis.'

'He won't escape me for long, although my empire is enormous. You mentioned good news?'

'It concerns Hattusilis, as it happens. Thanks to a reliable informer, I think I know where he is. But . . .'

'But what, Ahsha?'

'When Hattusilis is arrested, you will give me that guarantee that we shall conclude peace?'

'You've made a good choice, my friend. You can be sure that Egypt won't be disappointed. Where is the traitor hiding?'

'In the Yazilikaya sanctuary.'

*

Uri-Teshup himself led a small detachment, consisting of only a dozen men, to avoid alerting possible lookouts. A deployment of troops would have alerted them and given Hattusilis the chance to escape.

So it was the priests controlled by Putuhepa who had offered asylum to the late emperor's brother. Uri-Teshup would see that they were suitably punished.

Hattusilis had been unwise enough to stay near the capital, in a place that was easy of access; this time he would not escape. Uri-Teshup hesitated between summary execution and a sham trial. Having little taste for judicial procedures, even when well prepared, he opted for the former solution. Because of his position he had unfortunately to forgo the pleasure of slitting Hattusilis's throat himself, but he'd get one of his men to carry out this sordid task. When he returned to Hattusa, he would organize a grand funeral for Muwatallis, and he, his beloved son, would be his uncontested successor.

He would invade southern Syria with a well-drilled army, join up with the Bedouin, occupy Canaan, cross the Egyptian border and confront Ramses, who had committed the fatal mistake of believing in peace, as his ambassador had assured him.

He, Uri-Teshup, Lord of the Empire of Hatti! He had realized his dream, without needing the costly coalition formed by Hattusilis. Uri-Teshup felt strong enough to conquer Assyria, Egypt, Nubia and the whole of Asia; his fame would eclipse that of all other Hittite emperors.

The little troop approached the sacred rock of Yazilikaya, in which several shrines had been built. This was said to be the home of the supreme divine couple, the God of Storms and his spouse. Was not the second part of the new emperor's name, 'Teshup', that of the terrifying, fearsome god? Yes, he was himself the God of Storms, whose thunderbolts would strike down his enemies.

In the doorway of the sanctuary stood a man, a woman and a child: Hattusilis, Putuhepa and their eight-year-old daughter. The fools were surrendering, believing in Uri-Teshup's clemency!

He halted his horsemen and savoured his triumph. Ahsha had well and truly given him the opportunity to get rid of his last opponents. When this damned family was wiped out, he would have the Egyptian ambassador strangled, for he'd have no further use for him. To think that that innocent had believed in Uri-Teshup's desire for peace! So many years of patience, so many years of trials, finally to arrive at absolute power . . .

'Kill them,' Uri-Teshup ordered.

As the soldiers bent their bows, he felt intense pleasure. The treacherous Hattusilis and the arrogant Putuhepa, pierced with arrows, their bodies burned. What more delightful sight could there be?

But the arrows did not leave the bows.

'Kill them!' repeated Uri-Teshup, infuriated.

The bows were turned against him.

Betrayed! He, the new emperor, had been betrayed! That was why Hattusilis, his wife and daughter were so calm.

Hattusilis stepped forward. 'You are our prisoner, Uri-Teshup. Give yourself up and you will be tried.'

With a yell of fury, Uri-Teshup made his horse rear. Taken by surprise, the archers fell back. Seasoned warrior that he was, the prince broke resolutely through the circle and galloped off towards the capital. Arrows whistled past his ears, but none of them hit their mark.

44

Uri-Teshup galloped through the Lion Gate and on up to the palace, spurring his horse. Its heart gave out and it dropped dead at the top of the citadel from where the Emperor of Hatti had loved to gaze down on his empire.

The head of his private bodyguard ran up. 'What is happening, Majesty?'

'Where is the Egyptian?'

'In his rooms.'

This time, Ahsha was not indulging in the pleasures of love-making with a beautiful Hittite girl, but stood draped in a thick cloak, with his dagger at his side.

Uri-Teshup gave vent to his rage. 'An ambush – it was an ambush! Soldiers from my own army turned on me!'

'You must run,' recommended Ahsha.

'Run? What do you mean, run? My army will destroy that damned sanctuary and slaughter all the rebels!'

'You have no army.'

'No army?' repeated Uri-Teshup, taken aback. 'What does that mean?'

'Your generals respect the oracles and the revelations the gods made to Putuhepa, and have therefore sworn allegiance to Hattusilis. You have only your private bodyguard and one or two regiments which won't hold out for long. In a few hours you'll be a prisoner in your own palace, until the

264

triumphal arrival of Hattusilis.'

'It's not true. It's impossible!'

'Accept the facts, Uri-Teshup. Hatusilis has gradually taken control of the entire empire.'

'I'll fight to the bitter end!'

'A suicidal attitude. There's a better solution.'

'What is it?'

'No one knows the Hittite army better than you do, its actual strength, its weaponry, how it functions, its weaknesses.'

'Yes, but . . .'

'If you leave immediately, I have the means of getting you out of Hatti.'

'To go where?'

'To Egypt.'

Uri-Teshup was thunderstruck. 'You're mad, Ahsha!'

'In what other country will you be safe, protected from Hattusilis? Naturally, your right to asylum must be negotiated; that is why, in exchange for your safety, you must tell Ramses everything about the Hittite army.'

'You're asking me to be a traitor.'

'That's for you to judge.'

Uri-Teshup felt like killing Ahsha. This Egyptian had used him! But he was offering him the only possible way to survive – dishonourably, it's true, but still, to survive. And, what's more, he could harm Hattusilis by revealing military secrets.

'I agree.'

'That's the reasonable attitude.'

'Will you accompany me, Ahsha?'

'No, I'm staying here.'

'Isn't that rather risky?'

'My mission isn't finished. Have you forgotten that I'm seeking peace?'

*

As soon as the news of Uri-Teshup's flight was made public, the last soldiers who had remained loyal to him went over to Hattusilis, who was proclaimed emperor. The first duty of the new sovereign was to pay homage to his brother, Muwatallis, whose body was cremated on a gigantic funeral pyre in the course of a grand ceremony followed by a week of celebrations.

At the banquet that concluded the coronation ceremony, Ahsha occupied the place of honour, on Emperor Hattusilis's left.

'Permit me, Majesty, to wish you a long and peaceful reign.'

'There's no trace of Uri-Teshup. You have a genius for obtaining information, Ahsha. Have you heard anything about him?'

'Nothing, Majesty. You will probably never hear of him again.'

'I'd be surprised. Uri-Teshup is a bitter and obstinate man, who won't rest till he's had his revenge.'

'He lacks the means to achieve it.'

'A warrior of his calibre won't give up.'

'I don't share your fears.'

'It's strange, Ahsha, but I have the feeling that you know a lot about him.'

'That's just an impression, Majesty.'

'Did you by any chance help him leave the country?'

'The future may well have surprises in store for you, but I'm not responsible for them. My sole mission is to persuade you to engage in negotiations with Ramses, with a view to peace.'

'You're playing a dangerous game, Ahsha. What if I've changed my mind and am thinking of continuing the war against Egypt?'

'You know too much about the international situation to neglect the Assyrian danger, and you're too concerned for

266

your people's welfare to prejudice it in a pointless war.'

'Your analysis is shrewd, but should I accept it as the political vision that suits me best? The truth is of very little use when it comes to governing; war has the advantage of doing away with feuds and boosting the country's morale.'

'Would large numbers of dead mean nothing to you?'

'How could that be avoided?'

'By making peace.'

'I admire your obstinacy, Ahsha.'

'I love life, Majesty, and war destroys too many pleasures.'

'This world must displease you.'

'In Egypt a surprising goddess reigns, Ma'at, who obliges everyone, even the pharaoh, to respect the Rule of the universe, and to allow justice to exist on earth. That world does not displease me.'

'The fable is attractive, but it's only a fable.'

'You are mistaken, Majesty. If you decide to attack Egypt, you will find yourself up against Ma'at. And if you were victorious, you would destroy an incomparable civilization.'

'What would that matter, if Hatti dominated the world?'

'That's not possible, Majesty. It's already too late to stop Assyria becoming a great power. Only an alliance with Egypt will safeguard your territory.'

'If I'm not mistaken, Ahsha, you are not my adviser but the Egyptian ambassador – and you're looking after your own interests!'

'That's simply the way it looks, Majesty. Even though Hatti hasn't the attractions of my own country, I have become fond of it and don't wish to see it decline into chaos.'

'Are you really sincere?'

'I know a diplomat's sincerity is always open to question, but please believe me. Ramses' aim really is peace.'

'Do you speak in the name of your king?'

'Unreservedly. Through my voice, you can hear his.'

'Your friendship must be very strong.'
'Yes, Majesty, it is.'
'Ramses is fortunate, very fortunate.'
'That is what all his enemies claim.'

Every day for the last five years, Kha had gone to the Temple of Amon to spend at least an hour in the laboratory, where he knew all the texts by heart. As the years went by, he had had meetings with specialists in astronomy, geometry, symbolics, and other branches of sacred scholarship. With their guidance, he had learned how to find his way through all areas of understanding, and had advanced along the paths of knowledge.

In spite of his youth, Kha was about to be initiated into the first mysteries of the temple. When the court at Pi-Ramses heard the news, they were filled with amazement. Without any doubt, the boy was destined for the highest religious offices.

Kha removed the amulet he wore round his neck and the strip of cloth wrapped round his left wrist. He was led, naked and with closed eyes, into the crypt of the temple, to meditate before the mysteries of creation depicted on the walls. Four bullfrogs and four female snakes formed the primeval couples which had created the world; wavy lines suggested the waters of chaos from which the Principle had arisen to create the universe; a celestial cow gave birth to the stars.

Then the young man was led to the threshold of the Hall of Pillars, where two priests, wearing the masks of Thoth, the ibis, and Horus, the falcon, poured fresh water over his head and shoulders. The two priests dressed him in a white loincloth and invited him to worship the deities portrayed on the pillars.

Ten priests with shaven heads surrounded Kha. He had to answer a thousand questions on the hidden nature of the god Amon, on the elements of creation contained in the cosmic egg, on the meaning of the principal hieroglyphs, on the contents of the incantations for offerings and on many subjects about which only an experienced scribe could speak without making mistakes.

The examiners made no observations or comments. Kha waited a long time, in a silent shrine, for their verdict.

In the middle of the night, an elderly priest took him by the hand and led him on to the roof of the temple. He made him sit and gaze at the starry sky, the body of the goddess Nut, the only one able to transform death into life.

Raised to the rank of Bearer of the Rule, Kha could think only of the blissful days he would spend in the temple, learning all the various rituals. In his excitement, he forgot to recover the protective strip of cloth and amulet he had removed.

45

In Abu Simbel Setau had developed a real passion for the building project. He fired the workers with unflagging energy, so as to be able to offer the royal couple an incomparable monument. In Thebes, the construction of the Temple of a Million Years was progressing well under Bakhen's supervision. And the capital, Pi-Ramses, with its turquoise façades, was growing more beautiful by the day.

When Pharaoh returned to Pi-Ramses, Ahmeni laid siege to his office. He agonized over the possibility of having made the slightest mistake, and, using the gilded wooden brush-holder the king had given him, worked day and night, without a moment's rest. He was now almost bald and in spite of a healthy appetite a little thinner; he hardly slept, knew everything going on at the court, without ever putting in an appearance there, and persisted in refusing the honorary titles that were offered him. Although he complained of his weak back and aching bones, Ahmeni himself carried the confidential dossiers he needed to discuss with Ramses, without worrying about the weight of the papyri and the wooden tablets.

He was genuinely devoted to Ramses, to whom he felt linked by invisible, unbreakable ties. How could anyone not admire the work of the Son of the Light, who already had his place in the long list of dynasties as one of the most outstanding representatives of the pharaonic institution?

Ahmeni congratulated himself every day on having had the good fortune to be born in the century of Ramses.

'Have you come up against any serious difficulties, Ahmeni?'

'Nothing too serious. Queen Tuya has been a great help to me. When certain officials worked with bad grace, she intervened forcefully. Our Egypt is prosperous, Majesty, but we must not relax our efforts. A few days' delay in cleaning out the canals, a lack of care in calculating the numbers of cattle, indulgence towards lazy scribes, and the whole structure risks crumbling.'

'What is the latest word from Ahsha?'

Ahmeni puffed out his chest. 'Today I'm proud to say that our friend from our student days is a real genius.'

'When will he return from Hatti?'

'Well . . . he's staying on there.'

Ramses was astonished. 'His mission was supposed to be completed with the accession of Hattusilis.'

'He's obliged to prolong his stay, but he promises us a great surprise!'

At the sight of Ahmeni's enthusiasm, Ramses understood that Ahsha had succeeded in pulling off another dazzling feat. In other words, in spite of almost insurmountable difficulties, he had carried through the whole plan devised with Ramses.

'Majesty, will you allow me to open the door of your office to introduce a distinguished guest?'

Ramses assented, preparing to enjoy an unusual victory, brought about through the skill of his minister for foreign affairs.

Serramanna entered, pushing before him a big, muscular, long-haired man, with a chest covered with red hair. Angered by the Sardinian's action, Uri-Teshup turned round and brandished his fist at the giant.

'Don't you dare treat the legitimate Emperor of Hatti like that!' he shouted.

'And you,' Ramses interrupted, 'don't you dare raise your voice in this land, which is granting you hospitality.'

Uri-Teshup tried to hold the pharaoh's gaze, but succeeded only for a few minutes. The Hittite warrior felt the cruel weight of his defeat. To appear like this before Ramses, like a common fugitive . . . Ramses, whose power fascinated and daunted him.

'I'm asking Your Majesty to grant me safe refuge, and I know the price. I shall answer all your questions concerning the strengths and weaknesses of the Hittite army.'

'We must begin immediately,' said Ramses.

With the fire of humiliation burning in his veins, Uri-Teshup agreed.

The palace orchard was flourishing; a pomegranate, a juniper, a fig and an incense tree vied with each other in beauty. Iset the Fair loved to walk there with Meneptah. The eight-year-old boy's sturdy constitution astonished his tutors. He liked to play with Wideawake, the golden-yellow dog, who, in spite of his advanced age, submitted to the child's whims. Together they chased butterflies which they never caught. Then Wideawake had a good stretch and fell into a refreshing sleep. As for the Nubian lion, Invincible, he let Meneptah stroke him, at first somewhat begrudgingly, then trustingly.

Iset thought longingly of the time, already long past, when Kha, Meritamon and Meneptah had played in this orchard or in the neighbouring garden. Today, Kha was studying in the temple and pretty Meritamon, whose hand in marriage had already been requested by great dignitaries, devoted herself to sacred music. Iset recalled the over-serious little boy with his writing materials, and the beautiful little girl with her portable harp, which was too big for her. That was yesterday, and that happiness was now unattainable.

How many times had Iset seen Dolora again? How many hours had they spent talking about Nefertari, her ambition, her hypocrisy? It made Iset's head spin just to think about it. Tired, worn down by Dolora's persistence, she had finally decided to act.

On a low sycamore table decorated with paintings of blue water-lilies, she had placed two goblets containing carob juice. The one she would offer to Nefertari contained a slow-acting poison. When the Great Royal Wife died, in four or five weeks' time, it would not occur to anyone to accuse Iset. Dolora had provided her with the invisible weapon, declaring that divine justice alone would be responsible for Nefertari's death.

Shortly before sunset, the queen came into the orchard. She took off her diadem and kissed Meneptah and Iset.

'It's been an exhausting day,' she admitted.

'Have you seen the king, Majesty?'

'Unfortunately not. Ahmeni's still besieging him, and for my part I have a thousand and one urgent problems to settle.'

'Aren't you sometimes at your wits' end, what with the turmoil of public life and your ritual duties?'

'More than you can imagine, Iset. How happy I was in Nubia! Ramses and I were always together, every second was bliss.'

'And yet . . .' Iset's voice trembled.

Nefertari was curious. 'Are you unwell?'

'No, but I'm . . .'

Iset could no longer hold back the question which was burning her lips and her heart. 'Majesty, do you really love Ramses?'

A shadow of vexation momentarily passed over Nefertari's face, then gave way to a radiant smile. 'How can you doubt it?'

'At court, people whisper.'

'The court can no more help "whispering" than a magpie can be prevented from chattering. No one will ever manage to silence those people who make it their business to spread slanders and scandals. But you must have known that for a long time.'

'Yes, of course, but—'

'But I'm of humble origin and I married Ramses the Great: that is the source of the rumour. I suppose it was inevitable.' She looked Iset straight in the eye. 'I have loved Ramses since we first met, from the first second that I set eyes on him, but I didn't dare admit it to myself. And this love has continued to grow, and will endure beyond our deaths.'

'Was it you who insisted on a temple being built in your honour at Abu Simbel?'

'No, Iset. It was Pharaoh, who wished to celebrate in stone the indestructable unity of the royal couple. Who but he could have conceived such grand plans?'

Iset rose and walked over to the low table on which the two goblets were placed.

'To love Ramses is an immense privilege,' Nefertari went on. 'He is everything to me and I am everything to him.'

Iset's knee struck against the table; the two goblets overturned and their contents spilled on to the grass.

'Forgive me, Majesty. I am touched. Please forget my absurd, despicable doubts.'

Emperor Hattusilis had had the war trophies removed from the audience chamber of his palace. The cold grey stone walls, too austere for his taste, would be hung with brightly coloured tapestries in geometric designs.

Hattusilis was draped in an ample multicoloured length of cloth; he wore a silver collar round his neck, a bracelet on his left elbow, a woollen cap belonging to his late brother, and a bandeau round his head. Thrifty, and caring little for his appearance, he managed the finances of the state with a rigour that had never before been applied.

The principal representatives of the merchant caste entered the audience chamber one at a time, to submit to the emperor the economic priorities of the country. Empress Putuhepa, as the head of the religious caste, was present at these interviews and argued for a substantial reduction in the credits allocated to the army. In spite of having regained their privileges, the merchants were astonished at this attitude: was not Hatti at war with Egypt?

Using a tactic he had always found effective, Hattusilis proceeded one step at a time. He increased the number of individual interviews with the traders as well as with the senior officers, and insisted on the advantages of a prolonged truce, without ever uttering the word 'peace'. Putuhepa employed the same strategy in religious circles, and the Egyptian ambassador offered living proof of the improvement in relations between the two powerful enemies. Since Egypt was abandoning attacks on Hatti, shouldn't Hatti take the initiative and work towards a permanent end to hostilities?

But this fine edifice had been built on illusions, and now a bolt from the blue had destroyed it.

Hattusilis summoned Ahsha at once. 'I must let you know the decision I have just taken and which you will communicate to Ramses.'

'A proposal for peace, Majesty?'

'No, Ahsha. Confirmation that the war is to be resumed.'

The ambassador was thunderstruck. 'Why this sudden change of policy?'

'I have just learned that Uri-Teshup has asked for, and obtained, safe refuge in Egypt.'

'Is this small fact so shocking to you that it undermines everything we have agreed?'

'It was you, Ahsha, who helped him leave Hatti and take refuge in your country.'

'That's all in the past now, Majesty.'

'I want Uri-Teshup's head. That traitor must be sentenced and executed. No peace negotiations will be entered into so

275

long as my brother's murderer is not returned to Hatti.'

'He's under house arrest in Pi-Ramses, so you have nothing to fear from him.'

'I want to see his corpse burned on a funeral pyre, here, in my capital.'

'It is wholly unlikely that Ramses will agree to go back on his word and extradite a man to whom he has granted his protection.'

'You are to leave immediately for Pi-Ramses, to persuade your king and bring Uri-Teshup back to me. Otherwise my army will invade Egypt and I will capture the traitor myself.'

46

When the month of May was at its hottest, it was time to bring in the harvest, after the total of the standing crops had been calculated. Armed with sickles, the workers cut the golden ears from the stalks, leaving the stubble standing. The stout-hearted donkeys tirelessly transported the corn to the threshing floors. The work was hard, but there was no lack of bread, fruit or fresh water. And no overseer would dare prohibit the midday rest.

This was the time when Homer decided to write no more. When Ramses visited him, the poet wasn't smoking sage leaves in his snail-shell pipe. Wearing a woollen tunic in spite of the heat, he was lying on a bed under his favourite lemon tree, with his head resting on a cushion.

'Majesty, I didn't expect to see you again.'

'What is the matter with you?'

'Nothing except old age. My hand is weary, and my heart too.'

'Why didn't you send for the palace doctors?'

'I'm not ill, Majesty. It's only death, part of the harmonious whole. My cat Hector has left me. I haven't the heart to replace him.'

'You still have writing to do, Homer.'

'I have given the best of myself in the *Iliad* and the *Odyssey*. Since the hour of my final journey has arrived, why rebel?'

'We shall look after you.'

'How long have you reigned, Majesty?'

'Fifteen years.'

'You aren't yet experienced enough to lie convincingly to an old man who has seen many men die. Death has seeped into my veins, turning my blood to ice, and no medicine can delay its victory. But there is a more important matter, much more important. Your ancestors built a unique land, and you must see that you protect and safeguard it. What is the situation regarding the war against the Hittites?'

'Ahsha has carried out his mission. We hope to sign a treaty which will end hostilities.'

'How sweet it is to leave this country at peace, after having written so much about war. "The dazzling light of the sun falls on the ocean," says one of my heroes. "It sinks into the fertile soil and the black night comes, the dark night which those who are vanquished fervently desire." Today I am the one who is defeated and longs for the dark.'

'I shall have a magnificent House of Eternity built for you.'

'No, Majesty. I am still a Greek, and for my people the Otherworld is nothing but oblivion and suffering. At my age it is too late to abandon my beliefs. Even if this future does not seem very cheerful to you, it is the one for which I am prepared.'

'Our sages say that the works of great writers are more durable than the pyramids.'

Homer smiled. 'Will you grant me one last favour, Majesty? Hold my right hand, the one I wrote with. Thanks to your strength, it will be easier for me to pass over to the other side.'

And the poet passed away peacefully.

Homer was laid to rest under a burial mound, close to his lemon tree; in his shroud were placed copies of the *Iliad* and the *Odyssey*, and a papyrus describing the battle of Kadesh. Only Ramses, Nefertari and Ahmeni, all deeply moved, were present at the interment.

When the monarch returned to his office, Serramanna presented him with a report.

'I've found no trace of Ofir. He's probably left Egypt.'

'Could he be hiding among the Hebrews?'

'If he's changed his appearance and won their trust, why not?'

'What do your informants say?'

'Since Moses has been accepted as leader of the Hebrews, they've fallen silent.'

'So you've no knowledge of what they are plotting?'

'Yes and no, Majesty.'

'What does that mean, Serramanna?'

'It can only be a question of a revolt led by Moses and Egypt's enemies.'

'Moses has asked me for a private interview.'

'Don't grant it, Majesty!'

'What are you afraid of?'

'That he may try to kill you.'

'Your fears are unjustified.'

'A rebel is capable of anything.'

'Moses has been my friend since childhood.'

'He has forgotten that friendship, Majesty.'

The May sunlight flooded into Ramses office through the three large stone-framed windows; one of them looked out on to an inner courtyard where several chariots stood waiting. White walls, a straight-backed chair for the monarch and straw-seated chairs for visitors, a cupboard for papyri, and one large table comprised the austere furnishings. They would not have been disowned by Seti, on whose statue Ramses frequently gazed.

Moses entered. Tall and broad-shouldered, with his thick

hair, bushy beard and seamed face, the Hebrew looked like a man at the height of his powers.

'Sit down, Moses.'

'I prefer to stand.'

'What do you want?'

'I was away for a very long time, and had all the more opportunity to think deeply.'

'Did that lead to wisdom?'

'I was educated in the wisdom of the Egyptians, but what is that compared to the will of Yahveh?'

'So you haven't given up your ridiculous plans?'

'On the contrary, I have persuaded the majority of my people to follow me. And soon, all will be at my side.'

'I remember the words of my father, Seti: "Pharaoh must not tolerate either rebel or troublemaker. Otherwise it will be the end of the Rule of Ma'at and the advent of disorder; and this will bring misery to all, great and humble alike."'

'The law that Egypt observes no longer concerns the Hebrews.'

'So long as they live in this land, they must submit to it.'

'Grant my people permission to journey for three days into the desert to sacrifice to Yahveh.'

'The security reasons I have already explained to you force me to say no.'

Moses clutched his staff more tightly. 'I cannot accept this answer.'

'In the name of friendship, I am willing to forget your insolence.'

'I am aware that I address Pharaoh, the Lord of the Two Lands, and in no way wish to show disrespect. Nevertheless, Yahveh's demands remain and they will continue to be expressed through my voice.'

'If you drive the Hebrews to rebellion, you will force me to repress it.'

'I am aware of that, too. That is why Yahveh will use other

280

means. If you persist in refusing the Hebrews the freedom they demand, He will send down terrible disasters upon Egypt.'

'Are you trying to frighten me?'

'I shall plead my cause before your notables and before your people, and the infinite power of Yahveh will convince them.'

'Egypt has nothing to fear from you, Moses.'

How beautiful Nefertari was! Ramses marvelled at her loveliness as she supervised the rites for the consecration of a new shrine in honour of a distant goddess.

She, his sweet love, the one whose voice gave pleasure and uttered no vain word, she who filled the palace with her perfume and her grace, she who could recognize good and evil and never confuse them, was now held in high esteem as the Lady of the Two Lands. Wearing a six-strand gold necklace and a crown surmounted by two feathers, she seemed to belong to the world of the goddesses, where youth and beauty never faded.

In the eyes of his mother, Tuya, Ramses saw a certain happiness: the realization that the queen who had succeeded her was worthy of Egypt. Tuya's discreet but efficient assistance had allowed Nefertari to blossom and to find the right tone which characterizes great sovereigns.

The ritual was followed by a reception in honour of Tuya. Every courtier was anxious to congratulate the Mother of Pharaoh, who listened with half an ear to the usual platitudes. At last Meba managed to approach Tuya and the pharaoh. Smiling broadly, he sang the praises of Seti's widow.

'I consider your work at the Foreign Affairs secretariat unsatisfactory,' Ramses interrupted. 'In Ahsha's absence, you should have kept up a more regular correspondence with our allies.'

'Majesty, they promise you tributes of exceptional

quantity and quality! Rest assured that I've negotiated support for Egypt at a very high price. Many ambassadors request accreditation, to pay homage to Your Majesty, for no pharaoh's prestige has ever been more brilliant!'

'Have you nothing else to tell me?'

'Yes, Majesty: Ahsha has just announced his imminent return to Pi-Ramses. I intend to organize a fine reception in his honour.'

'Does his dispatch give the precise reasons for his return?'

'No, Majesty.'

The king and his mother moved a little way away.

'Is the peace continuing to be strengthened, Ramses?'

'If Ahsha has corresponded openly with Meba and has left Hatti suddenly, he is unlikely to be to bringing me good news.'

47

After a dozen long interviews with Uri-Teshup, Ramses had learned everything about the Hittite army, its favourite tactics, its weaponry, its strengths and weaknesses. The dethroned general had proved extremely cooperative, so anxious was he to harm Hattusilis. In exchange for this information, Uri-Teshup enjoyed a villa, two Syrian servants, food for which he quickly developed a taste, and close police surveillance.

Ramses was aware of the enormity and ferocity of the monster whom he had confronted with the fiery spirit of youth. Without the protection of Amon and Seti, his foolhardiness would have led Egypt to disaster. Even weakened, Hatti remained a formidable military power. An alliance, even limited, between Egypt and Hatti would find expression in a lasting peace in the region, for no one would dare attack such a united force.

Ramses was discussing this prospect with Nefertari, in the shade of a sycamore tree, when Ahmeni arrived, panting, to announce Ahsha's approach.

His long period of exile had not changed the head of the Egyptian diplomatic service. With his long, shapely head, well-groomed little moustache, eyes glinting with intelligence and supple limbs, he could seem supercilious and distant, and it was easy to think of him passing through life with supreme irony.

Ahsha bowed to the royal couple. 'I beg Your Majesties' forgiveness, but I haven't had time to bathe, have a massage and be perfumed. It's a sort of unwashed nomad who dares to present himself before you, but the message of which I am the bearer is too urgent to be sacrificed to my personal comfort.'

'So we shall postpone our congratulations till later,' Ramses said with a smile, 'although your return gives us the sort of pleasure which is engraved in the memory.'

'To receive the king's praise in my present state seems criminally disrespectful! How beautiful Egypt is, Ramses! Only a great traveller can appreciate its refinement.'

'Wrong,' retorted Ahmeni. 'Travelling distorts the mind. On the other hand, if you never leave your office and watch the seasons through your window, you can enjoy the pleasure of living here.'

'Let's postpone this argument, too, till later,' requested Ramses. 'Have you been expelled from Hatti, Ahsha?'

'No, but Emperor Hattusilis insisted that his demands be transmitted directly from the ambassador's mouth to Pharaoh's ear.'

'Do you bring me news of discussions leading to peace?'

'That was my dearest wish. Unfortunately I bring an ultimatum.'

'Is Hattusilis being as bellicose as Uri-Teshup?'

'Hattusilis admits that peace with Egypt would curb the Assyrian threat, but the difficulty is, in fact, Uri-Teshup.'

'The way you handled him was magnificent! It has enabled me to find out everything about the Hittite army.'

'Very useful in case of war, I agree. If we don't hand over Uri-Teshup, Hattusilis will continue the war.'

'Uri-Teshup is our guest.'

'Hattusilis wants to see his corpse burn on a funeral pyre.'

'I've granted Uri-Teshup refuge, and I won't go back on my word. Otherwise Ma'at will cease to reign in Egypt, to make way for lies and cowardice.'

'That's what I told Hattusilis. But he's adamant: either Uri-Teshup is returned to Hatti, in which case peace is possible, or the war goes on.'

'I am adamant too: Egypt won't trample underfoot the right to safe refuge. Uri-Teshup will not be returned.'

Ahsha slumped into a low-backed armchair. 'All these years wasted, all these efforts reduced to nothing. That was the risk we took, and Your Majesty is right. War is better than violation of a promise. At least we're better informed for fighting against the Hittites.'

'Will Pharaoh allow me to speak?' asked Nefertari.

The soft, calm voice of the Great Royal Wife delighted the monarch, the ambassador and the scribe alike.

'It was women who in the past freed Egypt from occupying forces,' Nefertari reminded them. 'It was women, too, who negotiated peace treaties with foreign courts. Tuya herself continued this tradition, setting me an example to follow.'

'What do you suggest?' asked Ramses.

'I'm going to write to Empress Putuhepa. If I can persuade her to start negotiations, perhaps she can persuade her husband to be less uncompromising.'

'The obstacle represented by Uri-Teshup can't be removed,' objected Ahsha. 'Nevertheless, Putuhepa is a brilliant and intelligent woman, more concerned with the greatness of Hatti than with her own interests. She won't be unappreciative of the fact that the Queen of Egypt herself is appealing to her. As her influence on Hattusilis is not inconsiderable, perhaps this move will have favourable results. But I shan't hide the difficulties of her enterprise from the Great Royal Wife.'

'You must forgive me if I leave you,' said Nefertari, 'but you will understand that I have very serious work to do.'

Ahsha watched with admiration as the radiant queen glided lightly away.

'If Nefertari succeeds in creating an opening,' Ramses told

his ambassador, 'you will return to Hatti. I shall never extradite Uri-Teshup, but you will obtain peace.'

'You're asking the impossible. That's why I love working for you.'

The king turned to Ahmeni. 'Have you asked Setau to return urgently?'

'Yes, Majesty.'

'What's happening?' Ahsha inquired anxiously.

'Moses believes himself to be the mouthpiece of his One God, this Yahveh who has ordered him to lead the Hebrews out of Egypt,' explained Ramses.

'Do you mean *all* the Hebrews?'

'For him it's a question of a people with a right to independence.'

'That's madness!'

'Not only is it impossible to reason with Moses but, what's more, he's turned threatening.'

'You sound almost afraid of him!'

'I'm only afraid that our friend Moses has become an enemy to be reckoned with,' declared Ramses, 'and I've learned not to underestimate my opponents. That's why I want Setau here.'

'What a waste!' lamented Ahsha. 'Moses was a strong, upright man.'

'He still is, but he has put his good qualities at the service of a dogma and an absolute truth.'

'You scare me, Ramses. That sort of war's more frightening than a battle against the Hittites.'

'We shall either win it or die.'

Setau put his broad hands on Kha's thin shoulders. 'By all the snakes on earth, you're almost a man!'

As they stood at the edge of the palace archery-range, where Ramses was to meet them, the contrast between the two was striking. Kha was a young, pale-faced scribe, of delicate appearance; Setau, square-headed, thickset and heavily muscled, with his mat-complexioned face unshaven, and wearing his usual antelope-skin tunic, looked like an adventurer or a gold-prospector.

Seeing them, one would never have imagined they were friends. Yet to Kha Setau was the master who had initiated him into knowledge of the Invisible, while Setau saw in Kha an exceptional person, able to reach right to the heart of the mysteries.

'I suppose you've done a lot of stupid things while I've been away,' grumbled Setau.

Kha smiled. 'Well, anyway, I hope I haven't let you down.'

'And you've been promoted.'

'I carry out some ritual duties at the temple, it's true. But I had no choice. And besides, I'm very happy.'

'Excellent, my boy! But, tell me, why aren't you wearing your amulet or your protective strip of cloth?'

'I took them off for the purification, in the temple, and couldn't find them afterwards. Since you're back, there's no more risk, particularly as the magic of the rites protects me.'

'All the same, you should wear some amulets.'

'Do you wear any, Setau?'

'Well, I've got my antelope-skin, you see.'

An arrow whistled past them and smacked into the heart of one of the targets, making them both jump.

'Ramses has lost none of his skill,' commented Setau.

Kha watched his father put down his bow – it was the one he had used at the battle of Kadesh, and only he could bend it. Kha thought the king had grown in stature: he was the very embodiment of authority. The young man prostrated himself before his father, who was also so much more than a father.

'Why did you arrange to meet us here?' asked Setau.

'Because you and my son are going to help me prepare for a fight in which my aim must be absolutely true.'

Kha said bluntly, 'But I'm no good at archery. I shan't be able to help.'

'It will be no ordinary fight, my son. The weapons will be our minds and magic.'

'Well, it's true that I officiate in the Temple of Amon, but—'

'The priests have unanimously chosen you as the head of their community.'

'But . . . I'm not even twenty yet!'

'Age isn't important; but in any case, I've rejected their proposal.'

Kha was very relieved.

'Some bad news has just reached me from Memphis,' Ramses went on. 'The High Priest of Ptah has died. I have chosen you, my son, to succeed him.'

'High Priest of Ptah? *Me?* But, that's—'

'That is my wish. In that capacity, you will be one of the notables before whom Moses wishes to appear.'

'What has he got in mind?' asked Setau.

'He says that, because I will not allow the Hebrews to venture out into the desert, his god is threatening to inflict hideous punishments on Egypt. The new High Priest of Ptah and my finest magicians will be able to show up this claim as a mere delusion.'

48

Accompanied by Aaron, Moses arrived at the entrance to the audience chamber of the Pi-Ramses palace, watched over by Serramanna and a guard of honour. As Moses passed, the Sardinian scowled menacingly. In Ramses' place, he'd have had this rebel thrown into a dungeon or, better still, sent into the heart of the desert. He trusted his instinct, and his instinct told him that Moses was bent on harming Ramses.

As he walked down the central aisle, between the two rows of pillars, Moses was pleased to see that the audience chamber was packed.

On the king's right sat Kah, wearing a panther-skin decorated with gold stars. In spite of his youth, his formidable mind and erudition meant that none of the priests had questioned his appointment as High Priest of Ptah. It was now up to him to prove his skill, by discerning the message from the gods and reproducing it in hieroglyphs. Everyone would be watching him closely: he must maintain the traditions handed down from the time of the pyramids, that golden age when the creative values of Egyptian civilization had been formulated.

Moses had been surprised by Kha's appointment, but now, seeing him close to, he recognized the young man's exceptional determination and maturity: he would undoubtedly prove a formidable opponent.

And what about the man on Pharaoh's left, Setau, the snake-charmer and chief magician of the kingdom? Like Ramses, he had been one of Moses' friends in their student days, as had Ahmeni, who was sitting further back, already prepared to note down the main points of the debates.

Moses forced himself to stop thinking of the years when he had worked for the greatness of Egypt. His past had died on the day when Yahveh entrusted him with his mission, and he had no right to mourn those times now lost for ever.

Moses and Aaron halted at the foot of the steps up to the platform where Pharaoh and his entourage were seated.

'What subject do you wish to debate before this court?' asked Ahmeni.

'I am not here to debate,' replied Moses. 'I am here to demand my due, according to the will of Yahveh: that Pharaoh gives me permission to lead my people out of Egypt.'

'Permission has been refused, for reasons of public safety.'

'This refusal is an insult to Yahveh.'

'To the best of my knowledge,' said Ahmeni drily, 'Yahveh does not reign over Egypt.'

'Yet His anger is terrible! My God protects me and He will perform miracles to demonstrate his power.'

'I used to know you well, and once we were even friends. In those days, you didn't live an illusion.'

'Those days are dead,' said Moses. 'Now, you are an Egyptian scribe and I am the leader of the Hebrew people. It really was Yahveh who spoke to me and I can prove it!'

Aaron threw his staff on to the ground, and Moses stared hard at it. The knots in the wood began to move, the staff began to ripple, and it turned into a snake.

Several of the courtiers shrank back in fright. The snake glided towards Ramses, who showed no fear. Setau leaped forward and seized the reptile by the tail. There were cries of astonishment at his action – and more cries when the snake changed back into a staff in his hands.

290

'I taught Moses that trick in the Mer-Ur harem years ago,' said Setau. 'It'll take a lot more than that to impress Pharaoh's advisers and the Egyptian court.'

He and Moses stared challengingly at each other: the last traces of their friendship died.

'In a week's time,' predicted the prophet, 'there will be another miracle, which will astound the people.'

Nefertari was bathing naked in the pool closest to the palace, guarded by Wideawake, who lay in the shade of a tamarisk tree. The water was always clear, owing to thin sheets of copper fixed to the stones, to plants that stopped any green slime forming, and to a system of irrigation channels ensuring constant fresh water; in addition, a special powder, made from copper which had been treated with acid, was regularly thrown into the pool.

At the approach of the Nile floods, the heat always became overpowering. Before beginning her audiences, the queen made the most of this delightful moment, when her body was refreshed and at peace and she could let her thoughts roam freely, light as egrets. She considered what she would say to the many supplicants, each believing their own request more urgent than anyone else's. To some she would offer words of comfort, to others she would speak sternly.

Wearing a gown with shoulder-straps attached just below her breasts, and with her hair hanging loose, Iset made her way silently towards the pool. Though she had always been called 'Iset the Fair', she felt almost plain next to Nefertari. The queen's every gesture was of incomparable grace, and in moments of stillness she was more lovely than any work by even the greatest painter who ever portrayed the ideal of feminine beauty.

After much hesitation, and a last conversation with Dolora, who was still as determined as ever, Iset had taken a final decision. This time, she would act.

291

Emptying her mind of all fear which might compromise her actions, Iset took one more step towards the pool. She must no longer be diverted from her goal.

Nefertari caught sight of her. 'Come and bathe.'

'I don't feel well, Majesty.'

The queen swam smoothly to the edge of the pool and climbed out up the stone steps. 'What's wrong?'

'I don't know.'

'Are you worried about Meneptah?'

'No, he's very well. Every day I'm more surprised at how strong he is.'

'Lie down here beside me on the warm tiles.'

'Forgive me, but I can't stand the sun.'

Nefertari's beauty was bewitching. Her figure was like that of the goddess of the West, whose smile lit up the next world and life here below. As she lay on her back, with her arms at her sides and her eyes closed, she was both near and inaccessible.

'What is it that's distressing you so much, Iset?'

Once again, Iset was assailed by doubt. Should she carry out her decision? Or should she run away and risk Nefertari taking her for a fool? Fortunately Nefertari was not looking at her. No, the opportunity was too good. She must not let it pass.

'Majesty . . . Majesty, I'd like . . .'

Iset knelt beside the queen, who, bathed in sunlight, did not move.

'Majesty, I wanted to kill you.'

The queen opened her eyes and sat up. 'I don't believe you, Iset.'

'Yes, it's true. I had to tell you – the burden was becoming unbearable. Now you know.'

'But why, Iset? Why did you want to do such a terrible thing?'

'I was told . . . I thought you didn't love Ramses and were

driven only by ambition. I was blind and stupid! How could I have listened to such despicable lies?'

Nefertari took Iset's hands. 'Everyone has moments of weakness. That's when evil tries to defeat our consciences and stifle all the goodness in our hearts. You didn't give in to evil – that's what matters most.'

'I'm ashamed of myself, so ashamed! When you bring me to trial, I shall accept my sentence.'

'Well . . . But who told you those lies about me?'

'I came to confess my wickedness, Majesty, not to play the informer.'

'In trying to kill me, what they really wanted was to injure Ramses. If you love him, Iset, you *must* tell me the truth.'

'You . . . you don't hate me?'

'You are neither ambitious nor scheming, and you have the courage to admit your mistakes. Not only do I not hate you, but I still respect you.'

Iset bowed her head and wept. Then she talked to Nefertari for a long time, easing her troubled heart.

Thousands of Hebrews had gathered on the banks of the Nile, joined by as many curious onlookers from various districts of the capital. Word had spread that through Moses the Hebrews' warrior god was going to perform a great miracle, proving that he was more powerful than all the gods of Egypt put together. If he did, then Pharaoh would have to give in to Moses' demands.

Against the advice of Ahmeni and Serramanna, Ramses had decided to take no action. To send the army and the police to disperse the crowds would have been to overreact. Neither Moses nor the Hebrews were disturbing public order, and the travelling traders were delighted to see these swarms of people.

From the roof of his palace, Ramses gazed down at the impatient throng. But uppermost in his mind were the terrible revelations Nefertari had just made to him.

'Is there not even the slightest doubt?' he had asked.

'No, Ramses. Iset told the truth.'

'I ought to punish her severely.'

'I beg you to be lenient with her. Yes, she nearly did something terrible, but it was for love. Anyway, no harm was done, and thanks to Iset we know Dolora hates you enough to commit a crime.'

'I had hoped she had conquered the demons that have been eating away at her heart all these years. But I was wrong. She'll never change.'

'Will you bring her to trial?'

'She would deny everything and accuse Iset of having invented it all. The trial would risk ending in a scandal.'

'So is she to go unpunished?'

Ramses had smiled. 'No, Nefertari. Dolora made use of Iset; we shall make use of Dolora.'

On the riverbank there was a stir and shouts broke out. Moses threw his staff into the Nile, and the water developed a reddish hue and a pungent smell.

The prophet collected some in a goblet and poured it on the ground. 'Witness this miracle! By the will of Yahveh, the waters of the Nile have turned into blood. And if His wish is not granted, this blood will spread into all the canals of the land and the fish will die. It is the first of the plagues from which Egypt will suffer.'

Then Kha collected some of the strange water, and fearlessly confronted Moses. 'It's nothing of the sort. What you've predicted is only the red tide of the Nile flood. For a few days this water will be undrinkable, and no fish must be eaten. If it is indeed a miracle, we owe it to nature and it's her laws we must respect.'

The big Hebrew bit back his anger. 'Those are fine words, but how do you explain the fact that my staff made the water turn blood-red?'

'You noticed the change in the water, and the strong current from the south, and timed your prophecy for the day when the red tide would appear. You know this land as well as I do: none of its secrets escapes you.'

'Until now,' thundered Moses, 'Yahveh has been content with warnings. Since Egypt persists in doubting, He will inflict other and more terrible plagues!'

49

Ahsha himself brought the letter to the Great Royal Wife, who was discussing the management of the granaries with Ramses.

'Here is the reply you were waiting for, Majesty. It comes from Empress Putuhepa in person. I hope its contents won't disappoint you.'

The tablet, wrapped in a precious cloth, bore Putuhepa's seal.

'Will you read it out, Ahsha? In the first place, you can decipher the Hittite script perfectly; and secondly, the information from Hattusa concerns you.'

To my sister, Queen Nefertari, wife of the sun, Ramses the Great:

How is my sister? Is her family in good health? Are her horses magnificent and strong? In Hatti, the summer months are here. In Egypt, will the Nile floods be good?

I acknowledge the long letter from my sister Nefertari, which I read most attentively. Emperor Hattusilis is extremely vexed by the presence in Pi-Ramses of the vile Uri-Teshup, an evil, violent and cowardly creature who deserves to be expelled and sent back to Hattusa to stand trial. Emperor Hattusilis proves inflexible on that score.

But is not the peace between our two countries such a great ideal that it justifies certain sacrifices? True, it is not possible to find a compromise as regards Uri-Teshup, and the emperor rightly demands his return. However, I have insisted he acknowledge that Pharaoh is right to honour his word. What confidence could we have in a sovereign who broke his promises?

So, although difficulties remain in the case of Uri-Teshup, why not suppose that they are resolved, so that we can proceed to draw up a treaty of peace? It will take time to draft this document, so it would be wise to begin discussions straight away.

Does the Queen of Egypt, my sister, share my thoughts? If she does, I ask that there be sent to us as soon as possible a high-ranking diplomat, one who enjoys Pharaoh's trust. I suggest Ahsha.

To my sister, Queen Nefertari, with my friendship.

'Unfortunately, we cannot accept this suggestion,' said Ramses regretfully.

'Why not?' asked Ahsha.

'Because it's a trap. The emperor hasn't forgiven you for getting Uri-Teshup out of Hatti, and he wants vengeance. If you go back there, we'll never see you again.'

'I interpret this letter differently, Majesty. Queen Nefertari presented convincing arguments, and Empress Putuhepa expresses her desire for peace. Given her influence on the emperor, this is an important step.'

'Ahsha is right,' said Nefertari. 'My sister Putuhepa has understood perfectly the meaning of my letter. There must be no more talk about Uri-Teshup. Instead, we must begin negotiating a treaty, with due attention to the contents as much as to the form.'

'The problem of Uri-Teshup won't just disappear,' objected Ramses.

'Let me make my position, and that of my sister Putuhepa, even clearer,' said the queen. 'Hattusilis demands Uri-

Teshup's return; Ramses refuses. Let them both remain firm and inflexible while negotiations proceed. Isn't that what is known as diplomacy?'

'I trust Putuhepa,' added Ahsha.

Ramses smiled. 'If you and the queen are in league against me, how can I resist? Very well, we'll send a diplomat – but it will not be you.'

'Majesty, it *must* be: the empress's wishes are virtually commands. Besides, no one else knows Hatti, and those we have to deal with, as well as I do.'

'Are you willing to take such a huge risk, Ahsha?'

'It would be a crime to neglect such an opportunity to conclude peace. We must devote all our energy to this task. Anyway, accomplishing the impossible has become the hallmark of your reign, hasn't it?'

'I've rarely seen you so enthusiastic.'

'I love pleasure and pleasures, and war doesn't lend itself to them.'

'I shall not conclude peace at any price, though. Under no circumstances shall Egypt be the loser.'

'I foresaw some difficulties like that, but resolving them is part of my job. First of all, we shall work for several days to settle all the details of an acceptable plan, then I shall visit some very dear lady friends, and then I shall leave for Hatti. And I shall succeed, since you insist on it.'

First it made an amazing leap; then it stopped less than a pace away from Setau, who was sitting on the bank of the Nile, watching with satisfaction as the waters changed and became drinkable again.

A second, then a third, then scores of them, lively and agile and in varied shades of green: huge frogs sprang out of the silt that the river had deposited on Egypt's soil, fertilizing it and thus ensuring food for Pharaoh's people.

From his place at the head of an imposing procession,

Aaron stretched out his staff and declared loudly, 'Since Pharaoh still refuses to allow the Hebrews to leave Egypt, here, after the water that changed into blood, is the second plague Yahveh inflicts on the oppressor: frogs, thousands of frogs, millions of frogs, which will go everywhere, into the workshops, the houses, the bedchambers of the wealthy!'

Setau quietly returned to his laboratory, where Lotus was preparing some new remedies with the venom of the splendid cobras captured around Abu Simbel. (The news from there was encouraging: the building work was making good progress.)

Setau smiled. Neither he nor Kha would have to do anything to combat this plague. Aaron should have consulted Moses before uttering a curse which wouldn't frighten a single Egyptian. At this time of year, the frogs' proliferation was quite normal – in fact, the people considered it a good omen. In hieroglyphs, the sign of the frog served to indicate the figure 'a hundred thousand', that is, an almost incalculable number, proportional to the abundance brought by the Nile flood.

Observation of frogs' development had led the priests of the early dynasties to see in them the endless mutations of life; so the frog, in popular awareness, had become a symbol both of successful birth, at the end of the many stages from embryo to infant, and of eternity, which survived through time and beyond.

The very next day Kha arranged for earthenware amulets, in the form of frogs, to be distributed free throughout the city. Delighted by these unexpected gifts, the inhabitants not only praised Ramses, but expressed gratitude to Aaron and the Hebrews, thanks to whom many a humble person had become the owner of a valuable object.

Ahsha put the last touches to the draft treaty he had drawn up with the royal couple. It had taken more than a month of

299

intensive work to finalise all the details, and it had proved invaluable to have Nefertari reread everything. As Ahsha had expected, Pharaoh's demands would make negotiations difficult. Nevertheless, Ramses had treated Hatti not as a defeated enemy but rather as a partner who would gain many advantages from this accord. If Putuhepa really wanted peace, the game should be playable.

Ahmeni came in with the magnificent amber-coloured papyrus, on which Ramses himself was to write the proposals. 'I've had a complaint from the inhabitants of the southern district,' he said. 'They say there's an infestation of mosquitoes.'

'In this season,' said Ramses, 'mosquitoes are always a pest if the rules of hygiene aren't strictly observed. Have they forgotten to drain a pond?'

'According to Aaron, this is the third plague inflicted on Egypt by Yahveh. Aaron is said to have stretched out his staff, struck the dust on the ground and turned it into mosquitoes. And you are supposed to see in this the hand of an avenging god.'

'Moses has always been obstinate,' Ahsha reminded them.

'Send a cleansing team to the southern district immediately,' Ramses told Ahmeni, 'and get rid of this scourge.'

The abundant Nile flood promised a happy future. Ramses celebrated the dawn rites in the Temple of Amon and then took a walk along the landing-stage, accompanied by Invincible, before turning back towards the palace: he had to compose a letter to Hattusilis, to accompany the peace proposals.

Suddenly he heard the thump of a staff on the tiled path. He looked round and saw Moses standing nearby. Invincible stared at the Hebrew, but didn't roar.

'Let my people go, Ramses, so that they can worship Yahveh as he wishes.'

'We have said everything there is to be said about that,

Moses.'

'Miracles and plagues have revealed the will of Yahveh to you.'

'I can't believe it's really my friend who says these strange things.'

'We are no longer friends! I am the messenger of Yahveh, you are a Godless pharaoh.'

'Is there no cure for your blindness?'

'You are the one who is blind!'

'Go your way, Moses; I shall go mine, come what may.'

'Grant me one favour: come with me to see the flocks of my Hebrew brothers.'

'What is so special about them?'

'Come, I beg you.'

With Invincible, Serramanna and a company of soldiers to ensure his protection, Ramses did as Moses asked. The Hebrews' flocks had been gathered together in a marshy area some ten miles from the capital. Thousands of horseflies flew round the animals, tormenting them without respite and making them bleat or bellow with pain.

'This is the fourth plague sent by Yahveh,' Moses revealed. 'I have only to disperse these animals and the horseflies will invade the capital.'

'A poor strategy. Was it really necessary to keep them in such a filthy state and make them suffer?'

'We must sacrifice to Yahveh rams, cows and other beasts the Egyptians consider sacred. If we celebrate our rites in your country, we shall arouse the peasants' anger. Let us go into the desert, otherwise the flies will attack your subjects.'

'Serramanna and a contingent of soldiers will accompany you, your priests and the sick animals into the desert. The other animals will be cleansed and taken back to their pasture. Then you will return to Pi-Ramses.'

'This is only a respite, Ramses. Soon you will be forced to allow the Hebrews to leave Egypt.'

50

'We must strike harder,' decreed Ofir, 'very much harder.'

'We succeeded in sacrificing to Yahveh in the desert, as He had demanded,' observed Moses. 'Ramses gave way, and he will give way again.'

'He must be near the end of his patience.'

'Yahveh will protect us.'

'I've another idea, Moses,' said Ofir. 'It'll take the form of a fifth plague, one which will do Ramses serious harm.'

'It's not for us but for Yahveh to decide this.'

'Of course, but perhaps we could lend him a hand. Ramses is stubborn, and the only thing that will make him give way is a clear sign from the next world. Let me help you.'

Moses agreed.

Ofir left the prophet's home and joined his accomplices, Amos and Baduch. The two Bedouin chiefs had continued to store quantities of weapons in the cellars of houses in the Hebrew district. They had just returned from northern Syria, where they had made contact with Hittite messengers. The magus was impatient to obtain fresh news, perhaps even instructions.

Amos rubbed his bald pate, which he had oiled. 'Emperor Hattusilis is furious,' he said. 'Since Ramses refuses to return Uri-Teshup, he's prepared to resume fighting.'

'Excellent! What does he want us to do?'

'The orders are simple. Keep the unrest going among the Hebrews in Egypt. Stir up disturbances all over the country, so as to weaken Ramses. Lastly, arrange for Uri-Teshup to "escape" and take him back to Hattusa. Or else kill him.'

Crooked-Fingers was a peasant who loved his plot of land and his herd of cows, a score of animals each more beautiful than the next, graceful and docile, even if their leader, Rusty, had a mind of her own and wouldn't let just anyone approach her. Crooked-Fingers spent hours chatting to her.

In the morning the mischievous Rusty would wake him by licking his forehead. Crooked-Fingers would try in vain to grab her ear, but eventually he always got up. Today, though, the sun was already high in the heavens when Crooked-Fingers left the farmhouse.

'Rusty! Where've you got to, Rusty?'

He rubbed his eyes, took a few steps into his field, and saw his cow lying on her side. 'What's the matter, Rusty?'

Her tongue hung out, her eyes were glazed, her belly was swollen. She was dying. A little further away, two cows lay already dead in the field.

Crooked-Fingers ran in panic to the village square to get help from the animal-doctor; but he was surrounded by a dozen farmers whose animals had also been stricken.

'An epidemic!' cried Crooked-Fingers. 'We must tell the palace immediately!'

When Ofir, from the roof of his house, saw a crowd of anxious, angry peasants flock past, he gathered that his orders had been correctly carried out: Amos and Baduch had created chaos.

Moses halted the farmers in the middle of the avenue leading to the palace. 'You are victims of the fifth plague Yahveh inflicts on Egypt,' he proclaimed. 'His hand will strike all the herds, the murrain will strike the great and the small livestock! Only the beasts belonging to my people shall be spared.'

Serramanna and some of his men were preparing to drive the peasants away, when Lotus galloped up on a black horse, and halted in front of them.

'You mustn't lose your heads,' she said calmly. 'It's not an epidemic. The cattle have been poisoned. I have already saved two milch cows and, with the help of the animal-doctors, I shall cure all the animals that haven't yet succumbed.'

The feeling of helplessness immediately gave way to hope. And when, soon afterwards, the minister for agriculture announced that Pharaoh would replace the dead animals at the state's expense, calm was restored.

Ofir and his allies still had enough poison to help Moses – but this time without telling him. Using an old recipe for magic, the prophet, following orders from Yahveh, had scooped up handfuls of soot from a stove and thrown it into the air, letting it fall like dust. The people on whom it had fallen would become covered with pustules. This sixth plague would be so terrifying that Pharaoh would have to yield.

Ofir had had another idea too. How better to impress the king than by afflicting those close to him? Amos, unrecognizable in a wig that covered his bald head and half his forehead, had delivered contaminated food to the cook who prepared meals for Ahmeni and his staff.

When Ahmeni brought in the day's dossiers, Ramses noticed a reddish rash on his friend's cheek.

'Have you hurt yourself?' he asked.

'No, but this rash is getting sore.'

'I'll send for Doctor Pariamaku.'

The palace physician, accompanied by a beautiful girl, came hurrying along, all out of breath. 'Are you ill, Majesty?'

'You know very well, dear Doctor, that I'm never ill. Please examine my private secretary.'

Pariamaku walked round Ahmeni, palpated the skin of his arm, felt his pulse, and pressed his ear to his chest.

'Nothing abnormal at first sight. I shall have to think.'

'What if it's ulceration caused by digestive trouble?' suggested the girl shyly. 'Should we prepare a remedy based on sliced sycamore seeds, aniseed, honey, terebinth resin and fennel, and use it both on the rash and as a philtre?'

Doctor Pariamaku tried to look important. 'Hmm, that's not a bad idea. Let's try it and see. Go back to the laboratory, my child, and have them prepare this remedy.'

The girl bowed nervously to the monarch and slipped away.

'What's the name of your assistant?' asked Ramses.

'Neferet, Majesty. Don't pay any attention to her – she's only a beginner.'

'She already seems very competent.'

'She only repeated a remedy I taught her. She's being trained, and I doubt if she's got much future as a doctor.'

Ofir was brooding. The little outbreak of ulcers had been cleared up, and Ramses still stood firm. Moses and Aaron kept the Hebrews under control, since any disturbances would have provoked Serramanna and the police into strong reaction.

To this setback was added loss of contact with Dolora. She had failed utterly. Nefertari was very much alive, and free of any ailment that might undermine her health. Feeling threatened, Dolora no longer dared come to the Hebrew district, even by night, so Ofir lacked direct information about court secrets.

This handicap did not prevent him from fanning the flame of rebellion among the Hebrews. A strong faction, united behind Moses and Aaron, was becoming a more and more formidable spearhead.

It would be dificult to organize Uri-Teshup's escape, for he was confined to his villa and was guarded day and night by Serramanna's men. In any case, Uri-Teshup's day was over and he was now a liability. Instead of taking rash risks, the best solution might be to let Uri-Teshup go missing, and thus to win Hattusilis's favour. Intelligent, cunning and ruthless, the new emperor seemed to be following in Muwatallis's footsteps.

However, Ofir still had one ally, whose treachery no one suspected: Meba. Although Meba was a mediocrity, he was the one who would help get rid of Uri-Teshup.

Ahsha kept his retinue to a minimum as, contrary to what he had told Ramses, he thought he had at best one chance in a hundred of being well received in Hattusa. To the new emperor he was a suspect who had allowed Uri-Teshup to escape punishment. Would Hattusilis's desire for revenge overrule his political sense? If so, he might well have all Ahsha's staff arrested, perhaps even executed, and that would force Ramses to launch an offensive to wipe out the affront.

True, Putuhepa seemed to favour peace, but it was doubtful if she would disagree openly with her husband's policy. The Empress of Hatti would not let herself be constrained by a dream: if negotiation proved fruitless, she would advocate confrontation.

A blustery wind, common on the Anatolian plateau, accompanied Ahsha and his escort to the gates of Hattusa. The impregnable fortress looked even more menacing than on his previous visits.

Ahsha delivered his credentials to a junior officer and waited patiently for a good hour near a side-gate, before being allowed to enter the city by the Lion Gate. He was taken not to the palace, as he had expected, but to a grey stone building, where a room had been prepared for him.

There were iron bars across the only window. Even to someone of optimistic temperament, the place looked like a prison. To outsmart the Hittites demanded skill and luck. A great deal of luck; and Ahsha was worried he might have used up the share fate had allotted him.

Shortly after nightfall, a helmeted soldier wearing heavy armour came for him. This time, he was escorted down a narrow alleyway to the citadel on which the emperor's palace stood. It was the moment of truth – if such a thing existed in the world of diplomacy.

A fire was burning in the hearth of the audience chamber, which was adorned with tapestries. Empress Putuhepa was enjoying the pleasant warmth.

When she saw him, she smiled and said, 'Would the ambassador of Egypt care to sit near me, here in front of the fire? The nights can be cold.'

Ahsha sat down on a plain chair, at a respectful distance.

'I greatly appreciated Queen Nefertari's letters,' went on the empress. 'Her thoughts are clarity itself, her arguments convincing, her intentions honest.'

'Am I to understand that the emperor is willing to open negotiations?'

'The emperor and I hope for specific suggestions.'

'I am the bearer of a document devised by Pharaoh and Queen Nefertari and drawn up by Pharaoh himself. It will serve as a basis for our discussions.'

'That is the initiative I hoped for. Naturally, Hatti has some demands.'

'I am here to listen to them, with the firm desire to reach an agreement.'

Putuhepa smiled again, and shed some of her formality. 'The warmth of those words is as pleasant as that of this fire. Tell me, Ahsha, were you worried by your rather chilly reception?'

'That would have been improper of me, wouldn't it?'

'Hattusilis has a cold, and has been confined to his bed for some time. My own days are very full, which is why I had to keep you waiting. But tomorrow the emperor will be well enough to begin discussions.'

51

The sun had not yet risen and Ramses was on his way to the Temple of Amon when suddenly Moses blocked his path. The king signalled the guard who accompanied him to do nothing.

'I must speak to you, Pharaoh.'

'Be brief.'

'Do you not understand that up till now Yahveh has been lenient? If He had wished, you and your people would have been wiped out. He, who knows no rival, has allowed you to live, the better to proclaim His omnipotence. Allow the Hebrews to leave Egypt, or else . . .'

'Or else?'

'A seventh plague will bring intolerable suffering to your country: a hailstorm of monstrous violence will bring death and injury to many! When I stretch my staff up to the heavens, thunder will roar and lightning will rend the skies.'

'Don't you know that one of the principal temples of this city is dedicated to Set, who governs storms? He is heaven's wrath and I shall use the rites by which I am able to appease him.'

'This time, you won't succeed. Men and beasts will die.'

'Let me pass.'

That afternoon, the king consulted the 'priests of the hour', who observed the sky, studied the movements of the planets and forecast the weather. In fact, they did predict heavy rain or hail, which might well destroy part of the flax crop.

As soon as the bad weather set in, Ramses shut himself up in Set's shrine and stood facing the god. The great statue's red eyes glowed like live coals.

The king could not oppose the will of Set and the fury of the storm clouds; but by communing with the god's spirit, he could lessen their effect and shorten the storm. Seti had taught his son how to converse with Set and channel the god's destructive force without himself being destroyed. It took immense spiritual energy to endure the confrontation and yield not a hand-span of ground to Set's invisible flames. But at last Ramses' efforts were crowned with success.

Meba was shaking with fear. Although he was disguised by a short wig and a heavy, badly cut cloak, he was terrified of being recognized, even in this dockside ale-house where only packers and sailors came to drink.

Amos took a seat in front of him.

'Who . . . who sent you?' quavered Meba.

'The magus. You are . . . ?'

'No names! Just give him this tablet. It contains information which may interest him.'

'He wants you to take care of Uri-Teshup.'

'But he's under constant guard!'

'The orders are definite. Kill Uri-Teshup. Otherwise we shall denounce you to Ramses.'

The Hebrews were beginning to have doubts. Seven plagues had been inflicted on Egypt, and still Pharaoh had not given in. Nevertheless, at a meeting of the council of elders, Moses succeeded in retaining their trust.

'What do you intend to do now?' one elder asked.

'Launch an eighth plague, one so terrible that the Egyptians will think their gods have abandoned them.'

'What will this plague be?'

'Watch the sky in the east, and you will see.'

'Shall we at last be able to leave Egypt?' asked another elder.

'Be patient, as I have been all these long years, and put your trust in Yahveh. He will lead us to the Promised Land.'

In the middle of the night, Nefertari woke with a start.

Ramses slept on peacefully beside her. The queen slipped silently out of the bedchamber and on to the terrace. The air was warm, the city silent and peaceful, but the Great Royal Wife's anxiety continued to increase. The vision that had frightened her did not fade, the nightmare still held her heart in a vice.

Ramses came up beside her and took her gently in his arms. 'A bad dream, Nefertari?'

'If that were all . . .'

'What are you afraid of?'

'Danger coming from the east, with a terrible wind.'

Ramses looked eastwards. He concentrated hard, as if he could see into the darkness. His spirit became one with the sky and the night, and was transported to the ends of the earth, from whence the winds came.

What he saw was so terrifying that he dressed hurriedly, had the palace staff and scribes woken, and sent for Ahmeni.

An enormous cloud, made up of millions – thousands of millions – of locusts, was blown towards Egypt by a fierce east wind. There had been locust swarms often before, but never on a scale like this.

On Pharaoh's advice, the peasants in the Delta had lit fires, into which they threw strong-smelling substances intended to deter the locusts. Some of the cultivated fields were covered with huge pieces of cloth laid like patchwork.

When Moses had announced that the insects would devour all the trees in Egypt and that no fruit would survive, the royal messengers had quickly carried news of the threat throughout the country. And today everyone was glad they had taken the precautions recommended by Ramses.

The damage was minimal; and people remembered that the locust was one of the symbolic forms adopted by Pharaoh's soul so that it might reach heaven in one gigantic leap. In small numbers, the insect was considered beneficial; only in vast swarms was it a threat.

The royal couple rode in their chariot through the country-side around Pi-Ramses, and stopped at several villages which feared a new onslaught. But Ramses and Nefertari promised that the scourge would soon disappear.

As the Great Royal Wife had foreseen, the east wind fell and was replaced by squally gusts which blew the cloud of locusts out to the Sea of Reeds,* beyond the cultivated fields.

'You aren't ill,' Dr Pariamaku told Meba, 'but all the same you should take a few days' rest.'

'This indisposition . . .'

'Your heart's in excellent condition, and your liver's functioning well. Don't worry, you'll live to be a hundred.'

Meba had pretended to be unwell, in the hope that Pariamaku would order him to keep to his room for several weeks, during which time Ofir and his accomplices might be arrested. But this childish plan had come to nothing. And to denounce them would be to denounce himself. He had no choice but to try to carry out his mission. But how could he get near Uri-Teshup without alerting the guards? His best weapon, when all was said and done, was diplomacy.

As soon as he saw Serramanna in one of the palace corridors, he went up to him.

* The marshy area to the north of the Gulf of Suez between the Red Sea and the Mediterranean (through which the Suez Canal was to be cut many centuries later). *Trans.*

'Ahsha has sent me a dispatch,' Meba said, 'ordering me to question Uri-Teshup and to obtain confidential information on the Hittite administration. Whatever he tells me must remain a secret, so we'll have to talk privately. I'll note down what he says on this papyrus, seal it and hand it to the king.'

Serramanna seemed put out. 'How long will you need?'

'I don't know.'

'Are you in a hurry?'

'Yes. It's urgent.'

'Very well, let's go.'

Uri-Teshup received the diplomat with suspicion, but Meba used all his charm and conviction to win him over. He didn't press him with questions, but instead thanked him for his collaboration and assured him that his future would soon become brighter. Uri-Teshup described his finest battles and even made a few jokes.

'Are you being treated well?' asked Meba.

'The food is good, the lodgings are satisfactory and I get some exercise, but I miss the company of women.'

'I think I can solve that problem.'

'How?' demanded the Hittite.

'Insist on a walk in the gardens at nightfall, to get the benefit of the cool air. In the tamarisk grove, near the side entrance, a woman will be waiting for you.'

'I think you and I are going to be good friends.'

'There's nothing I'd like better,' said Meba smoothly.

The weather was sultry, the sky grew dark: Set was once more displaying his power. The stifling heat and airlessness gave Uri-Teshup a perfect excuse to demand a walk in the gardens. Two guards accompanied him, but they let him wander freely among the flower beds, since he had no chance of escaping. Anyway, why would he try to leave the gilded cage where he was safe?

Hidden under the tamarisk trees, Meba trembled. Drugged

312

into a sort of trance by an infusion of mandrake, he had climbed over the surrounding wall and was prepared to strike. When Uri-Teshup bent over him, he'd slit his throat with a short-bladed dagger he had stolen from an infantry officer. He'd leave the weapon on the corpse, and the murder would be blamed on a band of soldiers bent on avenging all the Egyptian deaths Uri-Teshup had caused.

Meba had never killed anyone before, and he knew this deed would lead to his damnation. But he'd plead his cause before the judges of the Otherworld and explain that he'd been used. For the moment he must think only of the dagger and Uri-Teshup's throat.

He heard footsteps. Slow, cautious footsteps. His quarry approached, came to a halt, bent over . . .

Meba raised his arm to strike, but a ferocious blow to his head made everything go black.

Serramanna lifted the diplomat by the collar of his tunic. 'You stupid, incompetent little traitor! Wake up, Meba.'

There was no answer; Meba didn't move.

'Stop play-acting!'

Then he looked more closely. Meba's head was at a strange angle to his neck. Serramanna realized he had struck too hard.

52

There had of course to be an inquiry into Meba's violent death, and Serramanna had to undergo close questioning led by Ahmeni. The Sardinian was tense, fearing he'd be punished.

'The case is clear,' Ahmeni concluded. 'You suspected, correctly, that Meba had lied to you and intended to kill Uri-Teshup. You caught Meba red-handed and tried to arrest him, but he resisted fiercely, and in the ensuing struggle he was killed.'

The ex-pirate relaxed. 'That's a masterly report.'

'Although he's dead, Meba will be put on trial. There's no doubt about his guilt, so his name will be erased from all official documents. But one question remains: who was he working for?'

'He told me he was acting on Ahsha's orders.'

Ahmeni chewed the end of his writing-brush. 'To have someone kill Uri-Teshup, and rid Ramses of someone who'd become inconvenient . . . But Ahsha wouldn't have relied on a socialite and a coward. And what's more, he wouldn't have gone against the wishes of Ramses, who insists on respecting the right of safe refuge. No, that must be another of Meba's lies. I wonder if he was a member of the Hittite spy ring operating here?'

'But weren't they helping Uri-Teshup?'

'Today, the name of the emperor is Hattusilis and Uri-Teshup is just a traitor. By killing the new Lord of Hatti's sworn enemy, the spy ring was currying favour with him.'

'In other words,' said Serramanna, stroking his long moustache, 'Ofir and Shanaar are not only alive but still here in Egypt.'

'Shanaar disappeared in Nubia, and Ofir hasn't shown up for years.'

Serramanna clenched his fists. 'That damned magus is probably quite close to us! The evidence that he'd fled to Libya was planted!'

'Well, he's certainly shown that he knows how to stay out of our reach.'

'Not out of mine, Ahmeni, not out of mine.'

'Do you think you could, for once, bring in the suspect alive?'

For three interminable days, dense black clouds hid the sun over Pi-Ramses. In the eyes of the Egyptians, the disturbances caused by Set were mingled with perils brought by the messengers of the goddess Sekhmet, the harbingers of disease and misery.

Only one person could prevent things getting worse: the Great Royal Wife, the earthly embodiment of the eternal Rule, which Pharaoh nourished with offerings. This was a time when everyone rigorously examined their inner self and tried to correct any deviation from the path of righteousness. Taking upon herself the faults and imperfections of her people, Nefertari travelled to Thebes, to the Temple of Mut, to lay offerings before the statue of the formidable Sekhmet, and thus transform the darkness into light.

In the capital, Ramses agreed to receive Moses, who declared that the darkness covering Pi-Ramses was the ninth plague inflicted by Yahveh on the Egyptian people.

'Are you finally convinced, Pharaoh?'

'All you're doing is attributing natural phenomena to your god. That is your vision of reality, and I respect it. But I will not allow you to sow unrest among the people in the name of a religion. That attitude is contrary to the Rule of Ma'at, and can lead only to chaos and civil war.'

'Yahveh's demands are unchanged.'

'You and your followers, Moses, may leave Egypt and go and pray to your god wherever you wish.'

'That is not what Yahveh wants. *All* the Hebrew people must leave with me.'

'You will leave behind all the livestock, large and small, as they are for the most part on loan to you and are not your property. Those who reject Egypt have no right to enjoy her benefits.'

'Our animals will accompany us. Not a single head of cattle shall remain in your country, for each one is to be used in the worship of Yahveh. We need them to offer up sacrifices and burned offerings until we arrive in the Promised Land.'

Ramses stared at him. 'Are you saying you're going to become a common thief?'

'Yahveh alone can judge my conduct.'

'What kind of belief can possibly justify such conduct?'

'You'll never be able to understand. Just admit that you've lost.'

'The pharaohs have succeeded in suppressing fanaticism and intolerance, those deadly poisons which eat into men's hearts. Do you not fear, as I do, the consequences of an uncompromising and definitive truth, imposed by men on other men?'

'Obey the will of Yahveh.'

'Are threats and abuse all you can say, Moses?' asked Ramses sadly. 'What has become of our friendship, which once guided us along the path of knowledge?'

'That's past and dead. All I'm interested in is the future, and that future is the exodus of my people.'

Ramses stood up. 'Leave this palace, Moses,' he commanded, 'and never appear before me again. Otherwise I shall consider you a rebel and the court of justice will decree that you suffer the appropriate punishment.'

Blazing with anger, Moses swept out of the palace, ignoring the few courtiers who were prepared to greet him, and returned to his home in the Hebrew district.

Ofir was waiting there for him. The magus knew of Meba's failure and death, but the diplomat's last report contained an interesting piece of information: Kha no longer wore the amulet and protective cloth given him by Setau. True, Kha's role as High Priest of Ptah protected him from the forces of darkness, but Ofir thought it was worth trying his luck.

'Has Ramses given in?' Ofir asked Moses.

'He'll never give in!'

'Ramses doesn't know the meaning of fear. This situation won't be resolved unless we use force.'

'You mean an armed rebellion?'

'We've got the weapons.'

'The Hebrews would be wiped out.'

'Who's talking about an open revolt? We must use death – death will be the tenth and last plague inflicted on Egypt.'

Moses' anger at Ramses had not subsided. And, in Ofir's threatening words, he thought he heard the voice of Yahveh. 'You're right, Ofir. We must strike so hard that Ramses will be forced to free the Hebrews. At midnight on the night of death, Yahveh will pass over Egypt and all the first-born will die.'

Ofir had pinned his hopes on this moment. At last he was going to avenge the defeats the pharaoh had inflicted on him.

'Kha, Ramses' son and probable successor, is at the top of the list of the first-born. Up till now he has enjoyed magical protection which I have not been able to overcome. But now . . .'

'The hand of Yahveh will not spare him.'

'We must make sure we aren't suspected,' Ofir advised.

'The Hebrews must fraternize with the Egyptians as usual. But they must take advantage of this to steal a quantity of precious objects which we shall need during the exodus.'

'We shall celebrate the Passover,' Moses announced, 'and we shall make a red mark on our houses, with bunches of hyssop dipped in the blood of the cattle sacrificed for the feast. On the night of death, the Exterminator will spare those houses.'

Ofir hurried off to his laboratory. He was going to use Kha's stolen writing-brush to paralyse the young man and drag him down into oblivion.

The play of light and shadow on the garden made Nefertari seem even more beautiful. Mysterious and sublime, moving with the grace of a goddess among the shrubs and flowers, she embodied happiness itself. Yet, when he kissed her hand, Ramses immediately sensed that she was worried.

'Moses isn't done with his threats,' she murmured.

'He used to be my friend, and I cannot believe his soul is evil.'

'Neither can I: I respect him. But a destructive fire has taken possession of his heart, and that frightens me.'

Setau, looking deeply concerned, approached the royal couple. 'Forgive me, I'm accustomed to being blunt: Kha is ill.'

'Is it serious?' asked Nefertari.

'I'm afraid so, Majesty; my remedies aren't working.'

'Do you mean . . . ?'

'Don't let's deceive ourselves: he's been bewitched.'

The Great Royal Wife, daughter of Isis and the most skilled magician imaginable, hurried to Kha's rooms.

He was lying on a low bed, his face drawn and grey, and he could breathe only with difficulty. But, in spite of the pain, he showed impressive dignity.

'My arms are numb,' he told Nefertari calmly, 'and I can't move my legs.'

The queen laid her hands on his brow. 'I shall give you all my life-force,' she promised, 'and we will struggle together against this creeping death. I shall bestow on you all the happiness life has given me, and you shall not die.'

In Hattusa, the negotiations were making very slow progress. Hattusilis argued about every item of the draft treaty Ramses had drawn up, proposed different wording, fought hard with Ahsha, then reached a compromise in which he weighed every word over and over again. Then Putuhepa would add her comments and still more discussions would ensue.

Ahsha showed exemplary patience. He knew they were working for a peace on which depended the happiness of the whole region – and of a good part of the world beyond.

'Don't forget,' Hattusilis reminded him, 'that I insist on the return of Uri-Teshup.'

'That will be the last point to settle,' replied Ahsha, 'when we have agreed all the rest of the treaty.'

'You're a real optimist! But are you sure the Emperor of Hatti has total confidence in you?'

'If the opposite were true, he might not have become Emperor of Hatti.'

'By attributing ulterior motives to me, aren't you compromising the outcome of the negotiations?'

'Naturally you have ulterior motives, Majesty, and you are naturally trying to obtain a treaty that's weighted in Hatti's favour, not Egypt's. It's my job to keep the scales evenly balanced.'

'That's a delicate game, and you may yet fail.'

'The future of the world: that's what Ramses has trusted me with, and it lies in your hands, Majesty.'

'I am patient, clear-headed and stubborn, my dear Ahsha.'

'So am I, Majesty.'

53

Serramanna now almost never left the guardroom reserved for his men. The most he allowed himself was an occasional brief distraction with a girl brought in from the most reputable ale-house. But even this pleasure brought him no respite from his obsession: his opponent would inevitably make a mistake and he had to be ready to take instant advantage of it.

Kha's illness had plunged the Sardinian into deep despondency. Everything that concerned the king and those close to him upset Serramanna as if the reigning family were his own, and he raged at his inability to destroy Ramses' enemies.

One of his mercenaries came in with a report. 'Something odd is going on among the Hebrews.'

'What do you mean?'

'There are smears of red paint on the doors of their houses. I don't know what to make of it, but I thought you'd want to know.'

'You thought right. Find some excuse and bring Abner to me.'

Since giving evidence in Moses' favour, Abner had managed to avoid all contact with the authorities. When he was brought in, he kept his head down, visibly ill at ease.

'Have you done something wrong?' Serramanna asked angrily.

320

'Oh, no, my lord! My life is as spotless as a priest's immaculate white gown.'

'Then why are you trembling?'

'I'm only a poor brickmaker, and—'

'That's enough, Abner. Why have you messed up the door of your house with red paint?'

'It was an accident, my lord.'

'An accident that happened to scores of other doors as well? Don't take me for a fool.' The big Sardinian cracked his knuckles, making the Hebrew jump.

'It's . . . it's a new fashion!'

'Oh yes? Well, suppose I made it the fashion to cut off your nose and your ears?'

'You've no right . . . the court would convict you!'

'A case of circumstances outside my control,' said Serramanna. 'I'm inquiring into the use of sorcery against Prince Kha, and I wouldn't be at all surprised if you had something to do with it.'

Abner knew the judges would be very hard on anyone practising black magic and would hand down a heavy sentence. 'I'm innocent!' he protested.

'In view of your past history, that's hard to believe.'

'Don't do that to me, my lord! I've a family, children . . .'

'Either you talk, or I charge you.'

Between his own safety and that of Moses, Abner didn't hesitate for long. 'Moses has put a spell on all the first-born,' he revealed. 'On the night of calamity, they'll be killed by Yahveh. The Hebrews were told to put a distinctive sign on their houses, so they'll be spared.'

'By all the devils of the sea, this Moses is a monster!'

'Will you . . . will you let me go now, my lord?'

'You'd talk, you little snake. You'll be quite safe in prison.'

Abner nodded, satisfied. 'When will I be freed?'

'When is this "night of calamity"?'

'I don't know, but it's soon.'

When Abner had been taken away, Serramanna hurried to Ramses, who received him as soon as he finished his conversation with the minister for agriculture.

Nedjem was so distressed by Kha's illness – only Nefertari's magic was keeping the young man alive – that he scarcely had the heart to carry out his duties. But Ramses had persuaded him that the service of the country and the Egyptian public came before all other considerations, even personal tragedy.

Serramanna reported on what Abner had disclosed.

'He's lying,' said the king. 'Moses would never plan such an abomination.'

'Abner is a coward and he's afraid of me; but he was telling the truth.'

'A crime like that, the cold-blooded, systematic killing of the first-born . . . Such a horror could only have originated in a sick brain. That can't have come from Moses.'

'I recommend that the police be out in force in the city, to discourage the murderers from carrying out their plan.'

'Deploy the country police too.'

'Forgive me, Majesty . . . but shouldn't we arrest Moses?'

'He hasn't committed an offence; the court would acquit him. No, I must think of some other solution.'

'I'd like to suggest a tactic which you'll think terrible but which just might work.'

'You're being very cautious! Speak out, Serramanna.'

'Let it be known that Kha has only three days to live.'

The mere mention of such a terrible prospect made Ramses shudder.

'I knew I'd shock you, Majesty, but that news will force the murderers to act hastily – and I intend to make the most of their haste.'

The king needed only a few moments to reflect. 'See that you succeed, Serramanna.'

322

*

Dolora boxed her hairdresser's ears; the girl had pulled one of the locks of her magificent brown hair too hard.

'Get out, you clumsy fool!'

The hairdresser slipped away in tears. Immediately the chiropodist took her place.

'Remove the dead skin and paint my nails red. And be careful not to hurt me.

The chiropodist was very glad she had long experience.

'Your work is satisfactory,' said Dolora after a while. 'I shall pay you well and recommend you to my friends.'

'Thank you, Princess. In spite of the universal sadness, you make me very happy.'

'What sadness do you mean?'

'My first client this morning, a great court lady, has just told me the terrible news: Prince Kha is dying.'

'That's just a rumour, isn't it?'

'Alas, no! According to the palace doctors, Kha hasn't more than three days to live.'

'Hurry up and finish. I've things to do.'

This was a matter of the greatest urgency. Dolora felt she had no choice but to disobey the order to respect security. Not waiting to have her make-up done, she put on a nondescript wig and threw a brown cloak over her shoulders. No one would recognize her.

She threaded her way through idle onlookers as she hurried through the city, and turned off towards the Hebrew district. She dodged between a water-carrier and a cheese vendor, nervously pushed aside two little girls who were playing with their dolls in the middle of the alleyway, jostled an old man who was walking too slowly, and rapped five times on a small door painted dark green.

It opened with a creak.

'Who are you?' asked a brickmaker.

'A friend of the magus.'

'Come in.'

The brickmaker preceded Dolora down a staircase leading to a cellar lit by an oil lamp whose faint gleam shone on the sinister, hawklike face of the magus. He was clutching Kha's brush, which he had covered with strange signs and partially burned.

'What is so urgent that you've come here, Dolora?'

'Kha is going to die in the next few hours.'

'Have the palace doctors given up trying to cure him?'

'Pariamaku says death is imminent.'

'That's excellent news, but it changes our plans a little. You did well to let me know.'

So the night of calamity would occur sooner than foreseen. The first-born would die, beginning with Kha, and despair would fall on the people of Egypt. Terrified by Yahveh's power and anger, they would turn against Ramses, and there would be widespread rioting.

Dolora threw herself at Ofir's feet. 'What is going to happen?'

'Ramses will be swept away. Moses and the true God will triumph.'

'And our dream will become a reality!'

'A reality . . . yes, indeed it will. Dear Dolora, you were right to persevere.'

'Couldn't we prevent some of the . . . violence?'

Ofir raised Dolora to her feet, and took her face in his hands. 'Moses is the one who makes the decisions, and Moses is inspired by Yahveh. We must not argue with his decisions, whatever their consequences.'

A door was thrown open upstairs. There was a muffled cry, then rapid footsteps on the stairs, and Serramanna burst into the cellar.

He pushed Dolora aside, and butted Ofir, knocking him to the ground still clutching Kha's brush. The huge Sardinian slammed his heel down on the magus's arm and forced him to open his fingers.

'Ofir, I've got you at last!'

54

Setau entered Kha's bedchamber, threw the bewitched writing-brush on the floor and stamped on it furiously, reducing it to tiny fragments. Nefertari, who had kept Kha alive by unstintingly giving him of her own life-force, watched gratefully.

'The curse is destroyed, Majesty,' said Setau. 'Kha will mend rapidly now.'

Nefertari removed her hands from the back of the young man's neck and collapsed, utterly exhausted.

Doctor Pariamaku prescribed harmless tonics for the queen. Setau gave her a genuine remedy, which would restore to her blood the energy she had expended.

'The Great Royal Wife has gone beyond the limits of fatigue,' he told Ramses worriedly.

'I insist you tell me *all* the truth, Setau.'

'By giving her magic to Kha, she has deprived herself of many years of life.'

Ramses remained constantly at Nefertari's bedside, trying to give her the strength he himself radiated, the strength on which he had built his reign. He was ready to sacrifice it to let his beloved wife enjoy a long and happy old age, and light up the Two Lands with her beauty.

It took all Ahmeni's persuasion to make Ramses resume

the affairs of state. The king only agreed to discuss matters with his friend after hearing Nefertari say soothingly that she felt the night withdrawing from her.

'Serramanna has given me a long report,' said Ahmeni. 'Ofir has been arrested and will be tried for spying, black magic, attempted murder of a member of the royal family, and the murders of the wretched Lita and her servant. But he's not the only guilty one: Moses is every bit as dangerous. Ofir has disclosed that Moses intended to kill every single first-born in Egypt. If Serramanna hadn't followed the princess and thwarted this monstrous plan, we would now be mourning countless victims.'

From the oldest to the youngest, from the poorest to the richest, from the most worldly to the most naive, the Hebrews were astounded to see Pharaoh in person appear at the head of a detachment of soldiers commanded by Serramanna. The streets emptied, and people watched nervously from behind half-closed shutters.

Ramses went directly to Moses' home. Alerted by the noise, the latter was waiting in his doorway, his staff in his hand.

'We were not supposed to see each other again, Majesty.'

'This is our last interview, Moses, you can be sure of that. Why did you try to spread death throughout the land?'

'My sole concern is to obey Yahveh.'

'Your god is too cruel. I respect your faith, but I refuse to let it be a source of discord in the land bequeathed to me by my ancestors. Leave Egypt, Moses, leave with the Hebrews. Depart and go to live elsewhere, guided by your truth. You are not the one who asks to leave; it is I who command that you go.'

Wrapped in a thick cloak, Emperor Hattusilis looked down on his capital from the top of the citadel on which his palace was built.

His wife took him affectionately by the arm. 'Our land is harsh, but it is not without beauty. Why sacrifice it to rancour?'

'Uri-Teshup must be punished,' he declared.

'Hasn't he been punished enough? Imagine what it must be like for a ruthless warrior to be confined to his house in the land of his worst enemy. He's already mortally wounded in his vanity!'

'I have no right to give way on this point.'

'We can't delay much longer,' warned Putuhepa. 'The Assyrians' army is growing more and more threatening and they won't hesitate to attack us if they learn that our peace negotiations with Egypt have failed.'

'Those negotiations are secret.'

'Come, my dear, the Emperor of Hatti mustn't be naive! Messengers come and go continually between Hatti and Egypt, between Egypt and Hatti, and what was secret once is so no longer. If we don't conclude the treaty of peace as soon as possible, the Assyrians will find us an easy target, for Ramses will witness our collapse without lifting a finger.'

'The Hittites can defend themselves.'

'Since the beginning of your reign, Hattusilis, your people have changed greatly. Even the soldiers long for peace. And have you yourself any other aim?'

Hattusilis looked suspiciously at his wife. 'Is all this due to Nefertari's influence?'

'My sister the Queen of Egypt shares my convictions. She has persuaded Ramses to make no more war on the Hittites. Can we match what she has done?'

'Uri-Teshup—'

'Uri-Teshup belongs to the past. Let him marry an Egyptian; let him merge with Pharaoh's people, and disappear from our future!'

'You are asking a lot of me.'

'Isn't that my duty as empress?'

'If I back down Ramses will consider it a sign of weakness.'

'Neither Nefertari nor I will interpret your generosity in that way.'

'You two women seem to have taken charge of the foreign policy of Hatti and Egypt!'

'Why not,' said Putuhepa serenely, 'if that results in peace?'

During his trial Ofir talked at length. He boasted of having been the head of the Hittite spy ring in Egypt and of having made an attempt on Kha's life. When he described how he had murdered the unfortunate Lita and her servant, the jury realized that he felt no remorse and would not hesitate to kill again wiith the same callousness.

Dolora wept. Accused by Ofir of active complicity, she did not deny it but merely begged her brother for mercy. She blamed Shanaar, whose bad influence had led her astray.

The court's deliberations were brief. The vizier pronounced the verdict. Ofir was condemned to death: he must take his own life by drinking poison. Dolora's name would be suppressed, erased from all official documents, and she was to be banished to southern Syria, where she was to work on a farm, undertaking the heaviest drudgery as the farmer saw fit. As for Shanaar, he was condemned to death in his absence, and his name, too, would be consigned to oblivion.

Although still suffering badly from exhaustion, Nefertari had kept up her correspondence with Putuhepa. Invincible and Wideawake, the latter still playful in spite of his age, never left the queen's side, as if they knew their presence gave her back a little strength.

Whenever he could escape from the demands of his

country, Ramses returned to his wife's side. They walked in the palace gardens; he read her texts by the sages from the time of the pyramids. Each day renewed the great love that united them, this secret, unfathomable love, incandescent as a summer sky and tender as a sunset over the Nile.

Nefertari had to make Ramses leave her and resume his obligations to Egypt, keeping the ship of state on the right course, and replying to the thousand day-to-day questions asked by ministers and high officials. Thanks to Iset the Fair, Meritamon and Kha, who was now fully recovered, the queen's convalescence was surrounded with joy and youthfulness. She appreciated visits by Meneptah, who was a remarkably fine child, and by Tuya, who cleverly hid her own fatigue.

Setau and Lotus left for Abu Simbel again, on the same day that Ahsha returned to Egypt. They scarcely had time to congratulate each other before they were parted again.

Ahsha was immediately received by the royal couple and prostrated himself before Nefertari. 'I have greatly missed your wisdom and your beauty, Majesty.'

'Are you the bearer of good news?' she asked.

'Excellent news.'

'Is Hattusilis willing to sign a treaty?' Ramses asked suspiciously.

'Thanks to the Queen of Egypt and the Empress of Hatti, the matter of Uri-Teshup is almost settled. Let him remain in Egypt and merge into our society. There will then be no further obstacle to concluding an agreement.'

A broad smile lit up Nefertari's face. 'Have we really won the greatest of all victories?'

'Our principal support has been Empress Putuhepa. She was most touched by the tone of the letters from the Great Royal Wife. Since the beginning of Hattusilis's reign, the Hittites have seen the growing danger from Assyria, and we, their past enemies, will be their future allies.'

'We must act rapidly,' recommended Nefertari, 'in order to make the most of this brief period of grace.'

'I bring the version of the treaty proposed by Hattusilis; we must study it closely. As soon as I have your agreement and that of Pharaoh, I shall leave again for Hatti.'

The royal couple and Ahsha set to work. To his surprise, Ramses noted that Hattusilis had accepted most of his conditions – Ahsha had done an astonishing job, without ever betraying his intentions. And when Tuya, in turn, had finished reading it attentively, she gave her approval.

'Whatever is going on?' asked the Viceroy of Nubia as his chariot, drawn by two horses and driven by an experienced charioteer, approached the palace of Pi-Ramses through noisy, congested streets. This was not at all what one might expect when making an official visit to Pharaoh.

'The exodus of the Hebrews,' replied the charioteer. 'They are leaving Egypt under their leader, Moses, on their way to their Promised Land.'

'Why has Pharaoh agreed to this folly?'

'He has expelled them for disturbances to public order.'

To his amazement, the viceroy saw thousands of men, women and children leaving the city, driving their herds and flocks before them and pulling carts filled with clothes and provisions. Some were singing, others looked sad. Leaving the land where they had led a pleasant existence filled the majority with despair, but they dared not oppose Moses.

The viceroy was received by Ahmeni and taken to Ramses' office.

'What is the reason for this visit?' asked the king.

'I had to warn you as quickly as possible, Majesty. So I didn't hesitate to take a fast boat to report to you personally the tragic events that have cast a shadow over the territory in my charge. It was all so unexpected, so violent! I couldn't imagine—'

'Stop gabbling,' demanded Ramses, 'and tell me the truth.'

The viceroy gulped. 'A revolt, Majesty. A terrible revolt by tribes united in a coalition.'

55

Shanaar had succeeded.

Month after month, he had argued with the tribal chiefs, struggling over and over again to persuade them to join forces with their fellows and seize the biggest gold mine in Nubia. Although he proposed to pay them handsomely by distributing bars of silver, the black warriors had proved reluctant to defy Ramses the Great. They felt it was madness to oppose the Egyptian army, which, at the beginning of Seti's reign, had inflicted a crushing defeat on Nubian rebels.

In spite of many failures, Shanaar had persisted. His last chance of killing Ramses was to lure him into a trap. To do that, he needed the help of experienced fighters, who were eager to acquire great wealth and who weren't afraid of the pharaoh's soldiers.

At last Shanaar's perseverance had paid off. First one chief had given way, then a second, a third and several others. Then, unfortunately, new discussions were needed to decide who would lead the revolt. The discussions had degenerated into a brawl in the course of which two tribal chiefs and one Cretan mercenary were killed. Eventually, they agreed on Shanaar; although not a Nubian, he was the one who best knew Ramses and his army.

The guards responsible for supervising the mineworkers put up only a feeble resistance to the horde of black warriors armed with spears and bows. In a few hours the rebels had taken over the site, and a few days later they beat off the troops sent from Buhen to restore order.

Given the extent of the rebellion, Shanaar knew, the Viceroy of Nubia's only recourse was to report to Ramses. Shanaar knew, too, that his brother would come in person to subdue the rebels. That would be his fatal mistake.

Barren hills, granite outcrops, a narrow strip of greenery resisting the advance of the desert, palm trees with double trunks, a sky of the purest blue, across which flew pelicans, pink flamingos, crested cranes and jabirus . . . such was the magnificent land of Nubia. Ramses loved it, and its charm acted on him even now, in spite of the urgent worries that had brought the king and his army to the Far South.

According to the viceroy's report, the Nubian rebels had seized the principal gold mine. The consequences were likely to be catastrophic. On the one hand, the goldsmiths needed the precious metal to adorn the temples; on the other, the king used it for gifts to his vassals, to help maintain good relations with them.

Although he was sorry to be far from Nefertari, Ramses had to strike hard and swiftly, all the more so since he was certain – and this had been confirmed by the Great Royal Wife's intuition – that the instigator of this revolt was none other than Shanaar.

Far from dying in the solitary desert wastes, as had been believed, Shanaar had not only lived but contrived to spread unrest. Control of the gold would enable him to raise hordes of mercenaries, attack the Egyptian fortresses, and launch into a mad venture to conquer the Two Lands. Hatred and jealousy, nourished by repeated failure, had led him into a world from which he would find no escape: the world of madness.

Between Ramses and his brother, all ties of affection had

334

been cut. Even Tuya had not protested when the pharaoh confided his intentions to her. This fratricidal confrontation would be the last.

Several Royal Sons were at Ramses' side, impatient to prove their valour. Wearing long-sided wigs, pleated shirts with full sleeves and kilts with flaps in front, they proudly carried the banner of the jackal-god, 'the Opener of the Ways'.

When an enormous elephant blocked their path, even the bravest were tempted to flee. But Ramses advanced towards this living mountain and let himself be lifted up in its trunk and placed on its head between the two huge ears, which flapped merrily: proof, if any were still needed, of the divine protection the pharaoh enjoyed. Invincible took up station on the elephant's right.

Archers and footsoldiers alike were convinced that Pharaoh would hurl himself at the enemy lines, but Ramses had tents pitched, and set up camp some distance from the target. The cooks immediately set to work, weapons were cleaned, blades sharpened, donkeys and oxen fed.

One twenty-year-old Royal Son dared to protest. 'Why are we waiting, Majesty? A few rebellious Nubians can't stand up to our army!'

'You know little about this country and its inhabitants. The Nubians are formidable archers and unequalled as fierce fighters. If we believe ourselves already the victors, many men will die.'

'Isn't that the law of war?'

'My law consists of sparing as many lives as possible.'

'But the Nubians won't surrender.'

'Not under threat, certainly.'

'Do you mean we're going to negotiate with these savages, Majesty?'

'We must dazzle them. It's radiance which wins the victory, not the weapon in the hand. The Nubians are accustomed to laying ambushes, to attacking the rearguard and taking the enemy from the rear. We shan't give them that opportunity, because *we* shall surprise *them*.'

Yes, Shanaar knew exactly how Ramses would behave: he would charge straight ahead, down the only track that led to the mine. On either side of the site, sun-scorched rocks and hills would provide shelter for the Nubian archers. They would kill the officers, the Egyptian army would scatter, Ramses would be in despair, he would beg for mercy but Shanaar would slaughter him with his own hands.

Not a single Egyptian soldier would escape alive.

Then Shanaar would hang Ramses' corpse from the prow of his ship, make a triumphant entry into Elephantine, and then seize Thebes, Memphis, Pi-Ramses and the whole of Egypt. The people would rally to his cause and Shanaar would rule at last, while avenging himself on all those who had not recognized his worth.

He left the stone hut, formerly occupied by the foreman responsible for supervising the purification of the gold, and climbed to the top of the area where the gold-bearing ore was washed. Water trickled slowly down the slope leading to the clarification basin. Clarification was a tedious operation, requiring long patience. Shanaar thought about his own life; about the interminable years it had taken for him to free himself from Ramses' magic, to be able to defeat him and proclaim his own greatness! At this hour of triumph, he felt almost intoxicated.

A lookout waved wildly. Cries broke the silence, and black warriors, with feathers in their hair, began running in all directions.

'What's happening here? Stop this commotion!'

Shanaar hurried down from his promontory and grabbed hold of one of the chiefs, who was wandering around in panic.

'Calm down, that's an order! I'm in command here.'

The warrior pointed with his spear to the surrounding hills and rocks. 'Everywhere! They are everywhere!'

Shanaar advanced to the middle of the level ground, looked up and saw them.

Thousands of Egyptian soldiers surrounded the mine.

At the top of the highest hill a dozen men erected a platform on which they installed a throne. Then Ramses, wearing the Blue Crown, came and sat on the throne, his lion at his feet.

The Nubians could not take their eyes off the forty-two-year-old king, who, in this twentieth year of his reign, was at the height of his power. In spite of their courage, the warriors realized it would be suicidal to attack. The trap Shanaar had intended to lay was in fact closing in on him himself. The Egyptian soldiers had killed the Nubian sentinels and left the rebels no chance of getting away.

'We shall win!' shouted Shanaar. 'Everyone with me!'

The Nubian chiefs rallied. Yes, they must fight. One of them, followed by a score of men yelling and brandishing their spears, stormed up the slope towards the king. A volley of arrows pinned them to the ground.

One young fighter, more cunning than his comrades, zigzagged nearly to the foot of the throne. Invincible pounced and embedded his claws in the attacker's head. Ramses, his commander's sceptre in his hand, sat impassively on his throne. Invincible clawed at the sand, shook his mane and returned to lie at his master's feet.

Nearly all the Nubian warriors dropped their weapons and prostrated themselves as a sign of submission.

Shanaar began kicking the chiefs furiously. 'Get up and fight! Ramses isn't unbeatable!' When no one obeyed him, he plunged his sword into the back of an old chief. The old man convulsed wildly for a moment; then his death rattle sounded.

Appalled, the other chiefs shot looks of hatred at Shanaar. 'You betrayed us!' one of them shouted. 'You betrayed us

337

and you lied. No one can defeat Ramses, and you, you have brought disaster upon us!'

'Fight, you cowards!'

'You lied to us,' they all shouted.

'Follow me and kill Ramses!'

Wild-eyed and brandishing his sword, Shanar climbed back up the promontory from where he could look down on the water-tank and the gold-washing area.

'I am the master, the only Lord of Egypt and Nubia, I am—'

Ten arrows shot by the chiefs hit him in the head, throat and chest. He fell backwards down the slope and rolled slowly towards the clarification basin. His body landed in the mud and silt that the gentle water had washed from the gold.

56

The Hebrews' departure passed off without incident. Many Egyptians lamented the loss of friends and close relations who were involved in this mad venture. For their part, many Hebrews were afraid of crossing the desert with its thousand perils. How many enemies would they face? How many peoples and tribes would hinder the passage of Yahveh's worshippers?

Serramanna was furious. Before leaving for Nubia, Ramses had entrusted him and Ahmeni with the task of maintaining order in the capital. At the slightest disturbance caused by the Hebrews, the troops must act vigorously and at once.

Since the exodus had begun peacefully, Serramanna had had no excuse for holding Moses and Aaron for questioning. He was still convinced, though, that Ramses was wrong to spare the leader of the Hebrews. Not even a long, close friendship could justify such tolerance. Though he was going far from Egypt, Moses was still dangerous.

As a precaution, Serramanna had ordered a small band of soldiers to follow the Hebrews and send him regular reports on their progress. To his great surprise, the prophet had not taken the road to Sileh, which was dotted with wells and watched over by the Egyptian army, but had chosen a difficult road leading to the Sea of Reeds.* Moses had thus forestalled any attempts to turn back.

The big man's thoughts were interrupted by someone calling his name.

'Serramanna!' exclaimed Ahmeni. 'I've been looking for you everywhere. Are you going to stand staring at the northern road for ever?'

'Moses has done so much harm and he's getting away unscathed. I hate injustice.'

'Before he died, Ofir gave us one last interesting piece of information, as if he wanted to destroy himself completely, like a scorpion: two Bedouin tribal chiefs, Amos and Baduch, left Egypt with the Hebrews. They're the ones who supplied the Hebrews with weapons, in case there's fighting during the exodus.'

Serramanna punched his fist into the air. 'Hah! That's a serious criminal offence, so it's clearly my duty to arrest those two – and also their accomplice, Moses.'

'I thought you might reason along those lines.'

'I'm leaving immediately with some fifty chariots and I shall bring back those three beauties and throw them into jail.'

Ramses took Nefertari in his arms. Though she was wearing scarcely any make-up, his sweet love was more beautiful than ever, and her perfume was fragrant enough for a goddess.

'Shanaar is dead,' he told her, 'and the Nubian rebellion is over.'

'Will there be peace at last in Nubia?'

'The rebel leaders have been executed for treason – the

---

* Although the Old Testament (Exodus, chp. 14) speaks of 'the Passage of the Red Sea', a glance at the map shows clearly that Moses would not have travelled almost due south from the Nile Delta, so having to cross the Red Sea, but would have gone due east, as the direct way to Canaan, 'the Promised Land'. (*Trans.*)

villages they tyrannized held great feasts to celebrate. The stolen gold has been returned to me, and I've deposited part of it at Abu Simbel and the rest at Karnak.'

'How is the work going at Abu Simbel?'

'Very well, thanks to Setau. It's remarkable the way he infects everyone with his own energy.'

The queen could not put off any longer telling him the bad news. 'Serramanna and a company of chariots have left in pursuit of Moses.'

'Why?'

'Travelling with the Hebrews were two Bedouin spies in the pay of the Hittites. Serramanna wants to arrest not only the two spies but Moses as well. He has legal grounds for doing so, so Ahmeni didn't stop him.'

Ramses thought of Moses at the head of his people, striking the ground with his staff, leading the way, forcing those who faltered to continue, and beseeching Yahveh to show himself in the form of a pillar of fire by night, and a pillar of cloud by day. No obstacle would cause him to turn back, no enemy would frighten him.

'But there's good news too,' added Nefertari. 'I've just received a long letter from Putuhepa. She's convinced we shall succeed.'

'That's wonderful.' But Ramses spoke without conviction; his mind was elsewhere.

'You're afraid Moses will be killed, aren't you?'

Ramses didn't answer directly, but said, 'I hope I never see him again.'

'As for the peace treaty, there's still one delicate point.'

'Uri-Teshup?'

'No, a problem of wording. Hattusilis won't acknowledge that Hatti is solely responsible for the climate of war, and complains of being shown as an inferior, obliged to submit to Pharaoh's will.'

'Well, that's the truth, isn't it?'

'The text of the treaty will be made public, and future generations will read it. He can't afford to lose face.'

'He must either admit defeat or else be destroyed.'

Nefertari drew back a little and looked up at her husband. 'Must we really give up the chance of peace because of a few extreme words?'

'Even the slightest word counts.'

'Nevertheless, may I propose a new draft to the Lord of the Two Lands?'

'Taking into account Hattusilis's demands, I suppose?'

'Taking into account the future of two peoples who reject war, massacres and disaster.'

Ramses kissed her on the forehead. 'Shall I ever be able to resist the tact and eloquence of my Great Royal Wife?'

'Never,' she replied, resting her head on his shoulder.

Moses had flown into a volcanic rage and Aaron had had to hit several recalcitrants with his staff. The people were tired of travelling and wanted to return to Egypt, where they could eat as much as they liked and live in comfortable homes. Most of them hated the desert and couldn't get used to sleeping in the open, or in tents. Many were beginning to protest at the harsh life the prophet imposed on them.

Then Moses had cried out in a loud voice, enjoining the half-hearted and the cowardly to obey Yahveh and continue on their way to the Promised Land, whatever the pitfalls and the trials. And the long march was resumed, past Sileh and into a waterlogged countryside, where humidity hung in the air. Sometimes the Hebrews sank into the mud; carts overturned; leeches attacked men and animals.

Moses decided to call a halt not far from the border, near Lake Sarbonis and the Mediterranean. The region was dangerous, because the desert wind blew enormous quantities of sand on to ill-defined patches of water and created deceptive areas of 'land' which formed the Sea of Reeds.

No one lived in these desolate places, abandoned to gusting winds and the wrath of the sea and sky. Even fishermen avoided them, for fear of falling victim to the shifting sands.

A dishevelled woman threw herself at Moses' feet. 'We are all going to die here, in this wilderness!'

'You are wrong.'

'Look around you! Is this supposed to be the Promised Land?'

'Certainly not.'

'We will not go any further, Moses.'

'You certainly will. In a few days we shall cross the border and we shall go where Yahveh calls us.'

'How can you be so sure?'

'Because I have seen Him, woman, and He has spoken to me. Go now and sleep. There are still great tribulations ahead of us.'

Chastened, the woman obeyed.

Aaron came over to Moses. 'This place is horrible,' he said. 'I wish we were on our way again.'

'We need a long rest. Tomorrow, at dawn, Yahveh will give us the strength to continue.'

'Don't you ever have any doubts about our success?' asked Aaron.

'Never.'

Serramanna's chariots, accompanied by one of the Royal Sons, who was acting as Ramses' representative, had travelled fast in pursuit of the Hebrews. When he smelled the sea air, the ex-pirate breathed in deeply.

He signalled to his men to stop. 'Anyone know this place?'

An experienced charioteer spoke up. 'It's haunted. We mustn't disturb the demons.'

'The Hebrews came this way,' objected Serramanna.

343

'They can behave like lunatics if they want. But we should turn back.'

Smoke could be seen in the distance.

'The Hebrews' camp isn't far away,' observed the Royal Son. 'Let's go and arrest the criminals.'

'The Hebrews are armed,' Seramanna reminded him, 'and there are a lot of them.'

'Our men are trained soldiers, and our chariots give us the advantage. We can fire a volley of arrows from a good distance, and demand that Moses and the two Bedouin are handed over. If they aren't, we'll charge.'

Not without apprehension, the chariots set out across the marshes.

Aaron woke with a start. Moses was already on his feet, his staff in his hand.

'What's that rumbling noise?'

'Egyptian chariots.'

'They're heading straight for us!'

'It's all right. We've got time to get away.'

Amos and Baduch refused to venture into the Sea of Reeds, but the panic-stricken Hebrews agreed to follow Moses. In the darkness, no one could distinguish the water from the strip of sand any more, but Moses advanced unhesitatingly between the sea and the lake, guided by the fire that had burned in his heart since his adolescence, a fire which had become the desire for a Promised Land.

The east wind rose, meeting the desert wind and holding back the waters from the shallows. A dry passage was thus created, enabling the Hebrews to cross the Sea of Reeds.

By deploying, the Egyptian chariots made a disastrous mistake. Some sank into the shifting sands, others were lost in the marshes, through which invisible streams ran. The Royal Son's chariot got stuck in boggy ground, while Serramanna's crashed headlong into the two Bedouin, who had separated from the Hebrews, and crushed them, before getting bogged down in the sand.

By the time the chariots had been freed and his men, some of whom were wounded, rounded up, the wind had changed again. Heavy squalls, laden with humidity, launched huge waves which covered the dry passage again.

With rage in his heart, Serramanna watched Moses and the Hebrews get away.

57

In spite of all the care lavished on her by Neferet, who was proving to be an exceptionally gifted doctor, the Mother of Pharaoh was preparing for the great journey. Soon she would join Seti and leave earthly Egypt, whose happy future was almost assured. Almost, since the peace treaty with the Hittites had yet to be concluded.

When Nefertari came to join her in the garden where she was meditating, Tuya saw that the Great Royal Wife was full of excitement.

'Majesty, I have just received this letter from Empress Putuhepa.'

'My eyes are tired, Nefertari; you read it, please.'

The words the queen read in her soft, musical voice delighted Tuya's heart.

To my sister, the wife of the sun, Nefertari.

All is well with our two lands, I hope that your health, and that of those close to you, is flourishing. My daughter is in good health and my horses are magnificent. May it be the same with your children, your horses and Ramses the Great's lion. Your servant Hattusilis is at Pharaoh's feet and prostrates himself before him.

Peace and fraternity: such are the words which must

be uttered, as the Light-God of Egypt and the Storm-God of Hatti wish to fraternize.

   The ambassadors of Egypt and of Hatti have set out for Pi-Ramses, bearing the text of the treaty, so that Pharaoh may seal for ever our joint decision.

   May my sister Nefertari be protected by the gods and goddesses.

Nefertari and Tuya fell into each other's arms and wept for joy.

Serramanna thought he'd be crushed like an insect under Ramses' sandal. With a heavy heart, he prepared to be driven out of the palace, and he dreaded it. He, the former pirate, had become used to his life as an upholder of the law and a redresser of wrongs. Absolute loyalty to Ramses had given a meaning to his life and put an end to his wanderings. Egypt, which he had intended to pillage, had become his home. He, the voyager, had landed, and he felt no desire to set sail again.

   Serramanna was grateful to Ramses for not making him suffer a public humiliation in front of the court and his subordinates. The king received him in his office, alone.

   'Majesty, I made a mistake. No one knew this terrain and—'

   'What became of the two Bedouin spies?'

   'They were killed, crushed under the wheels of my chariot.'

   'Are you sure Moses escaped?'

   'He and the Hebrews crossed the Sea of Reeds, I'm certain of it.'

   'Well then, they've crossed the border, so let's forget them.'

   'But . . . Moses betrayed you!'

   'He's gone, and, since there's no longer any risk of him troubling the harmony of the Two Lands, let him follow his own destiny. Serramanna, I have an important mission for you.'

The Sardinian couldn't believe his ears. Was the king forgiving him for his failure?

'You are to go to the border, with two regiments of chariots, to welcome the Hittite ambassador, and ensure his protection.'

'That is a task . . . a task . . .'

'A task decisive for the peace of the world, Serramanna.'

Hattusilis had given in. Guided by his intuition as a statesman, Putuhepa's advice and Ahsha's recommendations, he had drawn up the text of a treaty of peace with Egypt that met Ramses' demands, and had appointed two messengers to carry to the pharaoh silver tablets bearing the cuneiform-script version of the agreement.

In a letter, Hattusilis promised Ramses he would display the treaty in the Temple of the Sun Goddess in Hattusa, provided the same was done in one of the great temples of the Two Lands; but the emperor was still unsure that Ramses would ratify the document without adding new clauses.

From the Hittite capital to the Egyptian frontier, the atmosphere remained tense. Ahsha was aware that he could not ask any more of Hattusilis; if Ramses showed the slightest dissatisfaction the treaty would be abandoned. As for the Hittite soldiers, they did not hide their anxiety that groups of dissidents might attack them, to prevent the messengers of peace from reaching their destination. Passes, gorges and forests appeared as so many traps, but the journey passed without incident.

When he caught sight of Serramanna and the Egyptian chariots, Ahsha heaved a great sigh of relief. For the rest of the journey, he would enjoy peace of mind.

The Sardinian and the senior officer of the Hittite chariot corps exchanged cool greetings. The former would have willingly wiped out the barbarians, but he must obey Ramses and carry out his mission.

For the first time, Hittite chariots entered the Delta and drove along the road to Pi-Ramses.

'What's happened about the revolt in Nubia?' asked Ahsha.

'Do you mean word of it reached Hattusa?' asked Serramanna anxiously.

'Don't worry, the news has been kept secret.'

'Ramses restored order, and Shanaar was executed by his own allies.'

'May peace be established in the North as in the South! If Ramses accepts this treaty, it will begin an era of prosperity on which future generations will look back with gratitude.'

'Why should he refuse?'

'Because of a detail which isn't exactly insignificant. But let's be optimistic, Serramanna.'

On the twenty-first day of the winter season of the twenty-first year of Ramses' reign, Ahsha and the two Hittite diplomats were shown by Ahmeni into the audience chamber of the Pi-Ramses palace, whose magnificence overwhelmed them. Instead of the bleakness of their warrior world, they found a colourful universe, uniting majesty with refinement.

The messengers handed the silver tablets to Pharaoh and Ahsha read the preliminary statement.

May a thousand deities, from among the gods and goddesses of Hatti and Egypt, be witness to this treaty which the Emperor of Hatti and the Pharaoh of Egypt lay down. The sun, the moon, the gods and goddesses of heaven and earth, of the mountains and the rivers, of the sea, the winds and the clouds bear witness to this.

These thousands of deities will destroy the house, the country and the subjects of the one who does not observe

*the treaty. As for the one who will observe it, these
thousands of deities will ensure that he prospers and
lives happily with his household, his children and his
subjects.**

In the presence of the Great Royal Wife and the Mother of
Pharaoh, Ramses approved the declaration, which Ahmeni
transcribed on to papyrus.

'Does Emperor Hattusilis acknowledge the Hittites'
responsibility for the acts of war committed in recent years?'

'Yes, Majesty,' replied one of the ambassadors.

'Does he accept that our successors are bound by this
treaty?'

'Our emperor's wish is that this agreement shall generate
peace and fraternity, and that it shall apply to our children and
to our children's children.'

'What borders shall we respect?'

'The River Orontes, a line of fortifications in southern
Syria, the road separating Egyptian Byblos from the province
of Amurru, which is considered a Hittite protectorate, the
road passing to the south of Hittite Kadesh, separating it from
the northern exit from the plain of Bekaa which is under
Egyptian influence. The Phoenician ports shall remain under
Pharaoh's control; Egyptian diplomats and traders shall
circulate freely on the road leading to Hatti.'

Ahsha held his breath. Would Ramses agree to renounce
for ever any claim to the Kadesh citadel and, in particular, to
Amurru? Neither Seti nor his son had succeeded in taking the
famous stronghold near which Ramses had won his greatest
victory, and it seemed logical that Kadesh should remain
under Hittite control. But Amurru . . . Egypt had fought hard
to keep this province; soldiers had died for it. Ahsha was

---

* This is the authentic text of the treaty preserved in the Hittite and
Egyptian archives.

afraid Pharaoh would prove uncompromising.

The king looked at Nefertari. In her eyes he read his answer.

'We agree,' declared Ramses the Great.

Ahsha was filled with immense joy.

'What else does my brother Hattusilis desire?' asked Ramses.

'A treaty of peace between our two lands, Majesty, and an alliance against anyone who attacks Egypt or Hatti.'

'Is he thinking of Assyria?'

'Of any people who might try to occupy the land of Egypt or of Hatti.'

'We, too, wish for this treaty and this alliance, which will allow us to maintain prosperity and happiness.'

Ahmeni continued transcribing with a firm hand, as the ambassador went on, 'Majesty, Emperor Hattusilis wishes also for the royal succession to be respected and safeguarded in both our countries, according to the rites and traditions.'

'It could not be otherwise.'

'Lastly, our sovereign would like to settle the problem of the return of fugitives to their own country.'

Ahsha feared this last obstacle. One single detail could bring the whole agreement into question.

'I insist that such fugitives be treated humanely,' declared Ramses. 'When returned to their own country, be it Egypt or Hatti, they shall suffer neither punishment nor abuse, and their homes shall be restored to them intact. Moreover, Uri-Teshup, who has become an Egyptian, will remain free to decide his own fate.'

The two ambassadors, having already received Hattusilis's agreement to these conditions, acquiesced.

The treaty could now come into force.

Ahmeni would submit the final version to the royal scribes, who would copy it on to the finest-quality papyrus.

'This text will be carved in the stone of several temples in

Egypt,' announced Ramses, 'notably in the Temple of Ra in Khmun, on the southern face of the east wing of the ninth gate at Karnak and on the southern side of the façade of the great temple of Abu Simbel. In this way, from the north to the south, from the Delta to Nubia, the Egyptians will know that they will live for ever in peace with the Hittites, under the eyes of their gods.'

58

The Hittite ambassadors were lodged in the palace, in quarters reserved for foreign visitors, and they shared in the rejoicing that swept through the Egyptian capital. They were able to observe Ramses' immense popularity, celebrated in a song taken up everywhere: 'He dazzles us like the sun, he restores us like the wind and water. He is like bread and fine fabrics to us. He is the father and mother of the whole country, the light of both banks of the river.'

Nefertari invited them to witness a ritual celebrated in the Temple of Hathor. At it, they heard the invocation to the goddess who could create herself every day, who brought into existence all forms of life, lit up all countenances, made trees and flowers quiver for joy. When eyes were turned to the Principle hidden in the gold of the heavens, the birds took flight in that moment of bliss, and a path of peace opened under the feet of humans.

Their astonishment over, the ambassadors joined in the festivities. They were honoured guests at a banquet at which they feasted on stewed pigeon, marinated kidneys, roast leg of beef, Nile perch, roast geese, lentils, garlic and mild onions, courgettes, lettuce, cucumbers, fresh peas, beans, stewed figs, apples, dates, watermelons, goats' cheese, fermented milk, round honey-cakes, newly baked bread, mild beer, and red and white wine. On this exceptional occasion, a

353

vintage wine was served. It had been put into earthenware jars on the sixth day of the fourth year of Seti's reign, and marked with the sign of Anubis, the master of the desert. The diplomats were amazed by the abundance and quality of the food, admired the beauty of the stoneware dishes, and eventually gave themselves up to the collective joy and joined in singing the praises of Ramses in Egyptian.

Yes, it really was peace.

At last, the capital slept.

In spite of the late hour, Nefertari wrote in her own hand a long letter to her sister Putuhepa, thanking her for her efforts and telling her of the wonderful times Hatti and Egypt were enjoying. When she had affixed her seal, Ramses gently laid his hands on her shoulders.

'Isn't the time for work over?'

'The day contains more tasks than hours, it could not be otherwise, and it is good that it is so – isn't that what you tell your senior officials? The Great Royal Wife cannot be exempted from the Rule.'

Nefertari's special festive perfume enchanted Ramses. The master-perfumer of the temple had used no fewer than sixteen ingredients, including scented reedmace, juniper, broom flowers, terebinth resin, myrrh and various herbs. Green eyeliner emphasized the beauty of her eyes, and a wig anointed with oil from Libya framed the sublime loveliness of her face.

Ramses removed the wig and let Nefertari's long, wavy hair flow loose.

'I am content,' she said, 'for we have worked for the happiness of our people.'

'Your name will be for ever associated with this treaty,' he promised her. 'You are the one who has built this peace.'

'Our fame is unimportant if we can see the days and rites in correct succession.'

The king slipped off the shoulder-straps of Nefertari's

gown and kissed her neck. She turned and their lips met.

'That's enough talking.'

The first official letter from Hatti, following the acceptance of the peace treaty, provoked a strong wave of curiosity and anxiety at the court of Pi-Ramses. Did Hattusilis want to go back on an essential point of the agreement?

The king broke the seal affixed to the cloth wrapping the tablet of precious wood, and read the message, which was written in cuneiform characters.

He immediately went to the queen's apartment. Nefertari was finishing re-reading the ritual for the spring festivities.

'A very odd message!'

'Has something serious happened?' asked the queen anxiously.

'No, it's a sort of appeal for help. A Hittite princess with an impossible name is indisposed. According to Hattusilis, she seems to be possessed by a demon which the Hatti physicians can't drive out. Knowing how talented our doctors are, our new ally begs me to send him one from the House of Life, to restore the princess's health and enable her at last to have the child she desires.'

'That's excellent news. The links between our two countries continue to strengthen.'

The king sent for Ahsha and told him the contents of Hattusilis's letter.

Ahsha burst out laughing.

'Why is this appeal so funny?' asked the queen in astonishment.

'I have the feeling that the emperor has unlimited confidence in our medicine! He's asking for nothing short of a miracle.'

'Our doctors are very knowledgeable and highly skilled.'

'Certainly, but not even they can restore the fertility of a woman, even a Hittite princess, who's over sixty years old!'

After a moment of frank hilarity, Ramses dictated to Ahmeni a reply to his brother Hattusilis.

As for the princess who suffers – especially from her age – we know her. No one can manufacture medicines which will make her conceive – unless the God of Storms and the Sun God so decide. So I shall send an excellent magician and a competent doctor.

Ramses immediately sent off to Hattusa a magic statue of the healer-god Khonsu, who travels through space in the form of the crescent moon. Who but a deity could modify the laws of the human body?

When the message from Nebu, the High Priest of Karnak, reached Pi-Ramses, the king decided to transfer the court to Thebes. With his usual efficiency Ahmeni chartered boats and gave the necessary orders to ensure that the journey was as quick and comfortable as possible.

All those dear to Ramses boarded the royal ship: Nefertari, resplendent as ever; Tuya, whose joy was evident at having lived long enough to see peace between Egypt and Hatti; Iset the Fair, deeply moved at being associated with the great festivities; his three children, Kha, now High Priest of Memphis, Meritamon the musician and sturdy young Meneptah; his loyal friends Ahmeni and Ahsha, who had helped Ramses build a contented kingdom; Nedjem and Serramanna, both loyal servants. The only ones missing were Setau and Lotus, who would come from Abu Simbel to join them at Thebes. And Moses . . . Moses who had disowned Egypt.

At the landing-stage the High Priest of Karnak in person welcomed the royal couple. This time, Nebu was really old, bent and walking with difficulty, and leaning heavily on his staff. His voice quavered and he suffered from crippling rheumatism, but his eyes were still bright and his air of authority as strong as ever.

The king and the High Priest embraced.

'I have kept my promise to you, Majesty. Thanks to the work of Bakhen and his team of craftsmen, your Temple of a Million Years is completed. The gods have granted me the joy of being able to gaze on this immense masterpiece which will be their home.'

'I shall keep mine to you, Nebu. We shall climb together up to the roof of the temple, and we shall gaze on the sanctuary, its outbuildings and the palace.'

The enormous gateway, whose internal face was decorated with scenes of the victory at Kadesh, the vast first courtyard with pillars representing the king as Osiris, a giant statue, thirty-five cubits high, depicting the king seated, a second gateway, illustrating the harvest ritual, the Hall of Pillars, sixty-one cubits deep and eighty cubits wide, the sanctuary whose reliefs illustrated the mysteries of daily worship, the great carved tree that symbolized the eternal nature of the pharaonic institution . . . So many wonders, which the royal couple admired with the greatest joy.

The festivities for the dedication of the Temple of a Million Years were to last several weeks. For Ramses, their high point was to be the ritual foundation of the shrine dedicated to his parents; he and Nefertari would pronounce the life-giving words carved for all time on the pillars of hieroglyphs.

Pharaoh had just finished robing in the 'house of the morning' when Ahmeni hurried in, his face drawn.

'It's your mother. She's asking for you.'

Ramses hurried to Tuya's apartments. She was lying on her back, her arms at her sides, her eyes half-closed.

He knelt beside her and kissed her hands. 'Are you too exhausted to take part in the dedication of your shrine?'

'It's not exhaustion. Death is approaching.'

'We must ward it off together.'

'I no longer have the strength, Ramses. And why should I try? The time has come for me to join Seti, and so this is a happy time.'

'How can you be so cruel as to abandon Egypt?'

'The royal couple reign; they follow the right path. I know that the next floods will be excellent and that justice will be respected. I want to leave in peace, my son, thanks to the peace which you and Nefertari have built and which you will cause to last. A peaceful land is so beautiful, a land where children play, where the flocks and herds return from the fields while the herdsmen play tunes on their flutes, where people respect each other, knowing that Pharaoh protects them. Preserve this happiness, Ramses, and hand on this Rule to your successor.'

Facing the supreme test, Tuya did not tremble. She remained proud and majestic, her eyes fixed impassively on eternity.

'Love Egypt with all your being, Ramses. Let no human feeling be stronger than that love, and let no trial, however cruel, divert you from your duties as pharaoh.'

Tuya held her son's hand very tightly. 'Pray, King of Egypt, that I may arrive at the field of offerings, the country of bliss, that I may settle for ever in that wondrous land of water and light, and shine there in the company of our ancestors and of Seti . . .'

Her voice faded in a breath as deep as the Otherworld.

59

Tuya's House of Eternity in the Valley of the Queens, a place of beauty and serenity, was close to Nefertari's. The Great Royal Wife and the pharaoh organized the funeral of Seti's widow, whose mummy would rest from now on in her House of Gold. Tuya would be metamorphosed into Osiris and Hathor, to survive through her body of light, which invisible energy from the farthest reaches of the heavens would resurrect each day. The ritual furnishings were placed in the tomb: human-headed vases containing her entrails, precious fabrics, jars of wine, vases of oils and unguents, mummified foodstuffs, priestesses' robes, sceptres, finery, necklaces and jewellery, gold and silver sandals and other treasures which would equip Tuya for her travels along the magnificent paths of the West and through the realms of the Otherworld.

Ramses tried to accept joy and sorrow with the same fortitude. On one hand, the wished-for peace with the Hittites, and the completion of his House of Ramses, his Temple of a Million Years; on the other, the departure of Tuya. The son and the man were grief-stricken, but Pharaoh had no right to betray the Mother of Pharaoh, who had been so steadfast that death itself seemed to have had no hold over her. He had to respect her last words to him: Egypt must come before his own feelings, before his joy or sorrow.

And so Ramses submitted to the demands of his office,

helped by Nefertari; he continued to steer the ship of state, as if Tuya were still present. He must learn to do without her advice and her suggestions. It now fell to Nefertari to assume the tasks Tuya used to undertake, and in spite of his wife's courage, Ramses was worried the burden was becoming too great for her.

Every day, after celebrating the dawn rites, the royal couple remained long in meditation in the House of Ramses, in the shrine dedicated to Tuya and Seti. The king needed to absorb the invisible truths created by the living stones and the hieroglyphs to which the language gave life. By communing with the souls of their predecessors, Ramses and Nefertari were filled with the secret light that sustained their thoughts.

At the end of the seventy days of mourning, Ahmeni deemed it essential to submit urgent matters to Ramses. Installed in the offices of the House of Ramses, with his small but efficient team of scribes, Pharaoh's private secretary was in constant contact with Pi-Ramses and spent every waking moment keeping up with the perusal of the dossiers.

'The rise in the floodwaters is excellent,' he told Ramses. 'The wealth of the kingdom has never been so great, there is no fault to be found with the management of our reserves of foodstuffs, and all the craftsmen are working diligently. Prices are stable and there is no threat of inflation.'

'What about the gold from Nubia?'

'Both extraction and supply are satisfactory.'

'Are you telling me that Egypt has become a paradise.'

'Certainly not. But we're trying hard to be worthy of Tuya and Seti.'

'Then why this hint of annoyance in your voice?'

'Well, Ahsha would like to talk to you, but he doesn't know if this is the right moment.'

'Anyone would think he'd instilled a sense of diplomacy into you. Tell him to meet me in the library.'

*

The library of the House of Ramses was worthy of the one in the House of Life in Khmun. Day after day, papyri and inscribed tablets arrived there, and the king himself supervised their classification. Without a profound knowledge of the rites, philosophical texts and archives, it was impossible to govern Egypt.

Ahsha was elegantly dressed in a linen gown of exceptional quality, decorated with coloured fringes. He went into raptures at the sight of the library. 'It will be a joy to work here, Majesty.'

'The House of Ramses will be one of the vital centres of the kingdom. Do you want to talk to me about a book of wisdom?'

'I just wanted to see you.'

'I'm in good health, Ahsha. Nothing can erase the loss of Tuya, and I shall never forget Seti, but both have traced a path from which I shall not deviate. Is it that the Hittites are causing trouble?'

'Absolutely not, Majesty. Hattusilis is all the more delighted with our treaty in that it has made Assyria retreat into her shell. The mutual defence agreement between Hatti and Egypt has made the Assyrians aware that any attack would bring immediate, massive reprisals. Many commercial contacts with Hatti are in hand, and I can confirm that peace will reign in the region for many years. Isn't your word as solid as granite?'

'Then why are you worried?'

'It's Moses. Are you willing to hear him mentioned?'

'I'm listening.'

'My spies have kept track of the Hebrews.'

'Where have they got to?'

'They're still wandering in the desert, in spite of growing protests. But Moses rules his people with an iron hand. "Yahveh is a devouring fire and a jealous God," he likes to say.'

'Do you know where he's making for?'

'The "Promised Land" is probably Canaan, but it will be difficult for the Hebrews to seize it. They have fought against the Midianites and the Amorites, and at the moment they're occupying the land of Moab. The peoples of the region are afraid of the Hebrew nomads, who they think are terrible pillagers.'

'Moses won't be deterred,' said Ramses. 'If he has to fight a hundred battles, he will do so. I'm sure he has looked down on Canaan from the top of Mount Negev and has seen a land flowing with honey and festive oil.'

'The Hebrews are dangerous, Majesty.'

'What do you suggest?'

'We must get rid of Moses. Without him, they'll return to Egypt, provided you promise not to punish them.'

'Put that out of your mind,' said Ramses firmly. 'Moses will live out his destiny.'

'As your friend I'm glad at your decision, but as a diplomat I regret it. Like me, you're convinced that Moses will achieve his ends and that his arrival in his Promised Land will upset the balance in this region.'

'Providing Moses doesn't export his beliefs, there's no reason why we shouldn't get on together. Peace between our two peoples will be a factor for balance.'

'You're giving me a good lesson in foreign politics and diplomacy.'

'No, Ahsha. I'm simply trying to mark out a path of hope.'

In Iset's heart, passion had given way to affection. She still loved and admired the king, but she had given up any idea of winning him. How could she compete with Nefertari, who grew lovelier and more radiant with the passing years? With maturity, Iset had learned to be at peace and to appreciate the happiness life offered her. Talking to Kha about the mysteries of creation; listening to Meneptah describing the way

362

Egyptian society functioned, a subject he studied with all the seriousness of a future ruler; conversing with Nefertari in the palace gardens; being close to Ramses as often as possible – she enjoyed treasures beyond price.

'Come,' the Great Royal Wife invited her, 'let us go sailing on the river.'

It was summer, and the floodwaters had transformed Egypt into an immense lake: it was possible to sail from one village to another. A scorching sun sparkled on the life-giving waters, and hundreds of birds flitted about in the sky.

The two women, seated under a white canopy, had anointed their skin with scented oil. Near them stood earthenware jars, keeping water cool for their refreshment.

'Kha has left again for Memphis,' Iset said.

'Are you sorry?'

'He is only interested in ancient monuments, symbols and rituals. When his father summons him to take over matters of state, how will he react?'

Nefertari patted her hand reassuringly. 'He's so intelligent that he'll know how to adapt.'

'What do you think of Meneptah?'

'He's very different from his brother, but the exceptional individual is already apparent under the young man.'

'Meritamon has grown into a wonderful young woman.'

'She's realizing my own childhood dream,' said the queen wistfully, 'to live in a temple and play music for the gods.'

'All the people revere you, Nefertari. Their love for you is as great as yours for them.'

'How you have changed, Iset!'

'I have let go; the demons of covetousness have left my soul. I am at peace with myself. And if you knew how much I admire you, what you are, the work you do . . .'

'Thanks to your help, Tuya's absence will be less hard for me to bear. Now that you're freed from the burden of the children's upbringing, will you agree to work at my side?'

'I am unworthy . . .'

'Let me be the judge of that.'

'Majesty!'

Nefertari kissed Iset on the forehead. It was summer and Egypt was in festive mood.

The palace of the House of Ramses was already as busy as the one in Pi-Ramses; in accordance with the king's wishes, the annexes to his Temple of a Million Years had already become the principal economic centre of Upper Egypt, working in partnership with Karnak. The House of Ramses, standing on the west bank of Thebes, would proclaim for all time the splendour of Ramses the Great's reign, whose greatness already impressed everyone.

It was Ahmeni who received the message signed by Setau. Breathless with excitement, the scribe dropped everything and went off in search of Ramses, whom he found in the huge pool near the palace: every day during the fine season, the king swam for at least half an hour.

'Majesty, a letter from Nubia!'

Ramses swam to the edge of the pool. Ahmeni knelt down and passed him the papyrus.

It only contained a few words, those that Ramses hoped for.

60

A head of the goddess Hathor in gilded wood, with the solar disc between her horns, adorned the prow of the royal couple's ship. The queen of the stars was also the mistress of navigation; her ever-watchful presence guaranteed a peaceful journey to Abu Simbel.

There the two temples celebrating the union of Ramses and Nefertari had been completed. Setau's message was unambiguous and he was not in the habit of boasting. In the centre of the ship, there was a cabin with a convex roof, resting on two pillars with capitals in the form of papyrus at the back and of water-lilies in front; openings allowed air to circulate. For the queen, who was in thoughtful mood, this voyage was in the nature of a special treat.

Nefertari hid her great exhaustion, so as not to alarm the king. She rose and joined him under the white sail stretched out in the stern between four posts. Invincible lay on his side dozing, with Wideawake wedged against his back; the dog was sunk in a deep, refreshing sleep but knew he was protected by the lion.

'Abu Simbel!' said Nefertari. 'No king ever made such an offering to a queen.'

'No king ever had the good fortune to wed Nefertari.'

'We're almost too happy, Ramses – it frightens me sometimes.'

'We must share this happiness with our people, with the whole of Egypt and the generations to come. That's why I wanted the royal couple to be present for all time in the stones of Abu Simbel. Not you and I, Nefertari, but Pharaoh and the Great Royal Wife, of whom we are but the ephemeral, earthly embodiments.'

Nefertari nestled against Ramses and gazed out at Nubia, that wild and splendid land.

The sandstone cliff, the domain of Hathor, came into sight, framing a bend in the Nile to the west. In the past, a strip of tawny sand had separated two promontories which cried out for the hands of the architect and the sculptor; and those hands had been at work, lovingly transforming the rock into two temples dug out of its heart and proclaimed by façades whose power and grace filled the queen with amazement. In front of the southern sanctuary were four colossal statues of Ramses seated, each forty cubits high; in front of the northern one, more huge statues of the pharaoh, standing and marching, framed a twenty-cubit-high statue of Nefertari.

Abu Simbel was no longer simply a landmark for sailors, but a transfigured place, where the inner fire of the human mind would shine out, immovable and immutable, in the gold of the Nubian desert.

From the bank, Setau and Lotus waved a welcome, as did all the artisans who surrounded them. The latter shrank back when Invincible walked down the gangway, but the king's tall figure dispelled all fears. The great cat walked on the king's right, the elderly yellow dog on his left.

Ramses had never seen such satisfaction on Setau's face.

'You can be proud of yourself,' he said as he embraced his friend.

'It's the architects and sculptors you must congratulate, not me. I simply encouraged them, so that they'd create work worthy of you.'

'Worthy of the mysterious powers who live in this temple, Setau.'

At the bottom of the gangway, Nefertari stumbled; Lotus went to her assistance and noticed that the queen seemed faint.

'We must continue,' insisted Nefertari. 'I'm quite all right.'

'But, Majesty . . .'

'We mustn't spoil the dedication celebrations, Lotus.'

'I have a remedy which may cure your exhaustion.'

Rough, uncouth Setau never knew quite how to behave in front of Nefertari, whose beauty fascinated him. He bowed to her, overcome with emotion. 'Majesty, I hope . . .'

'Let us celebrate the birth of Abu Simbel, Setau. I want this to be an occasion never to be forgotten.'

The chiefs of all the Nubian tribes had been invited to Abu Simbel to celebrate the building of the two temples. Wearing their finest bead necklaces and new loincloths, they kissed the feet of Ramses and Nefertari, then struck up a victory song which rose to the starry sky.

That night there was more delicious food than there were grains of sand on the shore, more pieces of roast beef than flowers in the royal gardens, countless loaves and cakes. Wine flowed like the abundant floodwaters, olibanum and other incense-resins were burned on altars erected in the open air. Just as peace had been established with the Hittites far in the North, so it would reign for long in the Far South.

'From now on, Abu Simbel will be the spiritual centre of Nubia and the symbolic expression of the love that unites Pharaoh and the Great Royal Wife,' Ramses told Setau. 'You, my friend, will summon the chiefs of the tribes here, at regular dates, for them to participate in the rites that make this land sacred.'

'In other words, you're allowing me to stay in Nubia so

367

that Lotus will remain in love with me.'

The mild September night was followed by a week of celebrations and rituals during which those taking part had a chance to wonder at the interior of the great temple. In the hall with its three aisles and eight pillars, against which stood the twenty-cubit-tall statue of the king as Osiris, they marvelled at the scenes of the battle of Kadesh and the monarch's encounter with the deities who embraced him, the better to communicate their energy to him.

On the day of the autumn equinox, Ramses and Nefertari entered the holiest shrine. When the sun rose, its light followed the main axis of the temple and lit up the inner recesses of the sanctuary, where four gods were seated on stone benches: Ra-Horus from the land of light, Ramses' *ka*, Amon, the hidden god, and Ptah, the builder. The last remained in the shadows, except at the two equinoxes; on those two mornings the light from the rising sun lightly touched the statue of Ptah, who spoke to Ramses from the depths of the rock: 'I am thy brother and companion; I give thee endurance, stability and power. We are united in the joy of the heart; I cause thy thoughts to be in harmony with those of the gods. I have chosen thee and I give effect to thy words. I nourish thee with life, so that thou mayest give life to others.'

When the royal couple left the great temple, Egyptians and Nubians alike uttered cries of joy. The moment had come to dedicate the second sanctuary, that of the queen, which bore the name 'Nefertari, for whom the sun rises'.

The Great Royal Wife offered flowers to Hathor so that the face of the queen of the stars should light up. Identifying herself with Sekhet, the patron of the House of Life, Nefertari addressed Ramses:

'Thou hast restored vigour and courage to Egypt; thou art her lord. Thou takest on the form of the celestial falcon, to spread thy wings over thy people. For them, thou art like a wall of celestial metal, which no hostile force can scale.'

'For Nefertari,' the king replied, 'I have built a temple in fine sandstone, hollowed out of the solid mountains of Nubia, to last for all eternity.'

The queen wore a long yellow gown, a turquoise necklace and golden sandals; on her blue wig was a crown in the form of two long, slender cow's horns clasping a sun, and topped by two tall feathers. In her right hand, she held the key of life; in her left, a flexible sceptre shaped like a water-lily rising out of the waters of the first morning of the world.

Smiling faces of Hathor surmounted the pillars of the temple of the queen; on the walls were ritual scenes uniting Ramses, Nefertari and the deities.

The queen leaned on her husband's arm.

'What is it, Nefertari?'

'I'm just tired.'

'Do you want us to break off the ritual?'

'No, I want to discover every scene of this temple with you, read every one of these texts, take part in every offering. For this is the dwelling you have built for me.'

His wife's smile reassured the king. He did as she wished, and together they brought every corner of the temple to life, right to the innermost shrine, where the heavenly cow, the incarnation of Hathor, appeared emerging from the rock.

Nefertari spent a long time in the semi-darkness of the shrine, as if the gentle goddess could dispel the cold that was infiltrating her veins.

'I would like to see the scene of the coronation,' she said to the king.

Here Isis and Hathor stood on either side of a statue of the queen, carved with almost unreal delicacy, and were infusing her crown with the life-force. The sculptor had glorified the moment when a woman from this world entered, still living, into the universe of the gods, to bear witness on earth to its reality.

'Hold me in your arms, Ramses.'

She was as cold as ice.

'I am dying, Ramses, I am dying of exhaustion, but here, in my temple, with you, so close to you, that we form one being, for ever.'

The king held her so tightly to him that he believed that he could hold on to her life, the life she had given unreservedly to those close to her, and to the whole of Egypt, to preserve them from evil.

Ramses watched Nefertari's calm, pure face stiffen and her head slowly droop. She showed neither rebellion nor fear as her breath was extinguished.

Ramses bore the Great Royal Wife in his arms, like a bridegroom carrying his bride across the threshold of his home to set the seal on their marriage. He knew that she would become an undying star, that her mother the sky would give birth to her again and that she would embark for the eternal voyage; but that knowledge could not ease the unbearable sorrow that tore at his heart.

Ramses walked towards the door of the temple; hollow-eyed, and with empty heart, he left the sanctuary.

Wideawake, the old golden-yellow dog, had just breathed his last, lying between the paws of the lion, who gently licked the head of his companion to heal him of death.

Ramses' suffering was too great for tears. At that moment, his power and his greatness were of no help to him.

The pharaoh lifted up to the sun the noble body of the one he would love for all eternity, the Lady of Abu Simbel, Nefertari, for whom the light shone forth.